A View from the Mountain

Jack Kestner

A View from the Mountain

Enjoy!

Pam Kestner

Clinch Mountain Press
Emory, Virginia
2006

Information may be obtained from the publisher:
Clinch Mountain Press
P. O. Box 117
Emory, Virginia 24327
shearer@clinchmountainpress.net
www.clinchmountainpress.net

First Printing 2006
Second Printing 2007

Book design by Kathy Shearer and Lisa Kestner Quigley

Jack Kestner's columns were originally published in the *Bristol Herald Courier* and are reprinted here with permission. All photographs were provided by the Kestner family unless otherwise indicated.

Printed in the United States of America by Inové Graphics, Kingsport, Tennessee

ISBN-13: 978-0-9724765-3-9
ISBN-10: 0-9724765-3-9

Library of Congress Control Number: 2006928720

Front cover: Jack Kestner with his favorite dog, Duke. Photo by Earl Neikirk, courtesy of the *Bristol Herald Courier*. Background: Fall view of Little Mountain and ranges to the south as seen from Jack's home, Mountainside, on Clinch Mountain. Photo by Jack Kestner.
Back cover: Winter view from Mountainside. Photo by Mike Quigley.
Title page: Photo by Jack Kestner.
Page 11: Photo by Mike Williams, courtesy of the *Virginian-Pilot/Ledger-Star*.

Contents

Preface and Acknowledgments

This is Dad's book—a fulfillment, we hope, of what he had once planned to accomplish. Through the years, his readers called or sent notes or stopped him in the checkout line at the grocery store to comment on a particular column. Then they would invariably ask when he was going to put his columns in book form. At some point, he took their interest to heart and got as far as creating a potential outline.

After his death in March 2005, we decided as a family that the time had come to publish that book. Which, out of nearly 900 columns, should we choose? Once again, his readers came through and helped point the way by sending us their favorite subjects or specific columns. We have included as many of their requests as we could. And Lisa has written brief introductions to each chapter that, in some cases, provide background information that Dad did not include in the columns.

Though Dad wrote the columns, this book would have never come to fruition without the enormous help and assistance from a number of people, whose contributions we greatly appreciate.

From the very beginning, Steven Kaylor and the staff of the *Bristol Herald Courier* have encouraged and supported our efforts to get this book off the ground. They generously provided us with the means to reach out to Dad's readers, allowing them to participate in the column selection. In addition, we are grateful for the use of staff photographer Earl Neikirk's stunning photographs of the Great Channels.

Dad's organization of his columns on his computer left much to be desired. We needed some way to locate and copy the files. Lowell Dale, an old friend of Dad's, graciously spent hours searching for files and downloading them onto disks, and countless more hours on the phone providing much needed technical support.

Without a doubt, the fact that we can hold this book in our hands today is largely due to the incredible efforts of Joe and Elizabeth Szczesny. Joe and Elizabeth are long-time fans of Dad's. Over the years they have copied, from various sources, all of Dad's columns. When they found out that we did not have any columns prior to late 1994, they sent us a copy of every single one. We will be forever grateful to them.

Connie Woods, who adopted one of the stray dogs Dad had picked up, played a pivotal role in formatting much of this book by taking the raw columns and creating digital files for us.

Two of Dad's former colleagues from his *Ledger-Star* days—Jack Dorsey and Gene Owens—helped us identify people in pictures and tracked down photographers. Kathy Musick, librarian at the Hayters Gap library, assisted by arranging a session with Kathy Shearer to review a collection of photographs for the book.

To Ken and Shirley Davenport, the two best neighbors anyone could ask for, our gratitude for helping fill in some missing pieces in the history of the Davenport farm. Charles Bartlett provided his geographical expertise to aid with picture identification.

Long-time friends Colleen Davenport Taylor and Mike Pierry, Jr. generously provided additional photographs and assistance. The *Virginian-Pilot* kindly allowed us to use old photos that had originally appeared in the *Ledger-Star*, Dad's former employer, and the U.S. Navy gave similar permission for a photo from its files.

To our publisher, Kathy Shearer, our thanks. Kathy believed in this book from the earliest days when Charles Kennedy first suggested a collaboration and brought us together. Her enthusiasm, energy, and keen editorial insights are a part of every page. Kathy's friend and colleague, Larry Richman, offered his erudite editing and organizational suggestions.

And, to all of Dad's readers who wrote kind notes and made thoughtful suggestions on which columns to use, we thank you. Your encouragement has been so important to the success of this project.

In closing we would like to share with you a few lines from a speech Dad once gave:

"One of the old Greek philosophers—Plato, possibly—said that every man before he dies should do three things: Sire a child, plant a tree, and write a book.

"At first glance, these appear wholly unrelated. Not so. For each promises a continuance, a piece of immortality here on earth. A child, a tree, a book. Each, presumably, lives on after we are gone.

"Maybe what Plato was suggesting is that we hedge our bets. If the child turns out to be a ne'er-do-well, or the tree is struck by lightning, the written word will still live forever."

Lisa Kestner Quigley, Pam Kestner-Chappelear, Tim Kestner
June 2006

Foreword

I had the great pleasure of meeting Jack Kestner at his mountaintop retreat. Call it editor's privilege. We have lots of columnists and correspondents who write for the newspaper. Jack was the one I most wanted to meet.

We munched on cheese crackers and sipped iced tea under the pavilion where his daughter was married. His dogs circled the area. The hummingbirds buzzed his feeders. Across the vista he pointed out landmarks invisible to the untrained eye. He noted where he tried to grow gardens—when the grazing deer could be kept at bay. On one visit he gave my wife and me a sack of homegrown potatoes to take home.

Jack was an engaging, gifted storyteller. In person and in written word. His greatest strength was capturing the essence of events the rest of us gloss over. He guided and prodded us to see the things we were otherwise oblivious to or too hurried to duly note. And he did so with an unsurpassed eye for detail and, always, with a sense of humor.

And that is why people from Southwest Virginia—and certainly further afield—treasured him as a rare and precious literary jewel mined from these hills.

His love of nature, Hayters Gap, 'The Great Channels,' of animals—especially mistreated ones—and, of course, his children and grandchildren, was strong. His knowledge of the outdoors captivated his readers and visitors. Women were charmed by his debonair gentility and rugged good looks.

Jack could write tough, determined journalistic pieces that set out to right wrongs and hold the guilty accountable. And he could write touching pieces that showed a heart as large as the blue sky over Clinch Mountain.

On these pages you'll find a collection of his many columns written during his career at the *Bristol Herald Courier.* They range from stories about the difficulty of raising his children—Lisa, Pam, and Tim—after his wife died in 1967, to watching as the Cuban Missile Crisis unfolded. From rescuing an underweight dog, to journeying to Antarctica.

Of living through dreadful snowstorms that left "cups of coffee frozen solid on the kitchen table" and of surviving being shipwrecked "on a deserted island with a beautiful woman."

I did not know it then, but later learned he and my father attended

9

Tennessee High School at the same time. Their pictures appear on the same page of school's the 1940 yearbook. And in later e-mails, he raised the possibility that his great-grandmother was Jane Kaylor—could it be that we were distantly related?

I'm not sure it matters. Because in his own way, Jack invited every reader into his home, his life, and to his mountaintop retreat as if they were family. He ushered us into his world. And what an amazing, entertaining, and thought-provoking world it was.

Steven Kaylor, Editor
Bristol Herald Courier

෪

Other books by Jack Kestner

Police Beat 1959

Fire Tower 1960

Jack Hale Kestner
1921-2005

This book is dedicated to his readers

The old Davenport farmhouse, the Kestners' home from September of 1977 through September of 1978.

Mountainside, on the south slope of Clinch Mountain.

1 ~ Returning to the Mountain

We begin with Dad's return to Clinch Mountain above Hayters Gap in Washington County, Virginia, because this was the vantage point from which he viewed his life and the world. Dad was born in the valley below and spent much of his childhood roaming the woods. Many years and many places would separate him from his beloved mountains, but when a colleague of his suffered a heart attack, he realized it was time to return to his "roots" and take up a simpler lifestyle.

In 1977, he retired early from his job as military reporter for the *Ledger-Star* in Norfolk, Virginia. It was a difficult decision to make since it meant leaving a career he loved and uprooting his children from the only home and way of life we had known. In September of 1977, we left our home in Chesapeake. Pam was 16 and Tim, 15. Lisa, at 19, remained in Norfolk to attend college.

Dad had considered several land purchases for his mountain home but the "Davenport Farm" seemed to be the right fit. Years ago the property was owned by his grandfather, Will Kestner, who sold it to Ran Davenport. When Ran died, the farm passed to his son, Moody Davenport, who deeded it to his children. Dad purchased the approximately 70 acres from Moody's children in 1976. In 1983, he purchased 70 additional acres on the farm's western boundary.

The old farmhouse on the Davenport property—unheated and without electricity—had not been lived in since the late 1950s. Dad believed—and convinced us—the stay would be a short one, four to five months, while our new home further up the mountain was being built. However, construction delays, brought on partly by the weather, resulted in a 13-month stay in the farmhouse during one of the coldest and snowiest winters on record.

During those early years, we often learned the hard way how things were done. But through it all, we grew as individuals and as a family. Time would tell that his decision was not only the right one but one that pulled the Kestner family together.

Using one of his beloved Underwood typewriters, Dad "pounded out" the experiences of those early years in a journal that he later used as a resource for his weekly columns, which he began writing in 1987.

 C3

Life is an Adventure

August 31, 1992

It'll be 15 years tomorrow since I climbed into a U-Haul in front of our home in Chesapeake and drove off with our worldly possessions, bound for a new life on the side of a mountain. In retrospect, I think I was probably nuts.

I had to be—quitting a job I truly enjoyed to take on early retirement; uprooting kids and removing them from schools and friends, trusting that somehow we could make a go of primitive living in an alien environment.

No waving at neighbors across the street or calling them on the phone. There were no neighbors—nor phone, nor television, nor refrigerator, nor any of the other amenities we'd been used to. It was back to the basics.

Earlier in the summer, we'd made several trips to get the old farmhouse ready to move into (no one had lived in it for nearly 20 years). Also, we had to transport odds and ends of construction items for the new house up on the ridge.

Since we were operating on a tight budget, all summer long I'd consulted the weekly *Tidewater Trading Post* looking for bargains in building material. One week, I struck a gold mine. A contractor in neighboring Virginia Beach had gone out of business and was trying to get rid of a panoply of items. Result: every window and screen and door and vanity in this house (with one exception) was bought at less than half price.

My kids, Pam and Tim, left Chesapeake in the Cutlass a day earlier than I did in order to make the first day of school at Patrick Henry. (Lisa was left behind, enrolled in college.) After school the first day, they arrived in time to help with the unloading of the van, and to arrange their rooms.

By dinner time, we were all pretty much exhausted. I don't recall what we had to eat but I do recall where I cooked it—over a campfire in front of that old farmhouse. It was where I continued to cook until cold weather set in. Although an ancient wood burning stove had come with the farmhouse, hot weather made it a little uncomfortable to use.

Anyway, campfire cooking lent a touch of romance to this initial phase of our adventure. Lord knows we needed a touch of something to take our minds off this inconvenience.

There were so many things that we took for granted during our life in suburbia—the only life the kids had ever known. Washing dishes, for instance. At a corner of the front porch, we propped up an old porcelain sink—and bragged about having the only outdoor dishwasher in Washington County.

On rainy days, which fortunately were rare, we cooked over a small butane grill. Then set the dishes out in the rain to wash themselves.

We ate on the porch, too, around an old table. When the dishes were done and twilight fell, we added wood to the fire and sat around it— laughing and talking and telling stories and singing. That was our nightly routine.

Except for occasional visitors, we had no company save ourselves and our dogs, Brette and Duke. Instead of TV, there were only the night sounds of whippoorwills and screech owls and katydids. None of the children had heard katydids before. In the blackness and utter silence of the mountain nights, their chorus was deafening. A blanket of sound.

When Pam returned to the mountain recently on a visit, the rasping of katydids again filled the night air. "You know," she mused, "whenever I hear them I always think of our evenings around the campfire."

So do I. Although it's a sad, autumnal sound, and a prelude to winter, it still evokes pleasant memories.

Yep, it was probably a crazy move to make—but I'm glad we made it. Helen Keller said it best long ago: "Life is an adventure—or it is nothing."

☙

The Road Taken   *June 30, 1997*

A few days ago, I brought up from the old farmhouse a totem of our adventure here on the mountain. It's a four-foot lithograph by landscape artist Harold Shelton. At least, I assume he's a landscape artist. To tell the truth, I don't know one artist from another, but at least this painting is a landscape. It's titled "Yesteryear."

An old barn is centered thereon, its wooden shingles badly in need of repair. The only other signs of human habitation are a couple of weather-beaten sheds. All the rest is simply mountain farm scenery.

There's a farm down near Brumley whose rugged boulders remind me of the ones strewn in the foreground. So does the blue of the mountains in the background. I don't know what area of the country Shelton used as a model but it could have been any one of several around here.

It was Southwest Virginia that I thought about when I first saw it in a Tidewater department store. If memory serves, it was on sale. I made the purchase and took it home and hung it in my bedroom where it would hit me when I got up in the morning.

Why? Well, I'd just bought this mountain farm and had requested early retirement from the Norfolk *Ledger-Star*. Since it was probably the most drastic decision I ever made in my life, I welcomed anything that would reinforce it.

I'm not surprised that I needed a little reinforcement. In retrospect, I can only marvel that I had the guts—or insanity—to go through with it.

Consider: There I was at the peak of a career in military writing, had two children in high school and a third scheduled to enter college in the fall. Taking an early retirement would mean fragmenting my retirement pay.

On the other hand, if I'd stay only ten more years, I'd not only have the satisfaction of utilizing the news sources and skills I'd been slowly developing, my kids would also be through their schooling. This certainly would add to the comfort level of my income. So, what made me engage in the "quit now" insanity?

I'm not sure. One thing was a feeling that I'd probably chicken out if I waited another ten years. If that happened, then my dream of returning to a mountain I'd loved as a child would never be realized.

Also, an incident occurred in the newsroom that probably nudged me down the road. Tom Reilly, the newspaper's political writer, occupied a desk right across from me. For a long while, he'd been marking days off the calendar toward his retirement. All his plans were complete.

However, shortly after arriving in the newsroom one morning, he suffered a massive coronary. Although rushed to the emergency room, he didn't make it. Tom had waited too long to retire.

So, I shrugged off the troubling financial aspects. The children and I had been coming up here camping for many years. They were enthusiastic about making it a permanent move. If I waited another ten years, they wouldn't be a part of the picture; they'd be out on their own.

So, when was the final decision made? Twenty years ago today, June 30, 1977, was my last day as a newspaperman—although I will always view myself as such. Two decades have gone by. That should be long enough to gain a perspective, so, was it a good decision or a bad one? Would I do it all over again, or would I wait?

Difficult questions, for they all involve "the road not taken" and that's a road nobody has ever been able to look down with assurance.

On the other hand, if I limit myself to the knowledge of the road I did take, yes, it was a good move, and, yes, I would do it over again within the same time frame. Fact is, if I'd waited another ten years, I doubt I'd have had the physical strength that was demanded during our first couple of years here.

Another thing about the timing—if we'd waited, I doubt that we'd have had such a happy convergence of assistance as we encountered 20 years ago.

Our builders, for one thing. Allen Rush and Raymon Grace had worked together before and fitted in perfectly on this house. And Lonnie Kidd and D. P. Henderson for all the earth moving.

Even the selection of which way the house would face was a fortuitous thing. Two long-time friends, Frank DeFriece and the late Craig Rockett, had come up for a visit even before the final touches were put on the road. Our talk turned to the house itself.

"I think I'll face it due east so that all our main rooms will get the morning sun," I said.

Frank and Craig demurred. "With a view like that straight down the ridge, you'd be foolish to face it any other way," they insisted.

So, that was the final choice. And a happy one.

And Harold Shelton's lithograph? When we arrived with all our chattel from Chesapeake, we attached it to the wall beside the fireplace in the old farmhouse. Later that winter, we stacked wet firewood beneath it to dry out.

They made up the dream and the reality, juxtaposed.

C（

Deprivation Balloting   *January 25, 1988*

Take a couple of kids in their mid-teens, remove them from the city and electrical gadgets they've known all their lives and what will they miss most? Six weeks after our arrival, I decided to find out. The date was October 11, 1977, recorded in my journal as the first day we had to scrape ice from the windshield of our Blazer.

While we sat around our sawhorse plywood table in the kitchen of that old farmhouse, I handed them a list of 27 electrically-operated items we'd taken for granted in our house in Chesapeake. I asked that they give each item a descending scale number based on how much it had been missed. And I joined in.

Rummaging through some junk a few days ago, I came across the faded pages of that "referendum." Unless I receive proof to the contrary, I plan to claim it as the first deprivation balloting ever held in Washington

17

County, VA.

Our unanimity astonished me. Eight items were named by all three of us to occupy the first six positions. Pam and Tim also astonished me. I thought for sure the television set would be either first or high on their list. Not so. The hot water heater came first with all of us.

For hot water, we'd been depending on a passive solar heater—an old copper water tank set in a glass-topped, foil-lined coffin on the roof above the kitchen. It was hooked up to our gravity-fed water supply. The solar worked great on clear, sunny days, but on cloudy days, and after the autumnal equinox, it was like someone had pulled the plug. "Warm" was the most it got, and frequently we had to strain the definition of warm to get that.

As weeks passed, it got even worse. Tim insisted on a shower before going to school, and one morning vowed there was ice in the tub. I didn't believe him, so I yanked back the shower curtain and shards of ice flew everywhere! I am inclined to credit this Spartan display of cleanliness to the fact he had recently discovered girls.

No. 2 on the ballot was hardly unanimous. Tim listed our stereo, Pam voted for the washer/dryer, and I voted for central heating. I can understand Pam's vote. Doing the laundry meant a 35-mile round trip to a laundromat in Abingdon. A boring wasted evening—so said we all.

Tim and Pam agreed on No. 3. Central heating. But this was before winter set in with zero-range temperatures for days on end when we seemed to do nothing but cut wood. Four Coleman lanterns had been supplying our light, so my vote went for the light bulb. I was getting sick and tired of filling them and pumping them up and carrying them from one room to another. On top of that, fuel was costing a dollar a day—just to get the equivalent of four 100-watt light bulbs!

The light bulb was Tim's choice for No. 4, while Pam picked the electric range/oven. Even after six weeks, we were still cooking on a campfire in front of the house. Romantic, but painfully inconvenient. I voted the refrigerator No. 4.

For position No. 5, television finally got a vote from Tim. Pam went for the refrigerator, while I cast my ballot for the dishwasher. For No. 6 spot, Tim picked the washer/dryer; Pam the light bulb, me the range/ oven.

On December 28, I held a repeat election. Lisa was on Christmas break and I wanted to include her. Also, we'd installed a hot water system—thanks to a neighbor, Ken Davenport, who had loaned us a water jacket for our cook stove—and I was curious about what effect that would have.

Everybody voted central heating as No.1. Everybody, that is, except Tim. Stereo, which had been his No. 2 choice, now rose to first place. I viewed his vote as stubborn intimidation aimed at me. He wanted a battery-operated cassette player.

A third and final vote was held March 8 when Lisa was home for the weekend. She still voted central heating No. 1, but with spring just around the corner, the rest of us named the light bulb.

Thus ended our great deprivation balloting. In retrospect, I can only say that it was much easier to vote on those items than it was to do without them for a year.

CS

Our First Christmas *December 25, 2000*

Even if Christmas is celebrated three days early, as ours was this year, its features remain the same—the sumptuous meal, the exchange of gifts, and reminiscing about Christmases past. We celebrated ours early so everyone could make it back to their respective homes in time for their own family celebrations.

It was our 23rd here on the mountain, and contrasted sharply with our first one, which was marked by frugality. We had overlooked several things in the construction budget for our new house, so money was scarce back then.

Lisa, who was attending Old Dominion University, didn't leave Norfolk until Christmas Eve. Pam and I picked her up that evening at the bus terminal in Glade Spring. The first thing she said was, "Never again do I ride the bus!" The trip had taken over 12 hours.

We piled into the Blazer and went on to Bristol to do last minute shopping. Pam and I dropped Lisa at the mall while we searched for a nearby laundromat to do the weekly wash.

Although we'd brought an electric generator to the mountain, we discovered it didn't have enough power to operate a full cycle of our washing machine. As a result, we began doing laundry when we went shopping.

Returning to the mountain, we found Tim sound asleep on the sofa. But a beautiful cedar had been erected in a corner of the living room. When we woke him up and asked where he'd found it, he said, "A deer led me to it."

We cleared the kitchen table and each of us took turns wrapping family presents by the light of a Coleman lantern.

That finished, we decorated the tree. Notably absent were strings of lights, but it looked just fine anyway. And looked even better when presents were scattered beneath it—including ones for Duke, our first Doberman, and Brette, Lisa's collie-shepherd.

Strange, I can't recall a thing about Christmas Day except that the weather was rather mild. It was a fraudulent indicator, for this would be the last clump of mild days before March. Maybe it's a good thing we didn't know what that winter had in store for us. If we had, there might well have been rebellion among the troops.

ﾒ

The Winter of '77 *February 13, 1995*

Heigh-ho, winter at last! Finally the white stuff decided to stick around for a while. And the thermometer stopped lying about the season. But who cares if winter took its time arriving? And the delightful part is that spring arrives next month. Whee! A limited amount of misery.

I'm only sorry we couldn't have swapped winters back in '77 when we moved into that drafty old farmhouse. That year we began sleeping under blankets in September, and discarded them only for warmer sleeping bags on cots in front of the fireplace. And we danced to that tune until March.

Snows—the first big one came during Thanksgiving weekend. Lisa had come visiting during a college break at Old Dominion University and almost didn't make it back off the mountain. There was always snow on the ground, at least on our north slopes, even when it melted off the roads.

Washington County probably set a record for school closures that year. I called Pam in Roanoke to see if she could remember the number of days she and Tim missed at Patrick Henry.

"I seem to remember that in January we only attended three days," she said. "February was better but not by an awful lot."

A lot of short days and long winter evenings. No electricity, no telephone. We did have a battery-powered radio but, without television, the children began reading in earnest—by the light of Coleman lanterns. One of our regular routines was filling and pumping up those lanterns before darkness fell.

We invariably began each day with sourdough buckwheat cakes and fried country ham. Pam was horrified when she put on 15 pounds. But

20

she now insists that not all of it was fat.

"Remember, I had to gather firewood with you guys," she pointed out. "Some of that 15 pounds was muscle."

Firewood, indeed, was a continuing problem. We stacked it in a downstairs bedroom and along one wall of the living room so we wouldn't have to open the outside door and let in blasts of cold air when we carried it in. Somehow, we never managed to accumulate more than a few days worth of wood—and not always that much. I recall the time we were out in a howling blizzard cutting up an old locust snag above the pond.

There were five bedrooms in that old farmhouse but we never slept in them that winter. We lived in the living room with its efficient fieldstone fireplace. And the kitchen.

Our kitchen table was a sheet of plywood resting on sawhorses. The kids did their homework on it, we ate off it, sharpened chainsaws on it, entertained visitors around it, and wrote letters on it—to friends back in Norfolk regaling them with the delights of primitive living.

There were days and nights on end when the thermometer hovered close to zero. Records were broken at Tri-Cities Airport and most certainly at that old farmhouse.

When we'd arrived at the end of summer, our refrigeration consisted of two big Igloo coolers out on the front porch. Every couple of days, we had to leave the mountain and bring in bags of crushed ice for our milk and butter and meats and fresh vegetables.

After a few weeks, ice became unnecessary. In fact, a little later, for the sake of convenience, we began placing perishables in one of our bedrooms. It was plenty cold enough.

Eventually, the situation reversed itself. Stuff started freezing in the bedroom, so we began placing it in cabinets under the sink. And even that didn't always work. If we let the fire in the kitchen stove go out, we'd get up the next morning and find cups of coffee frozen solid on the kitchen table. Ah, yes, those were the days—and nights.

Our water system froze 22 times, the last time on Easter weekend. I remember the date for the Norfolk *Ledger-Star* flew in a reporter and photographer to do a story on "back-to-the-landers."

William Ruehlmann, the reporter, got up during the night and went into the kitchen to get a glass of water. He must have been half asleep, for when he filled his glass he cut off the water—which we always left running to keep from freezing. Bill was embarrassed the next morning when we had no water to wash up with. But it was no big deal, for the pipes thawed out before noon.

We could afford to let water run since it didn't cost anything, being piped in from a branch that fed the pond. Trouble was, the polyethylene line lay on top of the ground. We had no choice but to let it run.

I recall one night I was taking a shower before bed, had soaped up, and, whiff! No water. Had to towel off, dress, and rush up to the intake. Too late. As I recall, it was several days before it thawed out.

In the meantime, the bathroom was out of service and we had to use the barn. One night as Pam went out the door, flashlight in hand, I heard her mutter, "I think I'd rather explode than keep on using that barn!"

We derived one minor benefit from the frozen intake pipe. When it began to thaw, it produced some of the most beautiful ice cubes you could imagine—bushels of them, cylindrical and crystal-clear. They tinkled merrily in my Bacardi and tonic.

The pond froze over during the final days of December and didn't thaw until March, which gives a pretty good idea of how much continuous cold we had. I recall a weekend when Lisa came visiting with friends we all had a ball sledding and skating on that pond in the moonlight.

A rough winter, yes, but it did have its plus side. Long evenings together in front of the crackling living room fire, or around the kitchen table, reading by the light of a hissing Coleman lantern.

If I had to pick a time in our lives when we truly became a family, that would be it.

ଔ

Planning the New House   *October 17, 1988*

When we first began drawing lines with a ruler on a yellow legal pad—lines that would eventually become a house—we really didn't know what we were doing. We only knew what we wanted to live in. As a result, when I laid the pad in front of Allen Rush a few months before we moved to the mountain, he had his work cut out for him.

"Well," he would say, sucking on his pipe, "this feature looks good on paper, but you just can't build it that way. It's not structurally sound." Then he'd point his pipe stem at another feature and say, "Now, this is a good idea; this will work out just fine."

And it did. And so did other gentle suggestions. He'd say, "Adding a sundeck over the porch roof will let you use natural long railings," or, "Offsetting that picture window will break up that boxy look."

It all worked out. Which was hardly surprising, since he'd spent his adult life building houses. I think Allen was secretly amused at our ground

22

rule of "no paint, no plaster." We insisted on fieldstone gathered from the farm and whatever natural wood was available.

Fortunately, an old tobacco barn had come with the farm. Its ancient adz-hewn logs of chestnut and oak would make an ideal facing for the ground floor.

The ground floor itself represented a radical departure from our plans. It was to have been our basement—dug, as it was, into the ridge. Instead, we decided it would be a shame to waste this fine natural insulation. A wise decision, for I've seen frost on the ground outside and 60 degrees inside—without heat.

The whole idea of the house reflected one basic premise: We wanted to live in the woods, but we wanted the comforts and conveniences of the city. Having our cake and eating it, too. Well, why not?

Another thing: Helping to build a house you're going to live in is an enormously satisfying experience. At least, it proved that way to me and the kids. From the fields and woods, we gathered good, honest stone for our master stonemason, Raymon Grace. And we served as Allen's carpenter's helpers—such as we were.

The end product isn't a showpiece, for it wasn't intended to be one. But liveable? I doubt I could ever live so contentedly anywhere else. Maybe because our own touches are there. Living in that old farmhouse while the new house was being built gave us ideas about what we wanted—and didn't want.

Although wood would also be used for heating in the new house, we learned the hard way how much heat is lost carrying it in—to say nothing of freezing our behinds off in the process. So we came up with an innovation—a "cold lock" wood chamber. Since we had an attached woodshed, and since our big fireplace boiler was on the ground floor below it, we devised a cellar door arrangement above a standby wood chamber—with access directly into the living/dining room. It holds enough wood to last a couple of days.

Another idea is probably my favorite in the whole house—an octagonal dining table, eight feet across, with a fountain in its center. It was an idea that evolved not only from a desire to produce an effect, but to fill vacuum. Since our living/dining room measured 24x26, we needed something to take up the space. What with the cost of the house, we weren't going to have money for new furniture.

Six months before we moved, Tim and I took a night course in carpentry—with the sole objective of building that table. It proved kinda complicated. Eight segments had to be cut and glued, then their 16 ends cut to a precise 22 1/2 degrees, then these fitted and glued into two transportable sections.

After we moved in, we cut a 10-inch poplar and used segments for legs. A good friend voluntarily had the critical portion made. This was a circular container made from boiler plate for the fountain, surrounded by an eight-inch planter. The outside circumference measures 12 1/2 feet.

A fall chore I always look forward to is going out and digging natural plants for that planter—stuff that will stay green all winter. Running ground cedar, galax, trailing arbutus, teaberry, rattlesnake plantain, Pipsissewa, ebony spleenwort. This year I even found a pair of waxy white Indian pipes, fairly rare around here.

What a fine table it is to hold a party around—the fountain splashing over rocks in the center, green plants arching above our plates. Even when snow is banked deep outside, it's like sitting by a mountain brook on a day in May.

ଔ

Dining room table at Mountainside.

Dowsing

A fine spring of water came with the old farmhouse on this farm. But it was located nearly half a mile below the spot on which we'd decided to build our house—on a high ridge that provided a view from the mountain. Before starting construction, we felt we should determine whether a well was feasible.

We mentioned this one day to Velty Davenport, who'd helped get the place ready for us to move in. Velty said one of his sons had the gift of dowsing. If we wanted him to come up and see if there was an underground water supply close by, he felt sure Wayne would oblige. We said we'd be delighted.

Wayne arrived one morning, cut a peach fork from a tree near the old farmhouse, and proceeded on up to our building site. There, he grasped a branch of the fork with each of his hands, knuckles turned inward, and began walking slowly across the ridge. The tip of the fork pointed straight ahead and level with the ground.

I walked along with him, intensely interested. It was the first dowsing I'd ever witnessed. I'd read a bit about it. Supposedly reliable people believed it. Still, the whole thing smacked a bit of mumbo jumbo.

As Wayne walked, I saw the tip of the fork begin to dip. His knuckles whitened as it went down, down—and finally pointed to the ground at his feet.

"Good water," he said. "Not near the surface, but there's plenty." Back and forth across the ridge he went, moving upward with each pass. And each time, as he drew near the spine of the ridge, the tip would bend increasingly until it pointed to the ground.

"You've got an underground stream coming in right at your northwest corner." Wayne said, after he had finished his sweeps. "It falls away from the ridge to the east, there, before it gets to your house."

That was good news. Or was it? Not for an instant did I question Wayne's sincerity. Nor, for that matter, the evidence of my own eyes. Still, sinking a well would cost at least a thousand bucks, maybe twice that. Should I invest such a sum on the say-so of a tree limb?

I decided to wait. Days passed. Then I heard of another dowser, Garland Snodgrass, who lived on the North Fork of the Holston. I drove up to see him. Without telling him about Wayne Davenport, I explained that we wanted to be sure of an adequate water supply before starting our house. We'd heard he was a good dowser. Would he take a whack at it? He said he would, and graciously returned to the mountain with me.

Garland cut a dogwood fork, not peach, but otherwise his technique was identical to Wayne's. And so were his results. He discovered the same underground stream entering our property at the same northwest corner, and traced it down the ridge until it dropped off to the east.

I was flabbergasted. The mathematical probability of this occurring by chance was simply astronomical. Confident that I needn't wait any longer, I called a well-driller in Chilhowie before returning to Tidewater (where I still had my house to sell before I could move).

The well-driller wasn't so confident. After looking over the site, he passed word that he wanted me there when he started drilling. He felt it highly unlikely that water could be found at any reasonable depth on that high ridge. He needed to know when to stop drilling. I passed word to keep drilling until he struck water.

So he started after lunch one day. In four hours, at a depth of 141 feet, he struck a vein of water bringing in an estimated 15 gallons per minute. Pressure caused it to rise 90 feet in the well. This was at the height of a severe drought when many area wells were going dry.

Since then, I've watched a couple of TV programs on the subject. One, filmed in England, used encephalographic equipment to show a switch from beta waves to alpha waves in the brain of the dowser while he worked.

Last year, there was a segment on ABC's "20/20" devoted to dowsing. At the end of the program, the young producer gave a summary. He said that while there were indications that dowsing occasionally worked, the weight of the scientific community was against it.

For days afterward, every time I heard my water pump come on I would recall that statement—and smile.

CB

The Beavers' Pond — *November 7, 1988*

One of the things we looked forward to in our move to the mountain was having our own swimming pond. Early on, we'd picked the spot—a marsh area with hills on three sides fed by a small branch and a wet-weather spring.

Fortunately, one of the hills contained a good grade of clay— essential for the core of the dam. When the rising water approached swimming depth, we built a diving platform against the side of the dam. Plus a raft. The latter turned into quite a project.

Almost a Blazer load of salt-treated lumber went into that thing. We built cages at each corner to house 55-gallon drums that would raise the raft floor to diving level. And added a ladder for water access. With a lot of grunting and heaving, we launched it and christened it the USS *Landlocked.*

We figured we now had a swimming pond with the fanciest equipment to be found anywhere on Clinch Mountain. The fact it was the only one on the mountain didn't detract from our claim.

Our first swim brought a shock. It was the coldest water I'd swum in since Camp Cherokee, or maybe Brumley Cove. Another shock came later. When the branch and wet-weather spring dried up, the pond's water turned from a lovely ice-green to mud hole-brown. Algae formed.

By the time the weather had warmed up enough to make the pond inviting, its waters weren't. Oh, we swam in it a few times. But before long, it simply became our favorite spot for observing wildlife. Mallards would drop in occasionally on their way south. One summer, a pair of wood ducks nested in a dead white oak on its border. Deer seemed to like the place.

Then, wholly uninvited, the beavers arrived. From whence, or why, we still don't know. Anyway, they provided a new dimension to our wildlife observations. Before long, we began referring to it as "the beavers' pond."

This year brought a dramatic change. The water level dropped steadily all summer—from the drought, I reasonably concluded. It finally reached the point where the beavers had to abandon their original lodge against the dam and move out into the pond to build subsidiary ones.

Then came the rains of September, and I rejoiced for the beavers' sake. Prematurely, it turned out. For the pond continued to shrink. Growing suspicious, I fought my way through thickets of bullbriars and honeysuckle and Spanish needles below the dam to see if a "worst case scenario" had occurred. It had.

About 50 feet below the rim of the dam, a spring was emerging. Something less than a gallon a minute, I estimated. Not much, but when it continued for 24 hours a day, week after week, the outcome was inevitable.

You know, I spent the better part of two afternoons with a mattock and shovel down there, sweating over rock piles and honeysuckle tangles, trying to find the source of the leak. And I still haven't found it.

Ironically, my digging came simultaneously with a massive effort by the two most powerful nations on earth to free two grey whales trapped in the ice off Point Barrow. There's a good chance that those whales by now are blubber in the hold of some Japanese fishing boat—and most certainly those beavers are going to continue cutting down my apple trees. Yet, no regrets on either side.

A few days ago, when I cranked up my Subaru with the heater turned on, smoke began billowing out of the vents and beneath the dashboard. I turned off the key and called Bobby Ratliff, my Abingdon mechanic. Bobby said I'd better bring it in, it sounded like a meltdown of the heater core. So I took it in and left it. When I returned to pick it up, Bobby laughed and pointed to a box half-full of debris. Field mice had packed the housing with nesting material, completely blocking the fan.

Maybe I should have suspected mice. Some time ago, I was breezing along Interstate 81 on my way to Bristol when I felt something on my ankle. I looked down and saw a large blacksnake slithering down from the dashboard. Obviously, he knew where to look for mice. I stopped and put him in the back, and released him when I returned to the farm.

Animals do their thing. Man does his. The interplay of their relationship is a very real aspect of the adventure we call Life.

CȜ

Apache   *August 21, 2000*

As compensation for being removed from the conveniences of city life to a remote electricity-less mountain farm, I'd promised Pam two things, a horse and a porch swing. It took me a while to get around to the swing but the horse came that first year.

Tim mentioned one day that one of his Patrick Henry chums had a young gelding for sale. Since I didn't know anything about horses, I contacted D. P. Henderson at Meadowview to see if he would look him over.

D. P., who had done all our backhoe work here on the farm, was a long-time horse fancier. He said he'd not only examine him but would take his truck along and haul him back to the mountain in case we decided to make the purchase.

Apache turned out to be a handsome animal. A pinto, or "paint," I believe they're called. He had only one noticeable physical defect, a cast in one eye that gave him a singularly baleful expression. Someone subsequently told us that Native Americans believed such a horse was possessed. I scoffed at the idea, but later I wasn't so sure.

Apache began to exhibit the forcefulness of his personality on his way to the mountain. Every time we'd pass another horse in a field, he'd neigh loudly like he was saying, "Hey, look at me, man, I'm movin', I'm movin'!"

We stabled him in the barn overnight, and early the next day went out to show some visitors our new acquisition. Duke, our first Doberman, accompanied us.

We gave Apache a few forkfuls of hay and he began munching on it. Duke stared at him a minute, then went over, took a mouthful of hay himself and began chewing. I kid you not.

Duke apparently viewed Apache (the first horse he'd ever seen) as an overly large dog, and he'd just be darned if any favoritism was going to be shown at feeding time. That marked the beginning of a strained relationship.

One day down at the pond, I witnessed a challenge between the two. It amounted to, Who is going to be the Alpha "dog" here on the mountain? Duke was standing in the road nearby, while Apache was up the road near a slight rise. My attention was drawn by the thunder of hoofs. I looked up in time to see Apache galloping straight for Duke.

Duke turned and stared at him but didn't move a muscle. At the last possible moment, Apache veered around him. Duke stared after him, then turned and walked away with great dignity.

The only time they seemed to be in agreement was on the subject of play. We were inside the old farmhouse one night when we heard a commotion outside—a rumbling, metallic noise, then Duke barking followed by the sound of hoof beats and Apache whinnying.

We rushed to the door and looked out. There, in the drenching moonlight, was quite a sight. Apache had apparently pushed over our rain barrel and nudged it until it started rolling down hill. He was racing along one side, Duke on the other. They were having a ball.

If Duke viewed Apache as a large dog, Apache obviously shared that view. He would stand on the front porch of the old farmhouse and stare in the window at the humans and dogs inside. Hey, those dogs are permitted inside, why not me?

Apache was great at entertaining himself. He would find an empty box, grip it with his teeth, stand on his hind legs and toss it into the air. I've never heard of a horse acting like that.

Apache seemed to have some sort of weird interest in Lisa. She'd come home from college on her Easter break, Pam and Tim were in school, and I'd taken the Blazer to Bristol on business. It was a balmy day so she decided to take a sun bath on the hood of our Cutlass.

She related later that she had a feeling someone was watching her. She opened her eyes—and found Apache's head directly above her. He made her feel so uncomfortable that, when he wouldn't shoo away, she dashed inside the house. She said Apache followed her onto the porch and tried to push the door open.

When it came time for her to meet the school bus at the foot of the mountain, Apache was grazing far enough away for her to jump into the car and head down the mountain. Apache followed at a gallop.

When she picked up Pam and Tim, she excitedly related her story. They scoffed—until they met Apache coming down the mountain road. They decided that Tim should take the Cutlass, return to the house, get a bag of carrots and lure him inside the gate.

"Lisa and I began walking up the road with Apache following right behind Lisa," Pam related later. "I could see her out of the corner of my eye. Suddenly, I saw both her feet leave the ground and heard her scream."

Pam turned in time to see Apache lift Lisa by her shoulder and toss her into a roadside ditch. Needless to say, they broke for the farmhouse where they barricaded themselves. I found some rather excited children on my return.

Even if Apache had been a good riding animal, which he wasn't (he never got enthusiastic about any project he didn't originate himself), the incident with Lisa made all three kids leery of him.

So, not long after we moved into our new house up on the ridge, we sold him. I've often wondered if he entertained his next family as thoroughly as he entertained us.

CB

Apache and the view through Hayters Gap.

A Few Failures *March 13, 1995*

Looking back over our "back to the land" adventure we planned nearly two decades ago, it's sometimes a little hard deciding whether it's been a success or a failure. Certainly, there have been failures.

I'm reminded of one every time I look at the view stretching out below. There's a green blob smack dab in the middle of it that I'd just as soon forget. The green blob is a patch of overgrown pine trees we planted some 15 years ago. Today, it stands as a living monument to the folly of entering an unknown enterprise.

When Tim and I got into the Christmas tree business we thought it consisted of sticking seedlings into the ground, then waiting seven or eight years—at which time we'd sell them for lots of moola.

It didn't quite work out that way. There was the little matter of keeping weeds mowed, and giving each tree an annual shaping with a big chef's knife. Just thinking about that shaping makes my right arm sore.

Finally, when the trees did reach maturity, came the chore of marketing—finding a spot to open a stand, then staying there day after day, evening after evening. Even when we shifted to selling them on the stump, one of us had to be here.

And the trees kept growing. So, who's interested in a 14-foot-tall Christmas tree, even for free? Head Start takes one every year for the Hayters Gap school, and some go to churches. But before long, only St. Patrick's Cathedral will be able to accommodate them.

One day, I sat down and estimated the time and money and labor we'd sunk into that project and came to the regretful conclusion that if we'd let those fields lie fallow we probably could have cleared just as much money selling wild thistles.

As far as our original plans were concerned, the biggest dead loss occurred right here in this house. When we were designing the house (my previous architectural experience was limited to building a work room on the corner of our back porch), a decision had to be made regarding the type of heating—oil, gas, electric, or wood.

Since we had acres of trees to run up the chimney, that wasn't a hard decision. The real puzzler was how best to use wood to heat a two-story house with four bedrooms. I couldn't find a commercial product that would do, so I designed one.

Using a combination of hubris and ignorance, I came up with an open metal fireplace with a wraparound water reservoir. I had no idea what its size should be, so I decided to err on the large side. Boy, did I!

31

The end product, welded in Norfolk by Zeke Davenport, was so big you could stand up inside it—and so heavy that Terry Hagy had to bring one of his wreckers from Meadowview to position it on the slab. But it worked beautifully. And inexpensively. Admittedly, it gobbled up an inordinate amount of wood, but it kept the house cozily warm for around $25 a year—the cost of chainsaw gas and upkeep.

Then one winter night the sundeck door blew open during a blizzard. Most of the upstairs baseboard pipes froze and burst. Since replacing them would mean tearing out large sections of downstairs ceilings, we opted instead for a small airtight stove in the living room. My masterpiece is now welded shut.

Yep, there've been failures. But I think maybe our main objective can be classed as a success. At least, according to Christopher Morley's definition:

"There is only one success—to be able to spend your life in your own way, and not to give others absurd maddening claims upon it."

Jack, Pam, Lisa, Tim and Duke gather at Christmas in 1984.

An aging Pocket Book I uncovered recently on one of my dusty shelves—no spine, its pages loose between crumbling covers—falls into the category of an old friend.

I first came across <u>We Took to the Woods</u> by Louise Dickinson Rich in 1944 in the parlor of the nurses' quarters at Goleta Marine Air Station near Santa Barbara. While waiting for my date to arrive, I read enough to decide to get a copy of my own.

Today, every time I re-read it, as I've just finished doing, I have to wonder if Joan's tardiness on that long-ago evening didn't result in a profound change in my life. Seemingly insignificant events have a way of doing that.

The author of <u>We Took to the Woods </u>has reason to know this better than most, for that's how she came to write the book. One summer in the '30s, Louise Dickinson, with her sister and several other young people, took a canoe trip among the Rangeley Lakes in the rugged northwest corner of Maine.

During a portage, they passed a man chopping wood. He was standing in the yard of the only dwelling they'd seen in several days, so they stopped to chat. It was a fateful encounter. The man, Ralph Rich, began writing to school marm Dickinson as soon as she returned to civilization. Within six months, they were married and had returned to Forest Lodge to live.

Her book is the story of their life there. For chapter headings, she uses questions most frequently asked by the friends she left behind— "Don't You Ever Get Bored?", "What Do You Do With All Your Spare Time?", "Do You Get Out Very Often?", and so on.

I suppose the same questions are asked of everyone who lives back of beyond. I get them myself, even though Clinch Mountain is hardly the Maine woods.

When I re-read the book, I had to ask myself if it hadn't played a subconscious role in prompting our move here over 19 years ago. Or was it the time I spent in Thoreau's <u>Walden</u>? Or neither?

I dunno. The cause and effect relationships in our journey through life can only be guessed at, although some are more clear cut than others. The fact I wanted to be a writer from mid-teen-hood onward can be traced, I'm convinced, to my mother reading aloud to my brother and me night after night for years.

Although a relative of the poet Emily Dickinson, Louise Dickinson

33

Rich didn't try her hand at writing until she took to the woods, and even then it was largely by accident. Just for the fun of it, she entered a story contest. She wrote about Maine guides. Her husband was one, so the material was handy. The story turned out better than she'd expected so she decided to submit it for commercial publication.

To her surprise, *Saturday Evening Post* snapped it up, and subsequently bought other stories. This supplied the answer to another frequently asked question, "How Do You Make A Living?"

I live today in a fairly snug house with modern conveniences, but our first winter on the mountain in an electricity-less old farmhouse found resonance in Mrs. Rich's book.

"In civilization, we try to combat winter," she wrote. "We try to modify it so that we can continue to live the same sort of life that we live in summer . . . We heat every enclosed space and then, inadequately clad, dash quickly from one little pocket of hot air to another."

But in the wilds of Maine (and even here on the mountain during that first winter), "Outdoors is just another, bigger, colder room. When we get up in the morning we dress with the idea that we'll be using this other room all day."

Every reader probably discovers authors who write of experiences that they themselves have had. I was amazed at the number I found in this book, even in little things.

For example, I thought I was probably the only fool in the world who, as a youth, memorized poetry and then repeated it to himself during long walks. Not so. Mrs. Rich did it, even using one of the poems in my repertoire—Swinburne's "Garden of Proserpine." Weird.

We also shared a traumatic event that happened in the same way. Each of us lost our mates from sudden, massive brain hemorrhages that came without warning.

The final question Mrs. Rich tackles is, "Is it Worth-while?" The chapter containing her reply follows Thoreau's "Where I Lived, What I Lived For." Certainly, it spells out eloquently what the choice of living remotely in the Maine woods, or by Walden Pond, or on the side of a mountain, can bring:

"We thought we came here because we liked the woods, because we wanted to find a simple, leisurely way of life. Now, looking back, I think that we were unconsciously seeking to find a lost sense of our own identity.

"Here, I dare to be myself. I don't see why it should ever again be important to me what I wear . . . I don't see why I should ever care again what people think of me.

"All ordinary people are trying to find the same things. They all want to be left alone to conduct their own private search for a personal peace, a reasonable security, a little love, a chance to attain happiness through achievement. It isn't much to want, but I never came anywhere near to getting most of those things until we took to the woods."

Mountainside in 1995. The family built the pavilion on the left for outdoor entertaining and as a place from which to enjoy viewing nature and the changing seasons. Jack hosted his Tennessee High School class reunion here and hung a plaque which reads: "Dedicated to class of 1939."

Hayters Gap about 1910. Jack's grandfather Will Kestner owned the store to the left of the Union Church and lived in the house at the far left. His grandfather Newt Sisk owned the store to the right, and lived in the house beyond it with the white fence. The competition between the two men settled down when Will's son Denton married Newt's daughter Pearl. The old Hayters Gap School is up on the hill above the Sisk farm. A panoramic version of this picture hung over Jack's kitchen table.

2 ~ Family History

At times Dad believed it was best to keep the door closed on the family closet. But at other times he would peer inside with great curiosity, pleasure, and pride.

His story can be traced back to the early days of Hayters Gap and the surrounding area. His mother's ancestors, the Sisks, immigrated to America from Ireland in the 1750s. A decade later, the Kestners arrived from Germany. Both families migrated to far Southwest Virginia, eventually settling in and around Hayters Gap on the south side of Clinch Mountain.

Dad's father, Denton Hale Kestner, was born in the Gap on April 19, 1885. Just yards away, his mother, Pearl Sisk, was born on September 12, 1887. Pearl was the oldest of four daughters; Denton, the oldest of six sons. Their parents eventually opened competing general stores in the tiny community.

Growing up together, Pearl and Denton became close friends, and the friendship developed into courtship and marriage. They had been married over 40 years when Denton died in the early '60s. They had two sons, Dad, born in 1921, and Bill, born in 1923.

The family's story was not unlike many others of that time and place— one of hard work and struggle, of close family ties and simple joys.

The Family Closet November 16, 1987

On a recent visit to the mountain, my daughter Pam, who works for the Council of Community Services in Roanoke while pursuing graduate work at Radford, was asking a bunch of questions on our family background—the age at which her mother and I got married, the ages of her grandparents when they were married, etc. When I asked her what this was all about, she said it was a "genogram" for one of her graduate courses.

"A genogram is a tool used in family therapy," she explained. "There are certain patterns that families get into, living patterns, and if a family counselor can establish these, sometimes they'll reveal the root of weaknesses and problems that travel from generation to generation."

Okay, Pam, I'll buy that. Still, this poking around in family closets can be dangerous. Like your great-great-grandfather on my mother's side, Timothy Sisk. Timothy, according to the written recollection of his grandniece, Carrie Matthews (who died last year in Galax at age 99), was among the early settlers of this area—born around 1765, before Washington County was a county.

He was a salt trader. He'd spend the winter at his log cabin on the North Fork of the Holston building flat-bottomed scows, then pole them upriver to Saltville where he'd fill them with salt and await the annual spring flood. When the water reached its proper stage, he'd set out on a long, perilous voyage down the Holston to the Tennessee, then down the Tennessee to Knoxville—a major frontier outpost in those days of the late 1700s and early 1800s.

In Knoxville, he'd sell his salt and scows, then walk home. There were no roads to speak of, so he'd follow the riverbank trails. This was where most of the people lived, and, in the absence of Holiday Inns, he'd spend the night with any hospitable family offering accommodations at nightfall.

This was Timothy's livelihood. This was his annual "cash crop" that, in later generations, would be replaced by burley tobacco. There were obvious hazards. Not only on the plunging trip downriver, but also returning afoot packing the cash proceeds from several months' work.

Since he had no timetable, his family wasn't too concerned when he was late returning one spring. But when spring stretched into summer, the dread grew that he wasn't coming back. With autumn, that dread became a certainty.

Timothy had left behind two sons, Ancil and Timothy (the latter lies buried some four miles west of where I now sit writing). When the younger

Timothy grew into young manhood, he followed in his father's footsteps—although probably not with his mother's blessings. He, too, went down the river and sold his salt and scows at Knoxville. He, too, followed the river trails back, spending nights at hospitable cabins.

At one such cabin, he introduced himself and was welcomed. In fact, their hospitality was overwhelming. The man of the house in particular kept insisting that he stay another night—then another, and another.

Finally, the young man declared that he must leave, that his mother would be worried since his own father had failed to return from just such a trip. Whereupon, the man of the house clutched him to his bosom and tearfully confessed:

"I am your father!"

The way Cousin Carrie told it, the elder Timothy had picked the wrong family to stay with—wrong, in that one of its members was a beautiful young girl. He'd stayed one night, then another, then another—and lost his heart. He forgot about his family back on the North Fork, married the girl, and started another family.

Genograms. Yes, Pam. I suppose there are family patterns. But I'm not sure I want you to trace your father's weakness to some river boatman of long, long ago.

❧

Boundary Line   April 20, 1998

When my grandfather Will Kestner surveyed the eastern end of the Washington/Russell boundary line back in 1924, he kept records in a set of four field books. I came across them several years ago but only gave them a casual perusal before re-storing them. However, when I came across them again recently, I sat down for a closer look.

Well, sir, the more I read, the more puzzled I became. Those notes raised all sorts of unanswered questions. For instance, why did a judge in each county order that the survey be conducted? And why was the line considered so important that the two counties established a joint commission, members from which accompanied the survey party along each step of its route?

Granddad states these things as facts without bothering to tell how they came about. In Book No.1, dated Monday March 5, 1924, he wrote:

"Met the full commission at the summit of the mountain west of Little Moccasin Gap. All eat dinner in the edge of the state highway, and begun the survey at about 1 p.m."

Washington County members of the commission were listed as Judge F. B. Hutton, W. J. Johnson and Prof. J. S. Miller from Emory & Henry College. Russell County members were C. T. Smith, W. Gose Gray and C. C. Bundy.

"All remained on the work until 4 p.m.," Granddad wrote, "then Hutton, Miller, Gray and Bundy went home, leaving Johnson, Smith, Kestner and their helpers to continue the work as directed by the judges of both counties."

There were still a dozen left. In addition to the two commissioners, Granddad had five lads in his surveying crew, plus another five in what he called the "tent crew."

Among the surveying crew was Leslie, youngest of his six sons, who was listed as front chainman. Rear chainman was Ben Roberson. There were also two "axemen," Arthur Grace and Robert Hite, whose unenviable job it was to hack a way through that mostly virgin forest. The fifth man was Pickett Johnson, father of Abingdon attorney and Virginia Delegate Joe Johnson. Granddad always sketched a little flag by Pickett's name when he entered it in his notes, so I must assume he was a "flagman."

I called Joe to see if he knew what the position entailed. He said he did recall his father reminiscing about that surveying adventure when he was a young man, but didn't recollect him mentioning what his job was. We agreed that most likely he held a forward post. Granddad would point out the direction of his next transit shot, then Pickett would go ahead with a cloth on the end of a stick and wave the axemen into proper alignment as they hacked their way toward him.

The five-man "tent crew" consisted of Wick Hite (the "foreman and cook"), Irvin Johnson, Garland Counts, R. C. Patrick and Graham Scyphers. Rather than call them the tent crew they should have been called pack horses. Not only did they have to cart a large tent, cooking utensils, and supplies from one camp site to the next, they also had to carry the stone "monuments" that were set at frequent intervals to mark the boundary.

A total of 213 of these were set along the 12-mile section of boundary between the starting point above Little Moccasin Gap and the gap in the mountain (properly called "Hayters Gap") where Route 80 crosses today. It's a pity that Granddad didn't keep two sets of notes, one for the official survey, the other as a diary to record their daily adventures. How did these mostly young men react to being out alone in what, at that time, was truly rugged country?

I also have to wonder what Granddad would have thought if he'd known one of his grandsons would one day be living a couple of miles below his survey line, and writing about it. He'd probably say, "Can't you think of a better way to waste your time?"

The survey took its first break, a three-day weekend, on Friday, May 16. Granddad made an entry, "Crew all went home Friday night except Calvin Fields and Stanley Fields, who were left with tent."

The next break came May 24 when Russell County commissioner C. T. Smith had to leave "to gather up wool for manufacturers, for which he is agent. Whole crew then disbanded and went to their respective homes, rejoicing over the anticipated rest spell until about the middle of June."

But they didn't work long when they returned. Granddad's terse note states, "Reason for quitting the work—commissioners could not agree on location of line."

Which brings us back to the original vexing question: What was so all-fired important about this boundary line? Sure, income from taxes naturally comes to mind, but with mountain land selling for less than $5 an acre in those days, such income couldn't have been very impressive.

The Stuart family of Elk Garden owned the bulk of the land on both sides of the mountain, so I called Abingdon attorney Rogers Stuart to see if he'd heard any stories about why this survey had been ordered to take place under such close supervision. He agreed that the question was intriguing, but he hadn't heard a thing.

So, it looks like once again I'll have to rely on my readers to satisfy my curiosity. If any old-timer out there has heard a story that might shed light on the subject, please let me know.

℘

Two Country Stores   *January 18, 1988*

Hanging on the wall of my kitchen is an enlarged photo of Hayters Gap, Virginia, the little community clustered in the valley below this mountain farm. The photo shows it as it looked around 1910. Surprisingly, there is much more cleared land and many more buildings than you find there today.

Prominent in the photos are two large general stores, sitting almost side by side. Two big stores to serve such a small community? How come?

The one across the road from the church was built by one of my grandfathers. He had clerked in a store near his birthplace at Holston, 12 miles to the west, before immigrating to Hayters Gap in the late 1870s. It was a wise move. Up until then, the nearest store for area residents had

41

been Meadowview—nine horse-and-buggy miles to the south. The store prospered. So much so that Will Kestner was able to hire a clerk, a young man of his own age named Newt Sisk, who lived only a few hundred yards up the road.

They apparently made a good working team. With Newt in the store, Will was able to devote more time to reading and the study of his true love, surveying. But somewhere around the turn of the century, a split occurred. Newt, a thrifty man, had saved his money, left, and built a nearly identical store on a piece of his own property a mere stone's throw away. Talk about close competition!

Obviously, the rift was bitter and rancorous. But it was mended in a rather unique way. The eldest of six Kestner sons married the eldest of four Sisk daughters. I'm not sure how I should feel at being a by-product of such a merger. Oh, well, they were childhood sweethearts.

Surprisingly, both stores prospered. That is, until Will made a fatal business decision. Credit was crucial to the operation of a country store in those days. A farmer was on the books much of the year, then paid off when he sold his crop of burley or corn or wheat. But some didn't. This finally pushed Will over the edge. He put up a "Cash Only" sign. It marked the beginning of the end.

However, the customers that Will lost, Newt gained. He built a series of warehouses that stretched nearly to the church. One housed nothing but feed and farm implements, another contained only coffins and vaults.

It is a little remembered fact, but embalming in those days could be had on the home delivery system. After an area death, stalwart neighbors would dig the grave in the family cemetery while members of the family picked out a casket in the Sisks' store. The undertaker, usually from Abingdon, performed his embalming rites in the living room. Then the body was moved into the parlor to lie in state. A preacher would deliver the obsequies there.

What a delight such a store was for a boy! On some evenings, local musicians would bring their homemade instruments off the mountain, sit around the pot-bellied stove, and bounce their homemade music off walls stacked with Buster Brown shoes and bolts of print cotton. It stocked just about everything—kegs of horseshoes, baby clothes, plug tobacco cut to order, blasting powder and fuses. (My cousins and I would fill pop bottles on the Fourth of July, set them on a fence post, light the fuses and run, shaking up the community in a highly satisfying way.)

And the smells! In winter months, the faint aroma of polecat always pervaded the premises from pelts on shingle stretchers. In the late summer and early fall, it was the fragrance of herbs drying on upstairs tables—

peppermint, mullein, lobelia, boneset, goldenseal. But the king of the herbs was ginseng root, fetching from $3 to $5 a pound—a fortune in those days.

My mother liked to tell the story of an encounter between her father and a local 'seng hunter. When Granddaddy weighed the dried roots, the total was nearly triple what it should have been. So he performed an on-the-spot autopsy—and found the roots cleverly impregnated with buckshot.

Mother said that Granddaddy turned to the man and remarked dryly, "This is the wildest 'seng I ever saw, Zeb—you had to shoot it to kill it!"

೧

Will and Dora Kestner, and their store, above, at Hayters Gap. Courtesy of Colleen Taylor.

Denton Kestner and Pearl Sisk enjoying a buggy ride before he left Hayters Gap for North Dakota. November 7, 1908.

Father ~ Denton Kestner   *June 10, 1991*

Driving back to the mountain the other afternoon, I was listening to NPR when a commentary by Daniel Schorr brought back a childhood memory of my father. Schorr's subject was smallpox. He said while no case of the deadly disease has been reported anywhere in the world since 1978, there are two countries which still retain their anti-toxins—America and the Soviet Union.

This, he said, is because each is fearful that the other may have stockpiled frozen strains of the virus for possible use in biological warfare.

Well, if you're going into the biological warfare business, smallpox is a nasty weapon to start with. Not only because of its virulence, but also its highly contagious nature. Over the centuries, severe epidemics killed 30 out of every 100 persons who contracted the disease.

Before the days of vaccination, it was the scourge of the American frontier. If a case broke out in a fort, that fort was required to fly a red flag from its staff. No one was permitted to enter or leave. Entire villages of Indians were wiped out in a single epidemic.

I have met only one person who claimed to have had smallpox—my father. In 1908, when he was 24 years old, Dad got itchy feet (it seems to have run in the family) and left Hayters Gap to homestead in North Dakota.

On the rolling plains near Plaza, southwest of Minot, he built a little one-room shack on his 160 acres and settled down to meet the five-year residency requirement.

When my brother and I were small, Dad used to entertain us with stories from that segment of his young manhood. Stories of Indians. Of how one showed up at his shack one cold winter day wearing an open shirt, and how, when Dad questioned him about the cold, replied: "Your face cold? No. Well, me all face."

And when the Indian asked for food, Dad only had some bacon to fry, and when the Indian ate it he shook his head and said, "Too many salt." Strange, the things that will stick in a kid's mind.

There were other stories about the annual planting and harvesting of wheat, of the vast teams of men and mules and equipment that moved from farm to farm. About how his main entertainment was walking—including the 12 miles into Plaza to pick up his mail and groceries and back in the same day.

Somewhere amid my stored junk I have his pedometer and compass—which, in the absence of roads, were prudent items to carry when cutting across trackless plains. But the story that has stuck in my mind with the greatest vividness is the one he told Brother Bill and me about his battle with smallpox.

As I recall, he related it matter-of-factly, without any attempt at dramatization. But he didn't have to. To come down with a deadly disease while living alone miles from civilization spoke for itself. When Dad grew ill, he didn't know what was wrong. But when the chills and fever and nausea kept getting worse, he knew he'd better find help—and the only medical help in the area was a country doctor in Plaza. Somehow, he staggered those 12 long miles into the village and into the doctor's office.

I can just imaging the doctor's shock—not only from the thought of a man walking all the way in that condition but also at the disease he had. Dad said the doctor was faced with a dilemma. He knew that a case of smallpox would most likely create a panic in the little community, but he also knew that here was a patient who would have to have medical attention for quite some time. So he compromised.

There was a vacant store on Plaza's main street. So, when night fell, the good doctor slipped my father—along with a cot and blankets—through the store's back door. I've forgotten how long Dad said he remained in that vacant building. But I do remember him saying that every evening the doctor would shove food and water and medicine through the back door.

His nights were passed in utter darkness, for even as much as a candle would have given him away. Dad said he spent the daytime hours lying on his cot staring through the dirty front windows, watching people pass up and down the street, wondering what their reaction would have been if they'd known a case of smallpox was almost in arm's reach.

I can't recall whether or not Dad speculated on how he caught the stuff, or whether any other cases were reported in the area, but, obviously, it was rather rare. Pockmarks are a common aftermath of the disease's severe scabbing, but Dad was left with only two deep pits—and a story with which to entertain his two young sons.

CȜ

Mother ~ Pearl Sisk Kestner   *May 10, 1993*

It struck me that I've never used this column for a Mothers' Day tribute. (Which really isn't surprising seeing as how I never was what you'd call a dutiful son.)

It's easy to say nice things about my mother. She was, putting it succinctly, the finest woman I've ever known, bar none. Never once in all the years I knew her did I ever hear her speak an unkind word about anyone. Never once did I hear her voice raised in anger.

Parents, of course, shape our lives. Or should. Even in their absence, they still mold us. We all swim in a gene pool. By and large, I'm grateful for my genes.

The shaping begins early. If my father hadn't brought home all those books for my mother to read aloud, I doubt very much that words would have become a major factor in my life. It's fitting, therefore, that the most cherished memento I have of my mother consists of words. Words she put on paper Aug. 27, 1913—nearly eighty years ago—and mailed to Plaza, North Dakota.

It's a good thing she did. Otherwise, I probably wouldn't be here. Dad noted on the envelope that her letter had been "Rec. Sat. Aug. 30, 1913." Since it had been posted at Hayters Gap, that's pretty fast service for a two-cent stamp.

He preserved the letter, and passed it along on his death fifty years later. On the envelope, he added a further notation: "It is absolutely a true and correct story of our lives."

Mother was twenty-six when she sat down to write. I wonder if she knew it would be the most important letter of her life. She began it, not

46

with the usual salutation, but in the fashion of the fairy tales she would one day read aloud to her two sons:

"Once upon a time, there lived near each other a little boy and girl in a beautiful fertile valley that was almost shut off from the outside world by the blue mountains that surrounded it.

"They shared each others' playthings during childhood days, and dreamed dreams that were to be realized when they became man and woman."

She, the eldest of four daughters; he, the eldest of six sons. The farmhouses they grew up in were only a couple of hundred yards apart. Together they went to a little one-room school that nestled beneath a towering oak at the western end of her father's meadow.

"What happy days these school days were," she wrote. "For they would plan each year to have their desks just opposite each other across the aisle. (Boys and girls sat on separate sides of the room in those days.)

"When spelling was exchanged for correction, this little boy and girl managed to get the others' papers, and there were never many words marked wrong.

"Sometimes the little boy would go out with other boys to chop wood, and he would never forget to go around on the side of the building where the little girl sat and knock on the wall to show her he was still thinking of her."

But, as children have a habit of doing, they grew up.

"By and by, the boy and girl grew to young manhood and womanhood, and were acknowledged lovers. Sometimes there would be a tendency to follow after strange idols but they always came back to the old love and were all the happier for the straying in that they found there was no one just like the other."

They talked of marriage, she noted, but "the time never seemed just right. There was always just a little more to be accomplished."

Then came a fateful day—"a day when the young man said to the young woman that he was going away to seek his fortune." And "the queerest, desolate feeling stole over her when she knew he was going out of her life for a time."

I can only imagine the days that followed when she had only her work in her father's country store to look forward to. Days that moved as slowly as the seasons, days that turned into months, and then years.

At first, their letters were "filled with love and devotion. He tells her all about this new country and of his success in business, but after a while his answers to her letters become less and less frequent.

"At last, he accuses her of inconstancy. This was her death warrant.

It is true that other young men have sought her society but she looks upon them all as simply her friends.

"He is the one among all for her. She has told him this but he doesn't believe it and replies that he has lost all confidence in her. An occasional letter is passed but it is not as it should be.

"They have given the best part of their lives to each other, and what has it amounted to? They have nothing to look forward to, only the joys of the past to console them now.

"They are drifting, drifting, and unless some unseen power stands at the helm, I wonder what will the ending be?"

Eight full pages in flowing Spencerian script, ending in a poem and signed: "With deepest love, from The Little Girl."

In effect, it was a gently worded ultimatum. And Dad must have read it that way. For clipped to the envelope was one of those photo-postcards that were popular a century ago. It was a photo of him taken while seated on a fake crescent moon in a photographer's studio.

Dad had scrawled on it: "Picture made in St. Louis, Mo. enroute home from North Dakota."

CS

The Oakland Six
December 5, 1994

When I told Abingdon photographer Mike Pierry that I had a box of old plate glass negatives dating back nearly a century, his ears started flapping. "Mind if I take a look?" he asked.

"Sure, if I can find the box," I replied. "I'd like to see some prints myself since I'm pretty sure they were made by my Uncle Floyd."

In a Hayters Gap family of six sons, my father was the first born, Floyd the third. He became interested in photography as a young man, attended some sort of photography school up in Minnesota, married a Minnesota girl, and moved to Washington, D.C., where he joined the staff of the Smithsonian Institution as a photographer.

Believe it or not, I didn't become familiar with his work until I went to Bermuda. After arriving in the British colony, it didn't take long to discover I'd have to supplement my meager newspaper salary if I wanted to live pleasantly. My friendship with Janie, social hostess at the Elbow Beach Surf Club, was a big help. She arranged lunchtime photographic sessions with tourists, and my income began to increase nicely.

Also, if a tourist couple would inquire about an afternoon of sail-boating, she'd give me a call at the *Mid-Ocean News*. If I didn't have any other commitment, I'd meet the couple at the Princess Hotel boat slip and we'd take off in my little sailboat, the "Foolish Venture II," for a trip around Darrell's Island, Grace Island, and back.

I'd furnish drinks and snacks and a running commentary. The tourists could have gotten the same information by reading Will Zuill's book on Bermuda history, but this would have denied them the embellishments my fertile imagination provided.

One such couple was from D.C. As a southwesterly breeze sent us skimming across blue waters, we began exchanging personal information. The man showed an interest in my last name. "Our chief photographer at the Smithsonian is a Kestner," he said.

"That would be my Uncle Floyd!" I said. After the usual "small world" comments, the man complimented Floyd's photographic abilities.

"We call him 'One Shot Kestner'," he said. "Whenever we have a picture for him to make, he takes just one. If we suggest taking another as a backup, he says, 'I believe that one will do it'."

Such frugality can probably be explained by those plate glass negatives. Today's film is so relatively inexpensive that photographers customarily shoot several frames to make sure they have a good one. However, if each shot involved a large glass plate that had been laboriously coated with emulsion, I can see how "old school" photographers would get in the habit of shooting only what they thought necessary.

Anyway, I finally located the box of plates for Mike. Unhappily, some were broken, and all were coated with decades of grime. Mike carefully cleaned the nonemulsion sides of the plates, then made contact prints. Results were amazing. After all those years, that emulsion still retained fine detail.

Most of them were obviously taken in the Hayters Gap area, although some contained people and backgrounds that I couldn't identify. (One was of my father asleep in bed. His kid brother must have sneaked up on him.)

The print I was happiest to get was made from a plate with a broken end. It's a family portrait—Granddaddy and Grandmother Kestner with five of their six sons, but the centerpiece is a 1913 Oakland Six open touring car. My father is sitting behind the wheel, his parents and Leslie in the back seat, Giles beside him on the front seat, while Roby and Floyd are standing on the running board. Only Wiley is missing. Maybe they drew straws and he had to take the picture.

Anyway, the photo holds significance for me. According to Roby, it was the first motor car in Hayters Gap. Owning it was my father's only claim to fame. I can't recall him ever talking about the Oakland, but

Roby had several stories to tell, including one about a hazardous trip over into Russell County on the old wagon road.

After making the prints, Mike was able to identify the auto from a book of old vehicles. He sent me a photo-copy and there's no question about its identity—the square lamps mounted on each side near the folding windshield, big tool box on the left running board, tonneau folded like an accordion behind the rear seat.

It was winter, and everyone was wearing overcoats. Snow on the ground, and tire chains on the Oakland's 12-spoke rear wheels. Paved roads didn't come to Hayters Gap until many years later.

Mike told me that the Oakland was the forerunner of the Pontiac, which was named after Pontiac, Michigan, where it was built. The Oakland was also built there, but it was named after the county in which Pontiac is located.

This particular Oakland probably ended up in the collection of rusting hulks behind Granddad's barn. As a boy, I used to go out there and steal ball bearings from their wheels to use as "shooters" when I was playing marbles.

I'll bet when Dad was proudly posing in his car, he never dreamed that one day he'd have a son who would get pleasure out of it, too.

First car in Hayters Gap: the 1913 Oakland Six. Kestners from left: Roby, Giles, Denton at the wheel, Floyd, Leslie, and parents, Will and Dora.

Cousin Fred's Model T *September 11, 1989*

Anybody want to buy an '85 station wagon cheap? No reasonable offer refused. The way I look at it, enough is enough. A few days ago, when a whine in its innards reached banshee proportions, I took it in for a medical consultation. Diagnosis: failure in the final drive of the differential. Estimated repair cost: from $1,200 to $1,650, depending on whether or not the torque converter is okay.

A financial shock, yes. But even more so because, earlier this year, I had to replace the transmission—at a cost of $1,372.79. Moreover, twice during the past year it had to be hauled in from Interstate 81—first for a broken timing belt, then for an electrical failure involving the fuel pump. Last winter, I had to bring a mechanic up here on the mountain when its brain (computer) suffered temporary paresis and had to be re-activated.

All in all, I figure my repair bill this year will amount to roughly $1,000 more than my annual salary during the first year I worked as a newspaper reporter. This, on a make of car blaringly advertised on TV as "Inexpensive—and built to stay that way!" Yeah, sure.

All of which got me to thinking about a kinder, gentler age. Specifically, I got to thinking about the Model T Ford. Now there was a car. When it broke down, it would sit there by the side of the road, like a plain but honest woman, and the driver would climb out and spit on his hands and pick up a wrench or a pair of pliers or a screw driver and fix it.

In those days, most car owners living in the country were their own mechanics. It had to be that way—although in every community there was always a guy who was considered top gun. Even if a Model T owner was only a fair to middlin' mechanic, chances were he could fix what ailed it, for the car had a beautiful mechanical simplicity.

My cousin Fred introduced me to the Model T. He'd bought it from somebody for $25—a not-inconsiderable sum in the mid-'30s, although this must have been nine or ten years after the last one rolled off Henry's innovative assembly line.

As I recall, Fred was too young to have a license. But that wasn't important to a country boy if he did his driving in a remote community like Hayters Gap. The paved road ended here.

Shortly after acquiring the Model T, Fred "got the feel of it" by taking it up on the schoolhouse hill, locking the steering wheel in a turn, shoving the throttle wide open, and spinning around in a circle until he threw the tires off. No big deal. In less than an hour—using only a jack, a tire tool and, possibly, a can of inner tube patching—it was as good as new.

There was no gas pedal. An accelerator arm was located on the right side of the steering column. As momentum was gained, the combustion rate was slowly increased by shoving up a "spark arm" on the left side of the column. That's how you built up speed.

The driver controlled the engine's performance, not the manufacturer. There was no gear shift. You pushed a floor pedal on the right side of the steering column to start out, then released it to go into "high." A pedal on the left was reverse.

There was no starter. You had to insert a crank in a hole just below the radiator. This would turn the crankshaft until combustion took place. A canvas top was part of the original equipment, but, by the time Fred acquired his, it was an open air two-seater—a true forerunner of the convertible.

Black was the only color that Model T's came in. Cousin Fred dressed his up by covering it with graffiti in white paint. Fred would take that Model T anywhere. Or try to. He tried to jump the creek in it one day and threw our cousin, Maiden, into the windshield and broke her arm.

He even became an entrepreneur in it. One day, we took it down on the North Fork to a watermelon patch and loaded up the back seat and peddled melons up and down the valley for ten cents each.

When Fred finally got his driver's license and started dating, he began driving his mother's new Dodge touring car. A Model T was hardly the vehicle to impress the girls. So, he got rid of the Model T.

All of the above is from memory, but I think it's fairly accurate. You can always remember the first girl you dated and the first car you drove.

Cȝ

Old Photos   *March 17, 1997*

Digging through junk in our woodshed loft, I recently came across a brown paper parcel bearing a notation in the handwriting of my father: "Miscellaneous lot of pictures, most of them old, put in here on Wed. Feb. 23, 1955. Dad."

They were old, all right, some dating back to the 1800s. Mostly portraits or snapshots of family members. Some, however, were of Hayters Gap landmarks. Among these was a snapshot of the area's first schoolhouse, a little one-room affair huddled under a massive white oak. Dad and Mother had become childhood sweethearts within its walls.

Some of the photos were so ancient their emulsion had eroded and faded to the point of rendering them worthless. Others, while faded, were

Blacksmith shop at Hayters Gap. Courtesy of Colleen Taylor.

still discernable. I was particularly fascinated by one, and spent the better part of an hour studying it with a magnifying glass.

A large group of people, some mounted on mules or horses, are posing for the camera in front of the old blacksmith shop located across the road from Hayters Gap church. At least, I assume it's the one at Hayters Gap. Certainly, it's a smithy, for the blacksmith himself is standing in the center of the group, holding the reins of a mule. I used to hang out there when I was a kid, and recall how delighted I was when the smith let me pump the bellows.

How do I know he's the blacksmith? His leather apron gives him away, plus the fact he's standing next to a "shoeing stand." This was an upright contraption, a little like a magazine rack, with troughs for shoes and tools, plus two boxes for nails mounted on top. When he was shoeing a horse, or mule, the smith moved it around the four quarters of the animal as he did his job.

The magnifying glass also revealed that the gentleman on the mule was headed for the grist mill down at the river bridge. How do I know? Because two flour sacks, presumably filled with grain, are swung across the saddle beneath him. Back then, that's how Hayters Gap residents got their meal and flour. I recall riding to the mill as a kid on one of my grandfather's mules, riding bareback with my cousin, Fred.

At the mill, Billy Akers, the miller, pulled the sluice lever, and water from the race began rotating the grinding wheel. Corn or wheat was fed into the hopper, and, presto!—out it came ready to be made into cornbread or hot biscuits. We didn't have to pay him. He simply took a portion of the grain, put the end product back into our flour sack, and off we went on our return voyage home.

How do I know the gentleman on the mule wasn't returning from the mill? Well, if his mule was in need of a shoe, it's safe to assume he had it done on the way there, not returning.

A tiny photo measuring only 2 x 2 1/2 inches resulted in an enhanced enlargement of my Granddaddy Sisk's house as it had looked at the turn of the century. On the right side of the house is an old smokehouse where my cousin A. J. cured family hams. It had been a dwelling originally, a dwelling occupied by Newt Sisk and his bride, Sallie.

That was the way things were done in those days. You built what you could afford and then, if you were thrifty and worked hard and prospered, you built a more substantial house nearby. His house pretty much followed the architectural fashion of the day—an upstairs porch with triple arches and scrollwork, duplicated below with another porch of the same pattern. It was once called a showplace, but then, Hayters Gap wasn't known for the opulence of its residences.

Drawn up in front of the white picket fence are two wagon teams. A friend of mine who admired the photo said they provide a Currier & Ives touch.

Ah, me, how time goes by. The only building in the photograph still standing today is the barn, which sat on a hill behind the house. It's still in fair shape to be around 100 years old.

I pass it every time I leave the mountain.

The Newt and Sallie Sisk home, where Jack was born, appears in the distance in this early view of Hayters Gap. The house is no longer standing. The blacksmith shop was just to the left of this view.

Jack plowing the old-fashioned way at the Sisk farm, about 1940.

Brothers Jack (left) and Bill Kestner with Ginger in Bristol, Tennessee, 1929.

3 ~ Salad Days

Dad didn't just reminisce—he wove tales. In his straightforward, conversational tone he recounted stories of his youth. A "youth well-spent" by most standards: days of adventure, of testing the waters, of goal setting, of looking forward to the future with an appreciation of his past.

He was born in his Sisk grandparents' home in Hayters Gap on September 29, 1921. Before entering school, he moved with his parents and his younger brother, Bill, to Bristol, Tennessee, where his father opened a real estate office. The Sisk and the Kestner grandparents remained in the Gap, where Dad continued to visit on weekends, holidays, and throughout the summers. His deep love for nature was first nurtured during these halcyon days in the woods.

His love affair with words also began during his early childhood. He credited his mother's nightly reading to him and Bill as the biggest influence in his becoming a writer.

Dad graduated from Tennessee High School in 1940, a year later than expected owing to a bout of the flu. From there he entered King College. He would jokingly refer to King as the place where his professional writing career began—he wrote for other students, guaranteeing a certain grade or there was no charge.

In 1942, he was accepted into the Navy's pre-flight cadet college program, first at the University of Virginia and then at the University of North Carolina. In 1944, he was discharged from the Naval Cadets when he contracted rheumatic fever. After leaving the service, he worked as an instrument man for an oil exploration company in Mississippi. He returned to UNC in 1946, graduating in 1948.

With his degree in English, Dad got his father's backing to enter the advertising business in Bristol. A one-man show, he would appear as vice-president of his company at town council meetings offering street trash cans on which he would be permitted to sell advertising. He would solicit ads from local businesses and then he would return later as the trash can installer.

With his pockets full from his successful venture, he headed to New Orleans where he published his first article in the *Times-Picayune*. Dad had found his calling.

ଓଃ

Brumley Cove

Funny how some places change while others seem to go on the same way forever. Brumley Cove, for example. Other than its headwaters—dammed to form Hidden Valley Lake—and the Royal Ambassador community at its mouth, it remains virtually unchanged from what it was half a century ago.

The cove is gouged into the side of Clinch Mountain some five miles west of Hayters Gap. It evokes more pleasant memories of my youth than any place I can think of. For one thing, it provided the only day of hooky from school that my father would authorize—the opening day of trout season.

We didn't bring many home. We cooked them on the spot. Since then, I've had many kinds of fish prepared in many different ways in many different places, but I can't recall any with the flavor of those fresh-caught trout, slathered in corn meal and fried in bacon grease over a campfire.

As my brother, Bill, and I grew older, we began climbing up in the cove. We named one camping site "Camp Rain-a-While" after being pinned inside a pup tent for three days and nights. Another was called "Camp Dysentery"—for obvious reasons—which probably came from drinking too much water from the creek, shrunken by the droughts of late summer.

Time passed. After World War II, several of my high school classmates and I made Brumley Creek our unofficial headquarters. We'd bring our dates on cookouts about a half-mile up in the cove to a site known as "The John Hayter Hole"—a deep, blue pool ringed by borders and ledges. Memorable occasions.

More time passed. One by one, the gang got married, or else immigrated to faraway places. We left Brumley behind.

Well, Brother Bill came a-visiting recently. While he was here, a neighbor in the valley called and said they'd come into possession of one of his boyhood diaries. She thought we might want to take a look at it. It turned out to be one that Bill had kept during our days at Camp Rain-a-While. Reading it made us wonder if we could find the place after all those years. So, after recruiting a friend from our childhood, we took off for Brumley.

We stopped off at the John Hayter Hole. It hadn't changed a bit. The thunderous rush of water into the pool brought with it a thunderous rush of memories. The ledges we'd dived from, the rocks we'd sunned on. It was like a stepping back into yesterday.

The road into the cove is actually the bed of an old logging railroad, so the climb is a long, gentle grade of some eight or nine miles to Hidden Valley Lake. But the road becomes a trail at the end of three miles. That's where walking gets rough, for that's where the impact of last year's terrible ice storm begins. It looks like some tipsy giant had sat down and played jackstraws with the trees.

On my last walk in Brumley those many years ago, two or three of the old railroad trestles remained. No more. It's all fording. I left Bill and our friend at one of the upper fords and went on alone, determined to find that elusive camp site.

It's difficult to convey the feel of Brumley—the sweep of its open reaches, its towering cliffs, its slopes covered with room-sized boulders from some long ago upheaval. Every season brings its individualization. At this time of year, it's a mass of wild flowers—geraniums lavendering the glades, yellow star grass pushing up around ancient crossties, pink lady's slippers, beds of painted trilliums. And always the white flash and pervasive roar of the creek.

It's hard to believe that a decade ago this entire cove and much of the lovely valley below came close to being converted into a massive hydroelectric system. And probably would have been except for the fierce determination of its citizens. The people of Brumley Gap today are just as warm and friendly as when I was a boy. But no one should mistake this for weakness. They hang tough. They played David and Goliath with a giant utility—and won.

I never did find Camp-Rain-a-While, even though I walked clear to the dam at Hidden Valley Lake. But I didn't mind. I found what I've always found.

Somehow, I have a feeling that when God gets a bit weary of witnessing how Man has messed things up, He takes a breather on the upper reaches of Brumley Cove. His touch is there.

☙

First Flight   *November 23, 1987*

I was whisked back in time over half a century recently when I looked down into the valley and saw a small private plane cruising so low I thought it was hunting for a place to land—in the same place another plane had landed on a Sunday afternoon in a long-ago autumn.

Cousins Fred and A. J. and other assorted kinsmen were sitting out on the front porch of my grandfather's house. The swing creaking while

Aunt Lil rocked as she read *True Story* magazine; the rest of us talking, waving at the occasional passing car and speculating on its occupants. A normal, ritualistic Sunday afternoon.

Suddenly, the sound of a low-flying aircraft brought conversation to a halt, then brought us to our feet when the plane appeared from behind the knob and circled the valley floor. Instantly, all us boys were out in the front yard waving. An airplane at Hayters Gap, VA., in the early '30s, wasn't rated much below the Second Coming.

The pilot flew low over the house, waggled his wings in recognition of our waving, throttled back, and brought the plane down for a short, bumpy landing in the stubble of an old wheat field just across the creek on the Johnson farm.

My cousins and I skipped across the creek like we, too, had wings. Then we just stood around the strange object, unbelieving. It was an open cockpit biplane with ripped and patched fabric, smeared windscreens, and a bent metal drag in place of a tail wheel. The three flyers who climbed out were equally dilapidated looking—old slacks, greasy leather jackets, scuffed helmets and goggles. One was a woman, as it became apparent when she took off her helmet and shook out her hair and smiled at us boys.

A crowd gathered in no time flat, among them one of the Johnson men who wanted to know if an emergency had brought the plane down. No, the pilot told him, nothing was wrong, they'd just landed "to see if any of you good people would like to take a ride in an airplane for one dollar—but we'll take you and your family up for free, of course."

Those were the early years of the Great Depression and money was scarce, but dollar bills began appearing as if by magic. My cousins were among the first to be strapped in. I remained behind, consumed with envy and sadness. I didn't have a nickel to my name.

By the time the fading sun had begun to climb the sides of Little Mountain, the flying trio had milked the crowd dry. The final ride of the day was announced by the young woman. Fred looked over at me.

"I wouldn't mind going again," he said. "I've got the money if you want to go." I didn't say a word. I didn't have to. Fred read it in my face.

I vividly recall how my heart raced as the pilot's partner strapped us into the cockpit, cautioning us not to hold onto the exposed control cables running along its sides. Then taxiing to the leeward end of the field, the turn upwind, the roar as the throttle was firewalled, the bumpy acceleration, and, finally, the ecstatic withdrawal from the earth.

Maybe it's just the hazy recollection of an impressionable 12-year-old, but it seemed to me that on this final ride the pilot climbed higher than he had with the others, and his dive toward the little dots of faces was steeper. I still recall the earth rushing up toward us, the delicious drain of blood as we pulled "G's" on the pull-out, the sudden weightlessness as we leveled off.

I never got over that first flight. When World War II came around, it seemed sort of preordained that I go into the Navy Air Corps—a career marked by its utter lack of distinction, unless I can count getting reprimanded for "dive-bombing" my girlfriend's house in Weston, West Virginia.

If I had gone into one of the ground services, would I have been killed, as were several of my classmates?

Idle speculation, but on such a whim as a barnstorming pilot's decision to make a few bucks by landing in a little mountain community, the course of a life could have turned.

03

Fairmount School   *March 25, 1996*

Over the years of writing this column I've received quite a few letters, but none that surprised me more than a recent one from Mary Hedrick. Miss Hedrick taught me fifth grade English at Fairmount School in Bristol. I hadn't seen or heard from her in well over half a century. An unexpected voice from the past.

The upshot was I dropped by to see her at her high-ceilinged, turn-of-the-century brick home on Sixth St. There she lives with a black and white cat named Katie. The house is next door to the Troutdale Dining Room, the building in which she was born over 90 years ago. So, Miss Hedrick has lived for nearly a century in one section of one block in one town. That's what you call roots.

The years have treated her gently. Although she says she doesn't see or hear well, she is still physically active and mentally sharp, and has far fewer wrinkles than I have.

We talked about our good days at Fairmount. And so they were. We agreed that schools then were a far cry from those today, but that it would be unfair to put all the blame on the system and its teachers.

Too many students now seem to arrive without a sense of discipline and responsibility. A half-century ago, these were instilled in their own homes. Correcting the absence has been dumped into the laps of teachers.

I don't remember any blare of trumpets and crash of cymbals when I enrolled at Fairmount in September 1927. I do remember that I was scared to death—scared at being ripped from the bosom of my family, scared at being thrust into a totally strange environment. And, if that wasn't enough, I was plucked from the class and held up for ridicule and scorn. At least, that's the way I looked at it.

You see, a pre-entrance requirement was vaccination for smallpox, and my father didn't believe in the procedure. "Introduce dead germs into my son's anatomy? No, siree!"

So, I was sent home where I remained until the school finally relented. I don't know how Dad talked Margaret Baumgardener, the principal, into re-admitting me. Maybe it was his argument that, "If everyone else's child is vaccinated, how can mine be at risk?" Re-entering the second time was worse than the first. I felt like a branded felon.

Most five-year-old boys (I didn't turn six until the end of the month) want nothing so much as to melt quietly into the school's woodwork. At the very least, they want to blend in with the rest of the class.

Small wonder I developed into the shy and timid man I am today. I don't remember much about that first year at Fairmount except that my little dog, Ginger, would walk me to school. She'd go as far as the entranceway on Maryland Avenue. Then she'd meet me there and walk me home at lunch. It marked my first encounter with the psychic abilities of dogs. Mother told me that Ginger would leave the house promptly at 11:45 a.m.

Nothing else about the first grade stands out. At least, nothing that is retrievable from my aging brain. Oh, yes, I did fall hopelessly in love with Carolyn Cowan. And continued my worship-from-afar throughout grammar school. As I recall, Carolyn was tacitly viewed by the boys as the belle of the first grade.

My seven years at Fairmount are mostly a blur, with an occasional blip. One blip is that of our history teacher (Miss Wingfield, I think) arranging a visit to Andrew Johnson's tailor shop in Jonesborough. Parents, including my father, volunteered transportation. Erskine Parks and David Powers were among those riding in our old A-Model Ford. I don't remember the tailor shop but I do remember the outstanding milkshakes at the drugstore where we had lunch.

Miss Viola Mathis (who, I am told, is still alive and living in Johnson City) taught art. It was a subject in which I had no special talent. My buildings and humans always came out the same height. In fact, they bore striking similarities.

Miss Mathis was athletically inclined, with a penchant for archery. One day, thinking to ingratiate myself and maybe get a better grade, I carried to her class the archery set I had received for Christmas. She stepped out of the school's west door, fitted an arrow to the string, assumed the bowman's stance, bent the bow in one graceful movement, and—crack!—snapped that sucker right in two.

Elsie Grubb taught fourth grade. We became friends. She and her sister, Alta, would visit my home on Florida Avenue and play the guitar and sing. When I was in service during WWII, Elsie wrote regularly and sent boxes of homemade candy. She was invalided by a car accident and had to retire from teaching. However, she kept writing poetry, and remained my good friend until her death.

The first line of our school song began, "Fairmount School is the best old school in town." Yes, it probably was.

ଓ

The Lumber Mill   *April 24, 1989*

Well, the minimum wage is back in the news again. Every time that happens, some old-timer always pops up and bores everyone to tears by recalling the pittance he worked for "when he was a boy."

So, let me tell you about the time I worked ten hours a day in a lumber mill for 25 cents an hour. I was either a rising junior or senior at Tennessee High that summer. Since I'd already decided on writing as a career (and was willing to settle for authorship of The Great American Novel), a typewriter, I figured, was a logical first step. Unfortunately, the nation was still embedded in the Great Depression, and a typewriter represented a hunk of cash. My parents simply couldn't afford one.

Then I recalled that one of the commissioners of the Boy Scout troop I was in also served as general manager of Cortrim Lumber Co. on Georgia Avenue Extension. When I approached Mr. Cooper for a job, he was doubtful. It was hard work, he said. Millwork was man's work. Finally, though, when I told him what I needed the money for, he reluctantly agreed to give me a try.

At the 7 a.m. whistle the next day, which some people in the area used to set their clocks by, Mr. Cooper escorted me through a bedlam of whining saws and screeching planes and the hot tannin smell of kiln-dried lumber. My work station was the receiving end of a ripsaw operated by a wiry, freckle-faced, red-headed guy with an enormous wad of tobacco bulging his cheek.

Mr. Cooper, I'm sure, walked me there as an act of kindness. But it was a mistake. For "Red" instantly sized me up as a kid who'd gotten a job by being a friend of the boss. So he set out to break me.

Red's job was to stand on one side of the ripsaw, walled in by dollies of lumber of varying lengths and types, and feed the contraption. He'd place a board on the apron, shove it against a guide abutting a conveyor belt, and the board would be ripped by a circular saw before being ejected on my side.

I, in turn, had to judge the length instantly, and whether it was oak or poplar or whatever. This was critical, for as I picked up the two pieces, I had to whirl back and get ready for the next two. If I hesitated, by the time I turned back I'd find pieces on the floor—and Red grinning delightedly.

Obviously, Red controlled both the selection of boards and the tempo at which they were fed. He could make things hard or easy. The easy, logical way was to feed sections of the same length and type over a period of several minutes before switching to another. This would let me establish a rhythm, which in turn would result in more work getting done.

But that didn't suit Red. No, siree, he was going to show up the boss's pet. As a result, every board he sent through was a different type and length. Which meant I had to continuously whirl from one side to the other. To make sure I was aware of his contempt, Red would generously coat an occasional board with tobacco juice.

When the quitting whistle blew at 5:30 p.m., I wasn't at all sure I'd be able to make it home—much less make it back to work the next day. Covered from head to toe with a fine patina of sawdust, I walked the long half-mile—all uphill—to the 900 block of Florida. There I found that Mother had a big dinner waiting on the table. But I couldn't eat. Every muscle in my body was screaming with fatigue. So I simply took a hot shower and went to bed.

Somehow, though, I made it back the next day. When I walked over to the ripsaw, Red grinned, spat on a board, and started all over again.

It was either that day or the next that one of the foremen dropped by. He stood behind Red, unobserved, and watched his not-so-subtle harassment. Finally, he tapped him on the shoulder and said, "Red, if I had a good dog, I wouldn't hit him over the head with you."

Well, actually, he didn't say "over the head." He used a more descriptive part of the dog's anatomy. Red got the message, and began to ease up.

At noon Saturday, I stood in line with the rest of the men and proudly drew my first pay—$13.75 for what was considered a normal 55-hour workweek. I'd already priced a portable Smith-Corona typewriter. Around a month later, when I'd made enough to buy it, I quit.

Which was probably just as well, for if I'd worked any longer I might have gotten so attached to the lumber business that I'd still be working with Red.

The Word Route   *October 19, 1992*

Words: In the beginning was the word.

My earliest memory is that of my mother reading to my brother and me. Not just occasionally, but night after night. If it hadn't been for that, I'd probably have wandered down some other vocational avenue. Which one, I don't know. Maybe training dogs, I've got such a great natural talent for it.

But all those words during all those formative years must have had their effect, for I was only a junior in high school when I decided I'd take the word route. It was in Miss Nininger's English class. We'd just finished Chaucer's <u>Canterbury Tales</u>, and she'd given us a weekend assignment of writing some sort of related short story.

My folks were visiting their folks here at Hayters Gap that weekend, and it was bedtime Sunday night before we returned to Bristol (naturally, I'd put off my homework until the last minute—exactly like I put off writing this column. Habits die hard).

But I'd worked out an idea in my head during the trip back, so I sat down on the edge of my bed and began scrawling in a loose-leaf notebook. A story about an airliner heading east above the Rockies, about the contrasting personalities of its passengers, about engine problems, and crash-landing in a mountain meadow—and how the passengers passed the time until their rescue by sharing stories of their past lives.

The first gray light of dawn was filtering through the bedroom curtains when I finished. I'd lost all track of time. Chaucer probably would have torn out his hair if he'd read the thing, but I experienced an emotion I'd never known before—a mixture of exultation and fatigue and pride and sheer amazement that I'd created something out of nothing. The watershed night of my youth.

That summer, I worked ten hours a day in a lumber mill to earn money for a typewriter—and used what little money I had left to build a "writing room," a cubbyhole beneath our back porch on Florida Avenue. My future was probably shaped within those papered walls.

Oh, not the future I'd visualized: the writing of books. That goal changed rather abruptly on a family trip to Tallahassee a couple of summers later.

En route, we laid over in Atlanta for several hours. I decided to visit the public library. I'd spent a lot of time in the one in Bristol, but it was only the ground floor of a remodeled private residence. Small and comforting.

Not so Atlanta. What an edifice! And the books—roomful after roomful, shelves stacked from floor to ceiling. The more I wandered around in that labyrinth, the more overwhelming it got. And then it hit me.

This place was a cemetery, and all those books were simply tombstones inscribed, "Sacred to the Memory of____", the author. Writers by the thousands were buried here. Did I want that? No, indeedy! I was a teen-ager who wanted to savor life, not spend it locked up in a room with a typewriter. Why, I hadn't begun to live!

I began making up for lost time a few days later when I left Tallahassee and went to Panama City—the first time I'd been removed from the protective environs of my parents. I got a job on a civil engineering crew at an Air Force base under construction, had my first drink of hard liquor, and settled down to serious dating. Why hadn't someone told me how much fun girls could be?

When I ran out of dating money, I sold the typewriter I'd sweated most of a summer to buy. A symbolic gesture, I figured. The burning of a bridge. It didn't turn out that way. As the twig is bent, so does it grow.

When I returned to college after the war, I bought another typewriter and wrote my first novel—an atrocious affair that went unpublished, but, nevertheless, was pure pleasure to write. That's the thing about words. You either enjoy the feel of them when you handle them, or you don't. If you do, you want to keep handling them.

So, when a new newspaper, the *Virginia-Tennessean,* was founded in Bristol and reporters were being hired, I jumped at the chance to take a "temporary" word job until I got around to writing The Great American Novel. To my surprise, I discovered I'd found my niche. The daily deadlines were lovely. They eliminated the isolation and sustained drive critical to the writing of a book.

Words are like stones. There are artists who can take a stone and turn it into a sculpture that delights and endures through the ages. Then there are the stonemasons who build bridges with them, and warm and homey fireplaces.

It can be fun being a simple wordmason.

CB

The Road Not Taken

A couple of interlocking events recently sent a wave of nostalgia washing through my system. One was the announced cut-back at Newport News Shipbuilding and Dry Dock Company, the other a PBS television special called "The American Aircraft Carrier."

The TV program was an hour-long recitation of daily life aboard a big flattop at sea. It featured the attack carrier *Independence*, launched at Newport News in 1959. Nineteen years earlier, I'd had a launching of sorts there myself.

When I graduated from Tennessee High in 1940, I wanted to go on to college and thence into some sort of writing career, but I also ached with a higher priority—to put behind the grinding poverty of the Great Depression that had dominated my life throughout the '30s. Maybe poverty is too strong a word. There was always food on our table and clothes to wear and books to read. But I'd had no money and now there was none to go to college. So I decided to go to work.

By chance, I learned of a summer course in welding at Virginia High. It was taught by a man by the name of Wilson who, with a brother, ran a welding shop in Bristol. I applied and was accepted. It was a long, hot summer. I spent it sweating behind an arc mask, learning how to run a smooth bead with an electric welding torch, how to braze, how to judge the properties of various metals.

Mr. Wilson, who had once worked at Newport News Shipbuilding (and still had contacts there), told his class that at the end of the course he'd select two students and personally take them there and get them jobs. It was a strong incentive. I was one of the selectees.

Thus it was, on a fine, sparkling morning in early September, we set out for Newport News. My first step out into the wide, wicked world to make my own way.

The next day, while Mr. Wilson was at the shipyard arranging our entry into the apprentice program, I decided to visit Virginia Beach and take a look at the Atlantic Ocean—oceans being noticeably absent in the Bristol area. So I caught a ferry to Norfolk and boarded a streetcar for the beach.

A half-century ago, the "boardwalk" at Virginia Beach was just that—a walk of boards extending up and down the beach, flanked by the canvas tents of refreshment stands and souvenir booths. One of these drew my attention. The sign on the tent flap stated that portraitist L. Pierre Bottemer would do a scissors profile and mount it on a souvenir card for 25 cents. I thought that would be a nice thing to mail my mother, who had been a bit sad on my departure.

While I sat on a stool and presented my 18-year-old profile, Mr. Bottemer mutilated a black square of paper with a pair of scissors. And asked questions—where was I from, what was I doing in Virginia Beach, what did I plan to do with my life? His manner was so friendly I found myself opening up to him, relating how I had hoped to go to college and eventually become a writer, but my family simply didn't have the money. So I was going to go to work at the shipyard.

He finished his snipping and drew up a chair and sat down. I can't recall his exact words but the thrust of them was simple: No one my age should give up on a dream so easily. I hadn't run into a brick wall, I had merely run into an obstacle, and obstacles could be overcome.

Riding the ferry back to Newport News, leaning on the rail and watching the Tidewater landscape drift by, I thought about the words of L. Pierre Bottemer. They must have been persuasive, for when I got back to my rooming house I told Mr. Wilson I'd be returning to Bristol and, I hoped, college.

That's the way it turned out. Somehow, the money was scraped together (I recall raking a lot of tuition-leaves on the King College campus.) Nineteen years passed, and I returned to Tidewater. As a writer, of sorts. At least, my by-line read, "*Ledger-Star* Military Writer." Up at Newport News, the big attack carrier *Independence* slid down the ways to join the fleet. We sort of joined together, for during the next two decades I was aboard her many times in many faraway places—the Caribbean, the Mediterranean, the Norwegian Sea, the South Pacific.

One day in the mid-'60s, I was walking down Norfolk's main street on my way to lunch when a sign in the window of a leading department store caught my eye. It said that L. Pierre Bottemer was doing portraits inside. Bottemer still alive! I was inside in a flash but had to wait for him to finish with a client. I introduced myself and fervently thanked him for his counsel a quarter-century earlier. The road not taken had undoubtedly been one of the turning points in my life.

Mr. Bottemer simply stared. He had no recollection of the incident whatsoever.

അ

Fiddling Around   *September 1, 2003*

Before I became a newspaperman, I'd fiddled around with other stuff. Fresh out of the Navy Air Corps, I'd gone to work down in Mississippi as an "instrument man" for an oil exploration outfit. Before the war, I'd worked in the Maps & Surveys Division of TVA as a lowly rodman and, fortunately, the two jobs were quite similar. Both involved running elevations with a level.

With the TVA, it was determining the potential shoreline of South Holston Lake. In Mississippi, it was establishing precise elevations for gravity meter stations. Day after day in the blazing sun, stripped to the waist, running a line among red clay hills.

I don't remember much about the little village of Magee where we were headquartered except that it had its fair share of pretty girls and was the scene of the only real fight I ever had in my life.

Four of us were driving around in a company car one evening, passing around a bottle of bootleg whiskey, when I said something that obviously irritated the guy seated in the back. He broke the bottle over my head. I took offense at this, seeing as how it was my bottle. I went over the back after him but he jumped out. I followed, tackled him, straddled him, and began rebuking him with my fists.

I was so enraged at the waste of all that good liquor that I wasn't aware he had kept the neck of the bottle in his hand and was slashing me with it. I've forgotten how many stitches it took to close all the leaks. Ah, well, the idiocy of youth.

Finally, I decided to take advantage of the GI Bill and return to college. I'd had one year at King but had fallen in love with Chapel Hill during pre-flight as a Naval Aviation Cadet. I applied, was accepted, and arrived in January, 1946. My memories of the place are a bit hazy but highlighted by cute coeds and the fact I graduated without knowing it.

You see, when I returned to college, I hadn't planned on getting a degree. There were subjects in which I'd always been interested and I simply wanted to wallow around in them—literature, writing, psychology, philosophy. However, when I'd had my surfeit of these, I began wondering how many courses I'd have to take to get a degree. At the registrar's office, I told the little old lady behind the counter what I needed to know and she disappeared into her files.

A few minutes later she returned and handed me a 5x3 rectangle of cardboard (I know that's the size for it's lying here on my desk). It bears the date of Jan. 22, 1948 and declares: "This is to certify that Jack Hale Kestner has completed the requirements of the curriculum prescribed for the degree Bachelor of Arts of the University of North Carolina."

What happened was that the university had given me credit for cadet courses I'd taken in pre-flight school—navigation, meteorology, etc. By weird coincidence, they precisely covered the blank spots in my curriculum.

Yes, there was rather wild celebration that night in Chapel Hill.

☙

The Dragonfly   *August 14, 1989*

I was down at the beaver pond the other day when a dragonfly zoomed in and landed on the stub of a dead limb. I gave him a low bow (well, as low as a body can make while sitting on a rock) and said, "Thank you."

He deserved my thanks. Forty years ago this month, dragonflies changed the course of my life. It's a rather involved story, but since it shows how an insignificant little thing like an insect can mold the future, I'm going to tell it anyway.

Late in July 1949, after finishing college and a boring year in an advertising venture, I hopped a Greyhound bus in Bristol for New Orleans. Why New Orleans? Well, the literature, for one thing. A couple of years earlier, Tennessee Williams had come out with *A Streetcar Named Desire*. And William Faulkner's <u>Mosquitoes</u> and <u>Wild Palms</u> had been set there.

But I suppose the main thing was itchy feet. And the New Orleans I'd read about was about as contrastive to Bristol as any city I could imagine. I found a little second-floor apartment in the heart of the French Quarter, a couple of blocks off Bourbon. At 619 St. Phillip St., to be exact (which is how my aging brain works; I can't remember what I had for lunch yesterday, but I can remember a street number from 40 years ago).

Those who have been to New Orleans know the motif of the Vieux Carré is the wrought-iron balcony overlooking the street. Well, I went out on my balcony one afternoon—probably to sip on a drink and watch the girls go by—and encountered a phenomenon. The air above the street was literally thick with dragonflies, more than I'd seen in the rest of my life put together.

Since I'd always had an intense interest in nature, and since none of the barflies in the neighborhood tavern could account for those rural dragonflies being in a big city, I took a streetcar out to Tulane University. There I introduced myself as a reporter from the *New Orleans Times-Picayune,* doing research on the dragonfly. Of course, I'd never been inside that newspaper—but this was before I developed the habits of probity and honesty that so characterize me today.

By pure luck, the dragonfly happened to be the favorite insect of the friendly entomologist whom the receptionist called out to help me. Not only did the professor tell me why hordes of them were occupying the French Quarter (something about the proximity to the Mississippi River and their breeding grounds), but also a wealth of other details.

Although dragonflies were called "snake doctors" here at Hayters Gap when I was a boy, the professor said they were called "skeeter-eaters" in the Deep South. He explained why. The first part of the dragonfly's life (known as the "naiad stage") is spent under water, during which it feeds on mosquito larvae. Then, when it becomes an adult, it catches adult mosquitoes in the air, thanks to a wonderful agility provided by four independently operating wings.

Even one dragonfly, he said, can dispose of literally dozens of mosquitoes a day, making it Mother Nature's most effective natural control. At the turn of the century, when mosquitoes were found to be the only way that the devastating plague of yellow fever was transmitted, all sorts of projects were launched to control them—including, the professor said, mass productions of the dragonfly.

On my way back to the French Quarter, I turned the story over in my mind and decided it was interesting enough to take a whack at. So I unlimbered my typewriter and pounded it out. The next day, I hunted up the office of the *Times-Picayune* and offered it to the editor of their Sunday supplement. He read it, looked up, smiled and said, "Sure we'll buy it."

"You will?" I asked—incredulous that anyone would actually pay money for words I'd stuck together.

Well, I only lasted a month in New Orleans before my money ran out. Money well spent, as I recall. Returning, penniless, to Bristol, I learned that Gene Worrell was in the process of establishing a newspaper to compete with the evening *News-Bulletin*. Although I still yearned to write The Great American Novel, I decided it would probably be necessary to eat occasionally during the interim.

Herman Giles, whom Gene had tapped as managing editor to get his new newspaper off the ground, asked what experience I had. I casually replied that one of my stories was currently featured on the supplement cover of one of the nation's leading newspapers—which was true. Of course, I neglected to add it was the only newspaper story I'd ever written. Anyway, I was hired—and went to work September 1, 1949, six weeks before the first copy of the *Virginian-Tennessean* rolled off the presses.

And that's why I always say thank you to the dragonfly.

Military reporter for the Norfolk Ledger-Star, *1959.*

4 ~ Newspaper Man

After his first article appeared in the *Times-Picayune* in New Orleans, Dad returned to Bristol—a timely decision on his part as the *Virginia-Tennessean* was hiring new staff for its upcoming launch as the region's second daily paper. Here, as a reporter, Dad found his professional home. The rush of approaching deadlines, the ever-changing locations, and the opportunity to connect with strangers were a perfect complement for his personality.

Two years later, in 1951, he left Bristol, lured away by the offer of a "dream job" as a reporter in Bermuda. In 1954, he married our mother, Thelma Elizabeth Atwood. Dad, our mother, and Lisa left Bermuda in 1959 when he was offered a position at the *Ledger-Star* in Norfolk, Virginia. As a military reporter for a region that was home to one of the world's largest military installations, Dad finally felt he was reporting the real news rather than the "soft stuff" of his assignments in Bermuda.

These are the years of his professional career that we remember the best. Our visits to the *Ledger* were always awe-inspiring for us children. A crowded newsroom filled with the low haze of cigarette smoke, the background clamor of what seemed like hundreds of typewriters, reporters rushing in and out—all convinced us that Dad had the most exciting job in the world.

Though he won many journalism awards, it was always the story that mattered most. Among his favorites was a piece he wrote on the last "drumming out" parade of the Marine Corps in the early '70s.

During a unit roll call, to the beating of drums, stripped of all his military insignia, a Marine is dismissed in disgrace from the Corps. In a later profile in the *Ledger*, Dad reminisced about the story and said: "I actually shed tears when I wrote that damned thing and when I was finished I knew it would do what I hoped it would." The story ran on front pages all over the world and the practice was ended.

Forty years ago this month, Bristol's newest newspaper was experiencing labor pains in an old warehouse on Shelby Street. An aging printing press had been discovered stored on a chicken farm near High Point, N.C. Since it was all the new enterprise could afford, it had been bought and hauled in and bolted to the floor over a new press pit. An entire staff of reporters (four, to be exact) had been hired and they were writing and stockpiling feature stories.

Sign painter Bob Marshall (who had a reputation as the town humorist) had also been hired to announce to the world that this was the home of journalism's newest baby. Bob had worked all morning on a ladder along the vast expanse of masonry that constituted the building's western wall, painting in letters ten feet tall. Then he broke for lunch.

We inside the building became puzzled when we noted most pedestrians passing our plate glass windows seemed to be laughing. Finally, one of us went outside to see what was going on.

What was going on was the sign Bob Marshall had painted. He'd been commissioned to paint simply, "Home of the Bristol Virginia-Tennessean." And he'd made a good start. But when he'd gone to lunch, he'd left a sign that read, "Home of the Bristol Virgin."

In a very real sense, that sign was accurate. Three out of four reporters had never worked on any newspaper before. Nor had our one-man photographic department, Harrison Hall. The entire newsroom staff was still in its 20s.

Herman Giles had been lured from Kingsport by Board Chairman Gene Worrell to mid-wife his new baby. Herman had the most experience of any of us—six whole years. He also had his hands full. Not only was he starting from scratch to produce a product to compete with a paper that had been a part of the community for 75 years, he had to do it on a limited budget with worn-out equipment. As if that wasn't enough, he had to do it while playing mother hen to a greenhorn reportorial staff.

If I remember correctly, it was quite a while before even a name was selected. There were all sorts of proposals, including one that it simply be called, *The Newspaper*. The proposer pointed out that this would bring us all sorts of free publicity, since people were always saying, "Well, I read in the newspaper the other day that . . . "

Somehow, Giles managed to whip his staff into shape, and the big day finally rolled around. The plan was to go to press on the evening of Saturday, Oct. 15, 1949, with a huge Sunday edition with which to blanket the city.

Herman and I were reminiscing recently, and he recalled several things I'd forgotten. It's easy to see why he would remember. That first edition almost didn't come out.

The head pressman had given repeated assurances that the press "would fly like a hummingbird."

"I told him that evening that he was right," Giles recalled wryly. "That press flew all over the place."

Among the other problems were stripped gears on a critical cutting

First press photo, for the Virginia-Tennessean.

cylinder, rendering the entire press inoperable. Giles loaded the cylinder into his car and hauled it to Kincaid's Machine Shop. After getting it brazed, he brought it back and it was re-installed. And the press ran beautifully. For about 15 minutes. Then, once again, the cylinder stripped its gears. Kincaid was called at his home and reluctantly agreed to come down.

"After he fixed it, he told us that he hoped it would hold, for he wasn't coming back," Giles recalled. "Fortunately, it held although the press kept breaking webs (sheets of newsprint). Also we had to keep making over plates."

As if this wasn't enough, somebody discovered that the oil pans on the main bearings had been installed upside down, rendering them incapable of holding critical lubricant. "We had to bring in dry ice and hold it over those bearings to keep them from heating and locking up," Giles recalled.

If anybody that night was sweating more than Herman Giles, unquestionably it was Gene Worrell. He'd persuaded some of the city's leading citizens (Jack Stone, Bill Tilley Sr., Jim Tilley, Bob Boswell, Rudy Burroughs, Nat Copenhaver, H. R. Bibee, Dave Weinstein) to invest heavily in the new venture, and several were on hand to witness the first press run.

That first edition was a big 64-pager. But the press only had a 32-page capacity, so two full runs had to be made. After being in labor all night and much of the next day, the area's newest baby was gaspingly delivered in mid-afternoon.

In retrospect, it was great to have been a part of that adventure—to be young and alive and totally involved. Many of that vigorous young team are long dead—Roy Elkins, Joe Hill, Dick Miller, Jim Dalton, Harrison Hall.

Maybe, somewhere, they have some new presses rolling. That would be heaven for old newspapermen.

○3

Bermuda   *September 2, 1991*

Yesterday marked a 40th anniversary for me. At 2 p.m. on Sept. 1, 1951, I boarded a plane at Tri-Cities Airport for New York, where I caught another flight for Bermuda. Events there shaped the rest of my life.

I suppose the main reason I left Bristol was itchy feet. I'd never been outside of the country, much less lived there. Moreover I was still making the same $45-a-week newspaper salary I'd started out on.

So, when I came across an ad in *Editor & Publisher* (a newspaper trade journal) for a berth as general reporter on the *Mid-Ocean News* in Hamilton, Bermuda, I responded with alacrity—alacrity and a one-paragraph resume and a sheaf of clippings.

A couple of weeks later, a letter arrived from Park Breck, the managing editor, saying I'd been selected. I was astounded. Why, I figured half the reporters in the U.S. would have applied for that job. Imagine, getting paid to live on an exotic British island. Wow!

Then I read a little further. My salary, Breck said, would start at 14 pounds sterling a week. I did a quick conversion into dollars and discovered this was just under $40. And I thought $45 was low! Reluctantly, I wrote Breck and declined the offer. But after mailing the letter, I suffered immediate doubts. What did I know about the cost of living over there? Maybe that was a fair salary. Maybe I'd turned down the opportunity of a lifetime.

Then, serendipity. A friend of mine, Johnny Bachman, casually remarked he was going to Bermuda on vacation. "You are! Well, will you do a little fiscal research and see if I can live on $40 a week?"

On Johnny's return, he looked me up and, with a broad grin, said, "You may not be able to live on it but you can sure have a lot of fun trying!" Then he told me about Bermuda. Within an hour, I was writing another letter asking if the job was still open. It was.

Stepping off that plane, I probably felt what Dorothy felt when she stepped out of her Kansas farmhouse into Munchkinland. Sparkling blue water everywhere, stately palm trees, white-coral roofs on pastel-colored houses, tiny cars and bicycles driving on the wrong side of the road, everybody wearing shorts.

The *Mid-Ocean News* was housed in an aging tree-fronted building on the side of a hill overlooking Hamilton Harbour. An afternoon daily, it competed with the separately-owned morning paper, *The Royal Gazette*. The *Gazette* practiced British-style journalism and was a bit on the stuffy side. We practiced American-style and were a lot sassier.

Still, there were British niceties to be observed—which I discovered in short order when Bermuda's Chief Justice, Sir Whatshisname, resplendent in crimson robes and powdered wig, ejected me from his courtroom for not wearing a coat and tie.

Well, how was I to know? After all, I'd just come from covering county court in Blountville where I'd seen men spitting tobacco juice on the floor and women openly breast-feeding babies (now, that would really have shaken up His Lordship).

As the only American male on the paper, I began covering U.S. forces stationed there—units at Kindley AFB, a Navy anti-sub squadron, and a Coast Guard Search & Rescue outfit. Pure happenstance. But it was destined to shape the bulk of my newspaper days, for I subsequently became a full-time military writer in Norfolk—for nearly 20 years.

Tourism was Bermuda's industrial nugget. Lots of big names in entertainment and commerce and politics coming down. Interviews with them provided a sizeable segment of our newspaper's daily content. I'd made friends with Janie, a social hostess at the Elbow Beach Surf Club (the island's newest and biggest hotel), and she would give me a call when VIPs arrived.

Janie was also responsible for my financial health. I'd discovered early on that $40 a week was simply not enough to cover the lifestyle to which I aspired. Certainly it wasn't enough to pay for a sailboat to take vacationing New York secretaries out on moonlit cruises on soft summer nights. So I had to find additional income.

Since I was a "comboman" (a reporter who makes his own photos), I frequently got requests for extra prints from guests I wrote stories about. And Janie handled these. Before long, I found myself going to Elbow

Beach at lunch to shoot guest-requested photos she'd arranged. This soon became a major portion of my income.

Janie also served as my ex-officio social secretary. She'd say, "Someone checked in today I'm sure you'd like to meet!"

Indeed, the Bermuda of 40 years ago was a splendid place for a carefree young bachelor. Words and women enshrined in a semi-tropical paradise. The best of all possible worlds. Ah, well. All good things come to an end, they say. But sometimes they shift to other good things. In my case, they shifted to marriage to a Bermuda gal, and a family.

Work, marriage, family. The three big shapers of our lives. They all happened in Bermuda.

୧୪

Jack and his wife, Thelma Atwood Kestner, on the South Shore of Bermuda in 1954, the year they married.

Flying into a Hurricane

For a while there, Hurricane Gilbert shoved even the political garbage of an election year onto a back burner. Which is proof, I suppose, that it's an ill wind that blows no good.

I'll have to admit to a fascination with hurricanes. It goes back to the early '50s in Bermuda when I flew with the Air Force into the eyes of two hurricanes, and experienced four on the ground. It was a time when both the Air Force and the Navy had begun flying hurricane reconnaissance—the Air Force out of Bermuda's Kindley Field, the Navy out of some place in Florida.

I was working for the *Mid-Ocean News*, a buddy of mine was working for the rival *Royal Gazette*, and we vied to become the first Bermuda journalist to make a hurricane penetration. By the flip of a coin, I won. Hardly a claim to fame, granted, but I can say that it made for an interesting day.

My clearance for the 53rd Weather Recon "Hurricane Hunter" Squadron arrived just after the third storm of the season, Carol, had been spotted east of the Leeward Islands. Our big WB-29, a modified version of the old World War II bomber of Hiroshima and Nagasaki fame, lumbered down the runway and roared off into predawn darkness. (The Navy was using modified Constellations, and lost one several years later during a hurricane penetration. As I recall, neither bodies nor wreckage were recovered.)

The only crew member on my flight whose name I recall was one of the pilots, Capt. Wally Taylor, and I remember him because we became friends, and he later served as best man in my wedding. Although Wally was officially listed as co-pilot, on this trip he flew in the left (command) seat. Carol was one of the more intense storms of the season, and he had more hurricane experience than anyone aboard.

We flew due south. The first part was routine. Then, two or three hundred miles from the storm's center, we entered dense clouds and began encountering turbulence. Over the intercom, the order was given to "button up"—to store or tie down all loose items.

The Air Force's normal flight plan for those early years was to penetrate at a relatively low level, enter the eye, take readings, get fixes, then exit at a high altitude. As our four big propellers chewed their way toward Carol's core, turbulence steadily worsened. Although it was mid-morning, we flew through an increasing twilight. It matched my increasing nervousness.

Some years later, I would take a couple of military flights that would be on the hairy side, including one in Antarctica when the skis of our C-130 broke through hidden crevasses as we took off from a glacier, and another in Vietnam on a dive bomb mission aboard an old A-1 Skyraider. But this one was different. On this one, I felt real fear.

At times we would run into rain bands and the whole aircraft would shudder. It was like flying through Niagara Falls. Nor was it comforting to glance through the Plexiglas and observe those long, tapered wings flapping like a bird in flight.

Every time I looked at Wally seated at the controls, my apprehension increased. For he was wrestling with the yoke like it was a living antagonist—pulling, shoving, turning. Feet pumping pedals, eyes glued to the instrument panel. The panel provided his only clue as to whether we were flying upside down or what.

I have no idea how long this incredible turbulence lasted (well, yes, I do—about one and a half lifetimes), but suddenly a flash of sunlight lit up the flight deck. We had broken the eye. And what a sight it was!

Imagine an immense coliseum, ten miles in diameter, whose seats are dirty, ragged clouds towering upward from a white-capped sea to a dizzying height. We were an intruding gnat, surrounded by a whirlpool of clouds. But the tension was broken, and the crew settled back with a collective sigh, relaxing into grins and conversation. Wally turned and gave me a wink—like, hey, piece of cake!

Back in the bomb bay, the dropsonde operator began releasing his babies—instrumented packages attached to parachutes. As they descended, they radioed pressure and temperature readings to the aircraft. Gilbert has the honor of providing an all-time low barometric reading for the Northern Hemisphere—26.13 inches. As I recall, Carol was something over 27 inches—still low.

We circled and climbed inside that spectacular eye, enjoying its fearsome beauty as we took precise navigational fixes. Since weather satellites were a long way down the road, this was the only way of pinpointing the storm's position, course, and speed.

That afternoon, we broke into one of Carol's high walls (encountering only moderate turbulence) and headed for the barn.

Believe it or not, we got socked by Carol a second time. After making a feint at the East Coast, she swung slowly to the northeast and partially side-swiped Bermuda. Two more hurricanes that year, Dolly and Edna, scored direct hits. I was glad I had my feet on the ground!

03

The "Foolish Venture"

I can't recall what triggered it, but I got to thinking the other day about a sailboat I owned many years ago in Bermuda.

The "Foolish Venture." I'd named it that partly because I figured that's what it would turn out to be, and partly because the "Sea Venture" was the name of the ship carrying English settlers to Virginia in 1609 that got wrecked on Bermuda and gave the islands their first settlers.

After I arrived in September 1951 and found living quarters, and bought a few pairs of shorts (the island's unofficial uniform), transportation was the next item on the agenda.

Cars weren't introduced until World War II. Before then, everyone rode bicycles, or horse-drawn carriages. Bermuda's narrow, winding roads were never designed for cars. And couldn't be widened because of space limitations. But bikes were ideal. And they gradually evolved from pedal bikes to motor-assisted bikes to full-sized motorcycles.

As a reporter on the *Mid-Ocean News*, I had to have transportation to get to my various assignments, so my first major purchase was a motorcycle. And it was fun. At least, it was fun for the nine months of the year when the temperatures were balmy. Cycling to a parish vestry meeting at night through a winter storm was another matter.

But land transportation covered only half of my requirements. For Bermuda is simply a collection of islands, some 300 of them, with the largest connected by bridges or causeways.

All the dry land amounts to only 21 square miles (about one twenty-fourth the size of Washington County); the rest is water. As a result, Bermudians are raised in and on the water. Most kids are swimming by the time they are walking. And a boat of some type is a standard family possession. Bermudians, who believe in living life at a leisurely pace, break up the week into two parts by closing shops and businesses at noon Thursday until Friday morning. Then just about everybody heads for water.

Ergo, even on my limited income, I had to have a boat. I found an old Bermuda racing dinghy, reasonably priced, built from native cedar. Since it had been designed strictly for racing, it had a dropkeel and carried an enormous amount of canvas. Tricky to handle but incredibly responsive.

Like most young men in Bristol, I'd done my courting in a car. In Bermuda, I discovered that a sailboat was a far superior contrivance. No gas to buy. Limitless "highways" to explore. Salt spray in the nostrils. No sound save the slap of water against the hull and the creak of halyards.

And moonlit nights were pure magic—the billowing white sails, the sparkle of moonlight in the bow wave, white rooftops floating dreamily in the distance.

My favorite spot in all of Bermuda was Grace Island. It reared its uninhabited acre or so of rock and wind-twisted cedars out in the middle of Great Sound. It was there that Jeff Fry, a reporter on the competing *Royal Gazette*, and I used to take our dates for Thursday picnics. And it was there that the "Foolish Venture" met her end.

We'd done our usual exploring and snorkeling in that unbelievably clear water, had feasted sumptuously, and were seated around a campfire of aromatic cedar when I noticed a line squall approaching from the southwest.

This posed a problem for an amateur sailor, which I certainly was. If we left at once, we might be able to beat it back to anchorage. But if the breeze died, we might be caught out in the sound in a storm of unknown strength. On the other hand, the "Foolish Venture" was attached to the island's rickety dock with only a bowline, the only line I carried. And there was no telling what kind of wind we'd get.

I opted to risk the boat rather than its crew. A wise decision, probably, for the squall, while of short duration, was a violent one. The wind shifted direction and smashed the "Foolish Venture" against the rocky shore.

So there we were. Marooned.

The nearest land was either Burgess Point, or the U.S. Naval Air Station that jutted out into the sound a couple of miles away. Then I remembered I had a flashlight, and that naval personnel manned the seaplane tower around the dock. Why, I could blink out an SOS signal and we'd be rescued in no time!

But then I was struck by a sudden thought: How many men would ever have the privilege of bragging in later life that once upon a time they'd been shipwrecked on a deserted island with a beautiful woman?

I've done many foolish things in my time, but I'm happy to report that signaling with that flashlight wasn't one of them.

Oh, well, a boat loaded with searchers came looking for us early the next morning, and took us home.

☙

Getting the Story   *June 11, 2001*

Back in '52 or '53 when I was a reporter for the *Mid-Ocean News*, a big story at the time was two Bermuda fishermen missing in their small boat. The U.S. Coast Guard and U.S. Air Force had launched a massive search that had gone on day after day, night after night. Front page news in both the daily papers.

Finally, after a week or ten days, the Coast Guard decided to abandon the search. They concluded that the boat could no longer be afloat. The Air Force, however, decided to give it one more whack the following day.

A spokesman at Kindley Field called to say the tiny craft had been spotted. A rescue vessel had been launched, while a press boat would be leaving Kindley to make a rendezvous in a couple of hours. I roared down to Kindley on my motorbike and found a reporter from *The Royal Gazette* already there. We climbed aboard the rendezvous vessel and headed out to sea.

I got some photos of the two as they came aboard. Although gaunt and haggard, in view of what they'd gone through they were in amazingly good shape. The *Gazette* reporter paired off with one, me with the other. One of the questions I asked was what day they had run out of food and water. The fisherman pulled a notebook out of his pocket and began thumbing through it.

"You mean you kept a diary of your adventure?" I asked incredulously. He nodded. I reached out for it and began thumbing through it, reading entries. Why, here was the summation of their entire ordeal. A gold mine!

"Can I keep this until tomorrow?" I asked. "I guarantee you'll get it back." He agreed and I shoved it surreptitiously into a pocket. Back on land, the *Gazette* reporter and I climbed on our bikes and roared off into the night. I'm sure he wasn't gloating inwardly like I was.

At some point between the west end of the island and my little hilltop cottage on the South Shore, the lights from an approaching vehicle blinded me. An instant after it passed, my headlight picked up something that my mind refused to accept. There, galloping straight at me, was a horse! I didn't have time to do anything except grit my teeth. My bike struck him dead center and stopped him dead in his tracks. Just to make sure, I catapulted over the handlebars and added my weight and momentum.

When I recovered my senses, the horse was gone, my bike was a mangled heap, and I couldn't raise one of my arms—plus I had an assortment of contusions and abrasions. There was a driveway leading up to the only house in the area so I stumbled up that and knocked on the door. A man in night clothes finally answered.

"Do you own a big horse?" I asked. When he nodded, I told him that the horse had been galloping down the middle of the road, I'd run into it and wrecked my bike. I wondered if it would be too much trouble for him to call a taxi. I was standing there, totally disheveled, dripping blood, and the first thing the man said was, "Is my horse okay?" Bermudians, I tell you.

When the taxi arrived, I briefly considered going to the emergency room at King Edward VII Memorial Hospital, but it was after midnight, and no telling how long they'd keep me. It could mean I'd have to write the thing in the office in the morning, and I had no idea how comprehensive the diary was. What it boiled down to was this—the story was simply too good to cram into a short deadline.

I spent the night going through the diary and writing. Although the fisherman's English might not have been impeccable, what the two men had experienced came through loud and clear. It would have been nice to have been able to record it by typing with both hands. A subsequent medical exam revealed a separated shoulder.

Our front page the next day was splashed with excerpts from the diary, photos of the men, and what I viewed as a story written in extremis, with only a bottle of Bacardi rum to serve as an analgesic. It will probably take a newspaperman to appreciate the motivating factor here. My paycheck that week didn't contain a penny more, but that was beside the point. The point was the story.

Well, actually I did receive pecuniary remuneration of a sort. Several weeks later, Ted Sayer, managing editor of *The Royal Gazette*, lured me away from the *Mid-Ocean News* by precisely doubling my salary.

I was told the story of the fishermen's diary had something to do with it.

⚜

The Norfolk *Ledger-Star*   *September 4, 1995*

On Friday, August 25, the last run of the Norfolk *Ledger-Star* rolled off the press. Its death came as no surprise. Decreased readership and the ascendancy of television have continued to wipe out major afternoon newspapers across the nation.

I'm only sorry I wasn't on hand to kiss it good-bye. The *Ledger* constituted the bulk of my newspaper career. The strange thing about it was that I didn't apply for a job there. Sheer luck, or whatever you want to call it, led me to Norfolk.

In the fall of '58, I came home from Bermuda for a visit with my folks. On arrival, my mother told me that a Cam Gregory in Norfolk had called and wanted me to call back, collect. Although I didn't know any Cam Gregory I didn't mind calling collect to find out what it was all about. Cam identified himself as personnel manager for Norfolk Newspapers. He said a reporter had applied for a job and had given as a reference Herman Giles of Bristol Newspapers.

He'd called Herman, who declined to recommend the reporter, so Cam asked if he knew of anyone he would recommend. Herman replied that a reporter in Bermuda who'd once worked for him was coming home on a visit—but he doubted that he'd leave Bermuda to go to Norfolk.

"Herman's right," I said. "I have a cushy job down there."

And so I had. I'd been hired away from the *Mid-Ocean News* by the Sunday *Royal Gazette* for a special feature-writing job that would have made most reporters' mouths water. My assignment was to cruise around the island looking for items of interest. I'd gather information, make my own photos, go home, write the story and process the pictures. When I collected a stack of stories and pix, I'd take them to the office and hand them to Editor Ted Sayer, along with a list of projects for the coming week. Then I'd pick up my pay check and leave.

Ten minutes a week in the office. Hey, you office-toilers, how'd you like to have those hours? Well, that's why I told Cam I wasn't interested.

But he persisted. "You'll be returning through New York, won't you? Okay, we'll pay for your airline ticket there via Norfolk. No obligation, but we would like to show you what we have here."

I thought for a moment and said, "Well, if you're fool enough to do that, I'll take you up on it."

I'd worked for five different newspapers but none with the large news-gathering organization I found in Norfolk. The *Ledger's* big newsroom was crammed with reporters specializing in their fields. The number and variety of copy readers and editors was also impressive.

Lunching with several reporters, I was even more taken by their talk. It reflected a high state of morale and pride in their work. Before I left, I told Tom Hanes, then managing editor, that I appreciated the offer and would think about it when I returned to Bermuda.

And I did. I particularly thought about it after my father-in-law bought us a house. He'd done the same for his oldest daughter, and, even-handed man that he was, insisted on doing it for his youngest. But I hesitated to move in. I had an uneasy feeling that if I did it would nail me to that British colony forever. I'd had a glimpse of what big city newspapering was like, and, while I had a peachy Bermuda assignment, it wasn't "hard" news, it wasn't significant, investigative reporting.

True, I'd grown fond of Bermuda's blue waters and pink sand beaches and the easy, unhurried life of Bermudians. I liked my salary and being my own boss. But I still felt that I'd be wasting an indefinable something if I stayed on. So, reluctantly, I gave notice. Some of my friends thought I had rocks in my head, and maybe I did. But, you know something? In all the years since then, I haven't had one moment of regret.

In Norfolk, I settled in comfortably on the military beat. Since Norfolk is the center of the largest military complex east of the Mississippi, it was arguably the best beat on the paper. At any rate, it satisfied my love of travel—from the South Pole to above the Arctic Circle and quite a few points in between.

Another satisfaction was the workplace itself. Wherever pleasant conditions are found, it generally means they have filtered down from the top through layers of management. The top in this case was the publisher, Frank Batten, Sr. A typical example of his relationship with his employees occurred when the *Ledger* gave me its customary farewell party on my retirement.

Batten had undergone surgery on his larynx and was recuperating at home. Although unable to speak a word, he wrote a letter, brought it to the party, and had managing editor Bob Dodson read it. It now hangs framed above my desk. The opening line:

"There is nobody sorrier than I that you are retiring except for many, many readers who follow your military writing . . ."

I was lucky enough to win a few journalism awards, but those plaques and citations hang in my closet. They reflect only technical skills. Batten's letter, and the circumstances of its presentation, reflect far more.

Yep, the old *Ledger* was a fine place to work.

CB

Lisbon 1962   *February 14, 2000*

There's one thing to be said about being snowbound. It provides an excuse for wading through a lot of stored junk, which in turn leads to a lot of discoveries. When I came across a brown manila envelope with "Portugal" scrawled on the outside, I had no idea what was in it until I dumped its contents onto the bed. Instantly, the old memory machine kicked in—my first military trip abroad.

There were odds and ends of memorabilia, including a flyer with the heading, "Cruzada Crista Internacional"—International Crusade for Christ. Where in Portugal I got that, I have no idea. There were also two letters from my wife c/o American Express in Lisbon, postmarked Norfolk Aug. 11 and Aug. 13, 1962, and one typewritten three-page letter from me to her written on Hotel Tivoli stationery.

The letters from Thel were probably typical of what any wife would write a journeying husband, i.e., emphasis on how the children were doing. Tim was only a month old when I left, Pam 16 months, and Lisa six years.

Naturally, she included news of our animals—Choo-Choo the turtle, Pretty Bird the parakeet, and Tykie the Dachshund. She wrote that one night at bedtime, she discovered Tykie missing. Finally, she found him asleep on the floor in the guest bedroom, his chin resting on one of my socks.

Lisbon had been the final destination for a bunch of U.S. newsmen covering a NATO exercise in the Bay of Biscay. We'd flown to the Azores where we'd boarded a destroyer which in turn had put out to sea and then high-lined us in Bo'sun's chairs aboard the aircraft carrier *Enterprise*. It marked the first deployment of the world's first nuclear-powered surface ship. *Enterprise* had been assigned a key role in the exercise, so naturally the Navy was eager to justify the most expensive (at that time) warship ever built.

In my letter home, dated 2 a.m., Wed., Aug. 15, 1962, I didn't devote much space to the military. Instead, I dwelled on the delight I was experiencing in the ancient city of "Lisboa." Even my hotel room rated half a page of copy.

"Huge, draped windows looking out on the main drag of Lisboa, the Avenida da Liberdade. Huge bed with a headboard that has all sorts of push-buttons for lights, etc. I like the system of putting light switches outside the room you're going into, like the bathroom. It makes sense. The bidet makes sense, too, although it hasn't been in use yet. The bath towel measures 5 ½ x 3 feet and weighs around 3 pounds. It hangs on 'S' piping which can be heated by steam with the turn of a knob.

"Air conditioning. Radio in the headboard. Elaborate cupboards. Sheets on top of the blanket as well as beneath. Quite a hotel room. And all for 160 escudos, or $5.61 a day. Boy, I could stay here forever!"

That evening, Bill MacDougall of the *Los Angeles Times*, Dan Partner of the *Denver Post*, and I decided to eat at what was reportedly one of the finest restaurants in Europe, the Tavares. We later agreed that it must be.

"Waiters in swallow-tail coats served us the meal," I wrote. "Beef tournedos and vegetables, followed by dessert, cheeses, and two brandies (the best I've ever had) in glasses the waiter warmed over an alcohol flame. And all for less than $5. I'm living it up!"

Well, what other reaction could you expect from a country boy in a furrin' land who suddenly finds himself eating high off the hog?

"After the meal, Bill returned to the hotel," I wrote. "Dan and I stood for a while at a statue near the Tavares where a small boy was playing a harmonica while two others were singing in Portuguese. Little girls and boys were dancing.

"One little girl about Lisa's age was dancing with another little girl about Pamela's age. All had a terrific sense of rhythm. It was a very nice scene and I hated to leave, but Dan and I had decided earlier we'd like to go dancing, so we hailed a taxi.

"The driver couldn't speak a word of English but seemed to understand from our sign language what we wanted. Wrong. He took us at the usual insane speed across town where he stopped and ushered us up to a second floor apartment where a woman immediately took us to a bedroom. Beautiful girls standing outside in the corridor.

"Dan and I said, 'No! No!' and made arm and hand motions to indicate we were interested in dancing and drinking rather than the entertainment she had, so the madam gave us her business card and let us leave.

"The taxi driver outside took us to some clip joint where we went down about 99 flights of steps and arrived at a room where a combo was playing its own version of American music. As soon as we sat down we were attacked by a couple of girls who demanded a bottle of champagne.

"Thank goodness I was with Dan, a solid individual, who demurred and told them we would only buy a drink at a time. Which we did. Even though it was a clip joint (costing us about $6 each before we left), I enjoyed it tremendously.

"The gal who had attached herself to me was from Madrid. Professional dancer type, she said, in pretty good English, and I believed it after dancing with her. We put on a floor show (thanks to her) which drew applause from all quarters."

Me? Putting on a floor show? I don't remember that and I don't believe it. Sitting up here, cocooned within a snowy landscape, it's also hard to believe that I once traveled to many exotic spots in the world. Now, in my old age, I'm glad I did. It's been over six years since I spent even one night away from this house.

Memories, memories.

ᘓ

Antarctica 1962 and 1963 June 19, 1989

The thing that got me to thinking about Antarctica was running across a batch of color slides—photos I'd taken in '62 and '63 while covering the Navy's annual "Operation Deep Freeze." Let's pretend it's November—Spring in Antarctica—and take a vacation on "The Frozen Continent." First, though, a bit of background:

The inhabitants of Planet Earth never have gotten along very well. Specifically, its governing bodies haven't. Can't agree on anything—political systems, economic systems, whatever. At least, they couldn't until the International Geophysical Year of 1957-58. It was then that 12 nations—including the U.S. and the Soviet Union—signed a 30-year cooperative agreement designating Antarctica an international laboratory.

The agreement stated that all nations would forego territorial claims. Instead, they'd simply establish stations and do research and cooperate scientifically. And so they have. For 30 years, it's worked beautifully.

Okay, so much for background. Now, let's get started. Our takeoff is from Harewood Field near Christchurch, New Zealand. Our aircraft is a big C-130 MATS cargo plane. Its normal landing wheels protrude from the skis we'll use when we land 2,200 miles to the south.

Enroute, we're introduced to the savage cold we'll be living in. Over a period of several hours, the temperature in the cavernous cargo hold is gradually lowered. As it is, we don layer after layer of thermal gear—30 pounds of it.

Some eight hours after take-off, we step out onto Williams Field—which is simply the frozen surface of McMurdo Sound. McMurdo Station is the American gateway to Antarctica. It's an ugly collection of Jamesway huts and warehouses and fuel storage tanks plunked down in the middle of wildly beautiful scenery. From it, American scientists fan out across the ranges and glaciers of western Antarctica to establish camps.

While the Arctic, north of Canada, is simply an ocean covered with a permanent layer of salt-water ice, the Antarctic, by contrast, is a vast land mass buried beneath enough fresh-water ice to cover the entire United States to a depth of two miles.

Geologists chip away at exposed cliffs, gathering rocks dating back 500 million years. Seismologists trace the course of ridges buried under thousands of feet of that ice. Other scientists study activity in the upper atmosphere. You may recall that it was one of these studies that first alerted the world to the hole in the ozone layer.

There's so much to do and see down here, all of us are soon suffering from what old Antarctic hands call "The Big Eye." Since the sun never sets, it's hard not to utilize the eternal daylight, so we soon acquire a glassy-eyed stare.

In addition to monitoring scientific projects, there are fun things to do—like spending an afternoon in the midst of thousands of Adele penguins at their rookery near Hallett Station. Or a box lunch picnic at Big Razorback Hill, an upthrust of volcanic rock in McMurdo Sound where Weddell seals have their breathing holes and whelping grounds.

It's kind of neat to sit there, munching on southern fried chicken, surrounded by a colony of barking seals and their pups, with an active volcano (Erebus) smoking in the background.

Lunch finished, we hike to Cape Evans and the hut where British Navy Capt. Robert Falcon Scott wintered over in 1922 before making his race for the pole. When Scott and his four companions failed to return, those remaining at the hut began a search the following spring—and found their frozen bodies within 11 miles of a food cache.

We enter the hut and find things exactly as Scott's party had left them—newspapers and magazines bearing dates in 1910; bags of flour and catsup and sugar, all perfectly preserved by the intense, dry cold.

The next day, we retrace Scott's route to the pole. But we do it the easy way, flying at 26,000 feet above the Beardmore Glacier up which Scott and his men had labored so painfully. We make the 825 miles from McMurdo to the South Pole in two hours and 42 minutes. It took Scott and his companions 79 terrible days—only to discover that the Norwegian explorer Roald Amundsen had beaten them there by a month.

Scott wrote in his sledge notes on that Jan. 17, 1912: "Great God! This is an awful place and terrible enough for us to have laboured to it without the reward of priority."

Awful, yes. Wildly beautiful, yes. And incredibly unique. The world's last unspoiled frontier. This year could mark a dramatic change. The 30-year, 12-nation agreement expires. Already there is talk of divvying up the continent among the signatories and exploiting it commercially.

Unhappily, for the past several years, Planet Earth has been gang-raped by a bunch of big business plunderers cynically waving the banner of free enterprise. Of course, there'll be solemn promises that adequate environmental safeguards will be taken—while Exxon continues its futile effort to clean up hundreds of miles of Alaskan shoreline.

It would be nice to keep one, just one, unspoiled place on this earth. A place devoted to the acquisition of knowledge for the betterment of all mankind—not just to satisfying the greed of a few.

☙

Antarctica, 1962. Mt. Erebus is in the background. Courtesy of the Virginian-Pilot/Ledger-Star.

The Cuban Missile Crisis Scoop 1962 *October 5, 1992*

Later this month, we'll be recalling the 30th anniversary of what some have termed the scariest week in American history—the Cuban Missile Crisis. I have a special reason to remember it. Purely by accident, I learned of the site of the crisis a full day before President John F. Kennedy startled the world with his announcement. Trouble was, my scoop never got published.

Shortly after noon on Sunday, October 21, 1962, a couple of dozen newsmen, mostly from Washington, took off in a press plane from Oceana Naval Air Station in Virginia Beach. We were headed for an overnight stop at Roosevelt Roads air station in Puerto Rico. Early the next morning we were scheduled to hop over to nearby Vieques Island to observe "PhibBrigEx," an annual multi-service military exercise.

The customary trip-long poker game for us military writer types began as soon as the wheels left the runway. Some time during the mid-afternoon, I got up for a stretch and a cup of coffee. Leaning against one of the Plexiglas windows, I glanced idly downward—and almost dropped my cup.

For there below was the nuclear-powered aircraft carrier *Enterprise*, the Navy's newest and finest, steaming briskly south with two destroyer escorts trailing astern. Boy! Only two days back, I'd spent hours trying to find out what in the world was going on with that big flattop.

Enterprise had returned to Norfolk from a brief deployment earlier in the week, and had shut down her nuclear reactors. Suddenly, she'd fired them up again and raced out of Hampton Roads so fast many of her crew were left behind. Even my most reliable sources couldn't say why. (Not surprising, since it was later revealed that the ship itself had sailed under sealed orders.)

That same day, and the next, there'd been a rash of speculative wire service stories. The president had interrupted a trip to return to Washington. Cabinet members were seen slipping into the White House. Rumors flew concerning a crisis in Europe, possibly Berlin.

Now, everything fell into place. The crisis wasn't in Europe. *Enterprise* was headed straight for Windward Passage. Which was bordered on the west by—Cuba! I hadn't a clue as to what had caused the flap, but, whatever it was, I assumed we were getting ready to invade.

Enterprise, I reasoned, was being sent to provide air cover (and possibly serve as an evacuation platform) for U.S. Navy personnel at our Guantanamo Bay Naval Station, located just below Windward Passage. Fortuitously, the amphibious assault exercise on Vieques had provided an ideal cover for the build-up of our military forces in the Caribbean. Beautiful timing! And, most beautiful for me, none of the other newsmen had been looking out their windows. I had a world-class scoop!

When our aircraft landed at RoosRoads, newsmen carried their luggage to rooms in the BOQ, then adjourned, as was their custom, to the officers' club bar. Not me. I broke out my portable and began pounding out my story. When finished, I turned it in to Bob White, head of Western Union in Puerto Rico, who was accompanying the exercise to make sure copy was expedited.

After dinner that evening, several of us gathered in the room of Navy Cmdr. Jack MacKercher, public affairs officer for our group. I casually mentioned to Jack that, no matter what happened on Vieques the following day, it couldn't top the story I'd already sent. Then I told him about *Enterprise*—and watched color drain from his face.

Since I'd known Jack for years, and had come to respect his Navy savvy, I decided we'd better talk. I jerked my head toward the BOQ balcony. Bob White followed us out.

"I gather that *Enterprise* is sensitive," I said. "Can you tell me, right now, that I've endangered national security?" MacKercher shook his head. "I can't tell you that, for none of us know that much about it," he said. "I've never seen such tight wraps. But since we don't know, it could."

What to do? Wire services and newspapers had been vying to learn the location of the rumored crisis. By pure chance, I'd found out. Quite a feather in my newspaper's cap. But it was awkward not knowing what effect this pinpointing might have on plans at the national level. Since I hadn't violated security in getting my information, it boiled down to a personal decision. A painful one.

I pulled out my notebook and scrawled a five-word message: "KILL *ENTERPRISE* STORY REPEAT KILL." I tore it out and handed it to Bob White, who rushed off with it. (When I returned to Norfolk a few days later, my editor told me that the "kill" message had been flashed through so fast it arrived at the office ahead of the original story.)

The following evening, I sat with other newsmen on the verandah of the Gramboko Hotel in St. Thomas, and listened to President Kennedy's description of Soviet missile emplacements in Cuba. My story wouldn't have affected a thing. I felt like kicking myself.

Oh, well, my decision actually paid off in the long run. For when word filtered up to the Pentagon, doors began opening that had previously been closed.

You never know.

CŞ

Seems like everybody and his little brother has a story to tell about where they were the day President Kennedy was shot. Dear Abby has even published a full-length book collection.

Well, my only claim to fame is that I may well have been the only person in the civilized world who didn't learn about it until nearly a day later. Here's how it happened:

In October 1962, I went to Antarctica to cover the U.S. Navy's annual support of scientific projects—"Operation Deep Freeze." During that visit, I not only fell in love with the wild beauty of Antarctica but also New Zealand, the jumping off point for "The Ice."

However, it's one thing to visit a place but quite another to stay there. After a few days of the bleakness and cold and utter isolation of McMurdo Sound, I asked an officer how in the world they got Navy men to volunteer to winter-over. He grinned.

"I'd say a lot of them volunteer just to spend time in New Zealand, going and coming," he replied. "New Zealand girls are the friendliest in the world!"

Well, yes, I'd noticed that. As a matter of fact, I liked both places so much that the following year I pulled a few strings and got my name on the roster for another trip down.

After the long flight from the States and a couple of days at the U.S. Navy Facility in Christchurch, our group boarded a ski-equipped C-130 Hercules and headed south. We were mostly newsmen with a sizeable sprinkling of VIPS, including one U.S. senator.

Things hadn't changed much at McMurdo, so I decided to break away from the group and develop stories on my own instead of taking the guided tour. A wise decision. More stories and more fun. As a result, when we returned to Christchurch, I figured I'd earned a vacation.

I decided that, instead of returning to the States with my group, I'd tour New Zealand and catch the next military flight. So, I rented a car and set out across the Southern Alps. My plan was to drive to Greymouth on the West Coast, then travel up the coast to Cook Strait where I'd catch a car-ferry to Wellington and explore North Island.

Thirty years ago, there was only one road leading to Greymouth across the mountains. The most charitable thing I can say about it is that it provided some interesting driving. The eastern section was in the process of being widened, but the western section was still in a pristine state— one-lane dirt. When you met a car, you pulled over as far as you could.

I'd gotten used to driving on the left side in Bermuda, but nothing had prepared me for a road like that. My side was the cliff side, and guard rails were notably absent. When I pulled over and stopped to let other cars pass, I'd find myself on the edge of several hundred feet of nothing. Needless to say, my nerves were somewhat frayed when I arrived in Greymouth.

After dinner that night, I wandered into the "parlor" of the bar (a uniquely British arrangement) and found that a group of Rotarians had just broken up their weekly meeting and were now having their customary pint of warm ale before wending homeward.

I began chatting with a guy who turned out to be the publisher of the local newspaper. When he learned I was a wandering American newsman (apparently they didn't get many in those parts) he asked if he could send over one of his reporters. I said, okay, and not long afterwards a young chap arrived. Although I was able to comment warmly about the unspoiled beauty of New Zealand and the friendliness of its citizenry, I'm afraid I was a bit blunt about that road across the Alps.

"If that road was in America, I said, "It would be condemned and closed to everything except foot traffic." Oh, well, at least I was quoted accurately—as I discovered when I read his newspaper at breakfast the next morning.

Thirty years have reduced the memory of my drive up the coast to a pleasant blur of rugged scenery and friendly people. It was late in the day when I reached the northern peninsula where I'd hoped to find lodging. But, for some reason I can't recall, I decided instead to return to Christchurch.

I do recall getting lost amid one rugged stretch of mountains, and finally arriving at the Navy facility in Christchurch just before midnight. I hit my bunk immediately.

It was mid-morning when I awoke. After dressing, I walked out and headed for the canteen. It was then I saw the American flag flying at half-mast at headquarters. I stopped a passing sailor and asked him why. He looked at me strangely.

"For President Kennedy," he replied.

"President Kennedy?" I repeated in wonderment.

The sailor shook his head. "Where have you been? He was shot and killed almost 24 hours ago."

CଓS

Most of the Thanksgivings of our lives fall into a pattern of family get-togethers, of homecomings with children, of laughter and good food. Not long ago, rummaging through a drawer, I found a handful of crumpled Vietnamese piasters—and was whisked back in time to a different Thanksgiving Day.

It was 1965, the year the United States became irrevocably committed in South Vietnam, the year when every major military complex in the U.S. began a drawdown to supply the men and tools of war. Since one of the nation's largest military complexes was centered in Norfolk, it was natural to be assigned to Vietnam. An enviable assignment, really. I didn't have to write think-pieces on the rightness or wrongness of the war, but simply stories about military men, particularly those from Tidewater, who had been caught up in it.

Not long after I arrived in Saigon, I headed for the island of Phu Quoc in the Gulf of Thailand. On the map it looked like a spinning top, its point resting on the 10th parallel, its northern beaches only five miles from the coast of Cambodia. The USS *Krishna*, from Virginia Beach, had dropped anchor there six weeks earlier to assume a key command role in IV Corps tactics.

"Operation Market Time," an all-out interdiction of Communist arms and supplies into the Mekong Delta, had just been launched. *Krishna* was to serve as floating headquarters for the Gulf of Thailand patrol, and as mother hen to a flock of 17 Coast Guard cutters and Navy Swifts.

Phu Quoc was only 200 miles from Saigon as the crow files, but to get to the *Krishna* I had to travel by an Australian Caribou transport aircraft, then an American weapons carrier, and, finally, a Vietnamese junk.

After a flight of less than two hours, the Caribou landed on a short concrete landing strip the Japs had built during World War II near the village of Du'o'ng on Phu Quoc's west coast. A couple of U.S. Army Special Forces sergeants met the aircraft to pick up cases of ammo and concertina wire. I rode with them in their weapons carrier to their compound in the village.

While waiting for a junk to make the final 15 miles down the coast, I chatted with Lt. Joe Parent, 27, of St. Louis, Mo., officer in charge of the 12-man "A" Team.

A few hours later, I was climbing the ladder of the *Krishna* to begin a truly interesting period of reporting in Vietnam. It was a journalist's dream. Stories were everywhere. I went on patrol aboard one of the 82-

foot Coast Guard cutters; studied operations of the Coastal Surveillance Center at An Thoi, the little fishing village at the tip of the island; spent the day with the ship's doctor at a clinic he had set up in the village.

I was struck by the strangeness of this segment of the war, removed as it was from the mainland. My quarters aboard *Krishna* were air-conditioned, and I ate in a wrought-iron and wood-paneled wardroom. Movies were shown nightly.

One night we were watching *Mutiny on the Bounty* when the lights suddenly went on. *Krishna's* skipper announced that the Coastal Surveillance Center had gone to general quarters. All of us rushed out on deck.

A parachute flare was floating lazily over the village. Red tracers arced through the night, and the thump of mortars could be heard. Alongside *Krishna*, the engines of the cutter Point Young coughed and came to life. I had to leap to its deck to catch it as it backed out.

We pulled in close to the compound and provided mortar illumination. The fire fight lasted for nearly three hours. Yet, when we returned to the *Krishna*, *Mutiny on the Bounty* had been restarted and Fletcher Christian had just made a landfall at Pitcairn Island. I took a hot shower and went to bed.

Joe Parent had invited me back to spend the day with his "A" Team. It just happened that the day I caught a junk ride up there was Thanksgiving. We strolled through the village and Joe chatted in Vietnamese with several of the residents. Since "A" teams are paramilitary, over half their time had been spent on civic action programs, so we took a jeep ride to inspect their projects—a dispensary, wells, houses, bridges, even a schoolhouse latrine.

They were a tough outfit, those Green Berets, but about as far removed from the flamboyant airheads of TV's long-running "A Team" as anything you could imagine. These were quite professional.

Thanksgiving dinner was served on a makeshift table in their blockhouse. Weapons were stacked against one wall, while in easy reach was a shelf of live grenades. The menu was canned hamburger steak, canned peas, and fried potatoes.

"Thanksgiving? Bah! Hum-bug!" one of the sergeants joked.

I've been lucky enough to have 22 Thanksgiving dinners since then. But it was the last one for Joe Parent. Out on patrol a few months later, he took a Viet Cong sniper bullet in his head. Although transferred to a hospital in Saigon, he never came out of his coma.

❧

Jack (right) aboard the aircraft carrier USS Forrestal, *Norfolk, May 1967. Courtesy of the U.S. Navy. The following month the* Forrestal *departed for Vietnam. With Jack is Frank Cramblet, then the Commanding Officer of Attack Squadron 65. He had taken Jack for a ride in an A6 aircraft. The vests the men are wearing contain survival gear, such as handheld radios and signal flares, to use in the event the aircraft they are aboard fails to operate properly and they have to eject. Parachutes were kept in the airplane as part of the seat.*

Jack (second from left) receiving the Slover Award for consistent excellence in news reporting at the Ledger-Star *from Frank Batten, the CEO of parent company Landmark Communications. On the left is Wayne Woodlief and on the right is Bill Sauder, both newspaper men with the same organization. Jack won three Slover Awards between 1964 and 1969, after which he retired from the competition.*

Jack interviewing Admiral Elmo R. Zumwalt (right), Chief of Naval Operations. Zumwalt granted very few interviews. After repeatedly being turned down, Jack requested a time—anytime—that he might be available. He was told to join Zumwalt for his 5 a.m. run if he wanted the story. Photo by Charlie Meads, about 1971.

Photos courtesy of the *Virginian-Pilot/Ledger-Star.*

Above, Pam, Lisa, and Tim on a camping trip with Jack at White Rock Cove near Hayters Gap, 1968.

"Pappy Jack" with his grandkids, 2003. From left: Olivia Chappelear, Lindsay Meredith, and Eliza Quigley.

5 ~ Single Dad

When our mother died suddenly in 1967, Dad found his life radically transformed. The shock of her death at 37 was initially muted by the immediate need of finding someone to care for us. He had a demanding career that required lots of irregular hours, not to mention lengthy trips throughout the world. His elderly mother lived eight hours away and his in-laws were on the island of Bermuda, so none of the more traditional options were open. Consequently, a parade of housekeepers marched through our lives—some surviving the experience better than others. All were interesting.

His parenting style was at times unconventional. Though our behavior was governed by military-style rules posted inside a kitchen cabinet, under his care we also learned and experienced things many of our peers didn't. For example, each evening that he was home for dinner it was served formally with candlelight, background music, and tiny sips of wine from crystal glasses. He was always creating some new dish and our dinner table was the most popular in the neighborhood.

Dad allowed us to indulge our "interior design" whims throughout the house and, among other decorating blunders, we ended up with a bright lavender kitchen accented with large multi-colored flower stickers from a fast food restaurant. How that house ever sold is a wonder.

He took us to the woods over and over again—teaching us to pitch a tent, build a fire, shoot a gun. He taught us wildflower names and snake identification. How to rest properly when we couldn't hike another step—and how to keep going when we thought we couldn't.

Through it all, the struggles and the sweetness, we emerged as a family bound together with ties deep and unwavering.

Dad fell in love each time a new granddaughter arrived—first Lindsay in 1989, then Olivia in 1993, and finally Eliza in 1998. They provided hours of entertainment and pride-filled moments for him. The girls loved to visit their Pappy Jack on his mountain, and always talk and reminisce about him with awe and wonder.

Our minds cleave to neat divisions of time—years sliced into seasons, centuries into quarters and halves—so I suppose it's only natural that I got to thinking the other day about this coming Friday. Friday will mark the 25th anniversary of a pivotal event in the life of our family—the death of a wife and mother.

I dug through dusty files and found the journal I'd kept, and correspondence dating from that period. Although parts of that January 10, 1967 evening were seared into my brain, much of the weeks and months that followed had been mercifully forgotten. Re-reading those yellowing pages brought it back. Death is too morbid, and bereavement too intimate, to base a column on. Still, excerpts may strike a responsive, albeit painful chord among some parents.

In a case of terminal illness, plans can be made in advance for child care. But Thel had dropped dead, literally and without warning, from a massive brain hemorrhage, leaving me with three children aged nine, five, and four. Which would have been bad enough in itself, but my job as a military writer had kept me away from home for long periods of time. As a result, child care had defaulted almost wholly into her capable hands.

I knew very little of the demanding routines of child rearing until I was forced to take the cold plunge as a sole parent—a fact brought forcefully to mind when I re-read a copy of a letter I wrote to the mother of a high school chum. Mrs. DeFriece had sent me a long letter of sympathy, and I replied on February 16—a day I characterized as "more or less typical" before detailing its evening activities.

"Home at five only to discover I had forgotten to buy Pam the kite I'd promised, so back to a neighborhood store with her and Timmy. Return home and start spaghetti sauce.

"Pam complains she doesn't feel well. Feel her forehead. Hot. Look for thermometer but can't find. Borrow one from neighbor. 101.8 degrees. Bed her down on sofa since spaghetti is at critical stage.

"Lisa sets table—a real little helper, that nine-year-old. Pammy insists on eating, but after a mouthful decides she wants soup instead. Fix soup while my spaghetti gets cold. Pam decides she doesn't want soup, she wants to lie down. Lisa clears table and washes dishes. Brother Bill has bought us a dishwasher and Lisa loves to use it.

"Take temperature a second time. 103 degrees. Call pediatrician. He prescribes a cool enema, four baby aspirins and since she's congested, a vaporizer.

"Enema is an interesting experience. Pam demands both Lisa and Timmy assist in the process—Lisa to read a story, and Timmy to hold her hand. Bathroom crowded.

"I attempt to administer amount prescribed by pediatrician. Evidently he had misjudged capacity of five-year-old for bathroom gets messed up. Clean floor while four-year-old continues to hold hand and nine-year-old to read.

"Turn down beds in meantime. Discover Timmy has somehow managed to spread a considerable wad of masticated bubble gum on bottom sheet. Get knife from kitchen and attempt to scrape. Gum designed for blowing and chewing or something, but not for scraping. Decide to change bed. Housekeeper has rearranged linen closet so can't find fitted sheet. Compromise by dusting gum area with talcum powder.

"Post-enema process completed. Give Pam a quick shower and put pajamas on. Tuck her in and try to find vaporizer. Finally locate in top of linen closet. But no vaporizer oil. Timmy recalls 'Mommy said all out,' so dress, drive to drug store, buy some. Hook up vaporizer, give aspirin, nose drops and cough medicine.

"Lisa and Timmy take shower. I towel off latter, put pajamas on and tuck in. He reminds Daddy that glass of ice water at head of bed has been forgotten. Fetch same. Tuck Lisa in.

"Thank goodness they're not sick every night, although if it's not that it's something else. Wherever Thel is, I'm sure she's having a good chuckle. She told me, but I didn't believe her."

Amazingly, the children survived it all. Oh, there were bad times, particularly in the beginning. Lisa, at nine, was the first to grasp the full implication of her loss. When I gathered them around me on the sofa and explained that their mother wouldn't be coming home, she burst out:

"It's not fair, it's not fair, now she won't get to see Pam and me get married!"

But kids have bounce. They even retain a sense of humor. One of my nightly responsibilities was listening to their bedtime prayers. On the evening we got a dachshund puppy (promptly named Josh), my journal says that five-year-old Pam concluded her prayer with:

"God bless Mummy, God bless Daddy, God bless Lisa, God bless Timmy, God bless ever'body in whole world. Make this a happy place for ever'body. Make it nice warm day tomorrow. Thank you for Josh. Hope he gets up in the night and piddles on Lisa. Ahh-men."

The Housekeepers

Although I shed nary a tear when Zoe Baird withdrew her name from consideration as the nation's next attorney general, I felt nothing but sympathy for what forced her to do it. Ms. Baird's sin was to hire a couple of immigrants (without working papers) to take care of her child.

She testified before the Senate Judiciary Committee that she'd first tried to hire Americans. Failing there, she had investigated and began the procedure for securing those papers. However, by letting the couple begin work before the procedure was completed, she broke the law.

Well, 26 years ago, I broke that same law. And, frankly, I've never had the least regret—or apology—for doing so. When my wife died suddenly, I was faced with the urgent need of finding someone to take care of our home and look after our children. If I'd known then that the next six or seven years would be a running struggle to fill that position— and keep it filled—I'd probably thrown up my hands in despair.

It began with the first person I hired, on the same day I went back to work. Returning to my newspaper office from an assignment in Virginia Beach, I swung by the house to see how things were going. The new housekeeper was sitting on the living room floor with her boyfriend listening to records. It was mid-afternoon, but Pam and Tim hadn't been fed their lunch. Lisa said later that the housekeeper and boyfriend had been closeted in a bedroom when she got in from school and didn't come out until shortly before I came home. That was the end of No. 1.

No. 2, as I recall, was Zelma, a pleasant country girl from North Carolina. Zelma weighed well over 300 pounds which eliminated any housework. At least, the work didn't get done. And she was a terrible cook. So Zelma departed.

Not long afterward, I had a call from my father-in-law in Bermuda. Knowing how desperately we needed a housekeeper, he'd been advertising and interviewing. "I think I've found someone," he said. "She's a little young, but she seems mature. And she likes children. If it's alright with you, I'll get her an airline ticket."

Of course, it was alright with me. But the next day it struck me that we hadn't discussed her immigration status. Didn't she have to have a work permit? I called INS to see. Yes, indeed, she did! But how long will that take? Well, only a few months—unless there's a hitch of some kind. A few months! I needed someone now. It wasn't a question of evading the law, it was a question of urgency. I decided to let her come anyway.

Anna was young. Nineteen. And knew absolutely nothing about cooking. But she got along beautifully with the kids, so I decided it would be prudent for me to continue cooking in exchange for a full-time babysitter. It didn't last. When Anna took the children to Bermuda for the summer, she began neglecting her duties and had to be let go. So, when the kids returned to Norfolk, it was back to Square One.

Although time has mercifully clouded my memory, somewhere along the line we got Annie. Annie was an African-American woman, who, by far, was the hardest working, most reliable of them all. Trouble was, she had a family of her own and had to leave at five. No weekends. But, time and again, she saved our necks.

Travel was critical to my job as a military writer. I'd planned another tour of Vietnam, but the high casualty rate among newsmen forced me to admit I'd be risking making orphans. Oh, well, at least I could report on state-side training.

When a large joint exercise of Navy and Marines was launched in the swamps of South Carolina (to simulate jungle fighting in Vietnam), I went along—even though it meant being incommunicado for several days. Our housekeeper at that time was a middle-aged widow. The kids weren't particularly fond of her, but she seemed reliable.

When I emerged from the swamp, I immediately called home. It wasn't the housekeeper, but Annie who answered. Seems like a nephew of the widow had gotten into a brawl, had been critically stabbed several times, so she simply up and left to take care of him. Lisa had called Annie, who agreed to stay with them until I returned. What a jewel!

In an attempt to find someone permanent, I made one final foray into the realm of illegal "furriners." My travels had brought me into friendly contact with newsmen throughout Western Europe, so I selected one from each country, sent them an international money order, and asked that they place an ad in a local paper.

The response was overwhelming. Scores of letters. And photos galore—including some in bikinis (I assumed they were letting me know they were willing to take my children to the beach). I ended up hiring an Irish lass who worked with deaf children in a school north of Belfast. Helen Deidre Fitzmaurice. Helen lasted longer than anyone. In fact, she came close to becoming a member of the family.

Maybe it's just as well she didn't, for I'd probably still be wondering if I hadn't taken a drastic step just to get a permanent housekeeper.

Hunting through a storage box for a sheaf of misplaced correspondence, I came across a folder that yanked me back 30 years in time, to the day my wife died. The folder contained items stemming from that event. There were notes and letters and homemade valentines from Tim, Pam and Lisa, plus several disintegrating sheets of rules and regulations.

Although I'd been a father for nine years, I only became one in the true sense of that word when Thel died. I'd spent so much time traveling around the world as a military writer, and even when home had devoted only a fraction of the child-care time that she had. As a result, when I was suddenly plunged into the role of sole parent, I quickly discovered she'd been doing about 95 percent of the work.

And a fine job she'd done, too. There couldn't have been a better mother. Which was my salvation. I really don't know what I'd have done if she'd left me with a bunch of unruly kids. Happily, they weren't.

On the other hand, I hadn't been home enough to know how she'd accomplished this. I wasn't sure what her rules had been. So, I decided I'd have to make up my own. I knew I'd probably make mistakes, but concluded it would be best to err on the side of being too strict. In that respect, I succeeded.

Perusing those crumbling pages, which I'd posted above the washing machine in the kitchen, I'm surprised all three children didn't run away from home. The regulations read more like those of a boot camp than a household.

As they grew older, the rules changed, of course, but before any were implemented, I lifted all three kids to the top of the refrigerator. It was a procedure I used not only to assure their undivided attention but also to avoid talking down to them. After explaining the do's and don'ts, I let them decide on appropriate punishment for infractions. That way, there could be no argument.

Timmy, to the horror of Pam and Lisa, was a hanging judge. He thought restrictions should be handed out for the least misdemeanor.

There were two ironclad rules: "All housekeeper instructions will be followed without argument. If questioning her judgment, do what she says anyway and talk it over with me when I get home."

Second, "No leaving house or yard after dark without permission. Must report home at twilight." Then came a bunch of stuff that can only be classified as "chicken regs":

"All school clothes will be hung up immediately after coming home.

Shoes will be placed in cupboard or room . . . Any mess created by eating in kitchen will be cleaned up before leaving . . . Dirty linen and socks will be placed in clothes basket, other clothing hung up . . . Bikes will be placed on back verandah at end of day . . . No waking each other up (or me) on sleep-in days except emergency . . . Homework to be done as soon as change clothes after school . . . Teeth must be brushed after breakfast and dinner." And so on. Fourteen of those things.

There was also a full page of daily household chores for each child. Well, some were twice-weekly, some once a week. A full page of them. I tell you, if I'd been a kid faced with such ordinances and proscriptions, I think I'd have rebelled. They didn't.

Enough of rules and regulations. It was the content of the other items in the folder which held my attention the longest. Some tugged at my heart. There were notes written by each child over the years, notes addressed to their Dad, notes that revealed their growth and my growth with them. A family trying to make a go of it without a mother.

Only once did the children encourage me to get married again, and that was to Helen, the little Irish gal who came over in the summer of 1971 to serve as housekeeper. When she returned to Newtownabbey after her first eight-month stay, nine-year-old Timmy wrote her regularly, relating all the family news. She subsequently sent me those letters.

In one dated March 26, 1972, he wrote, "I got in a fight with Jack Darden he got a black eye and he clawed me with his finger nails and it swoled up then I went to docters to get a tetnes shoat two nurses could not hold me down. But ween the docter walked in then I did not have a chance.

"I still wish you were my mother. I miss you saying God bless the child. The child isn't well and darling is sad. Nothing is good going on since you left."

Pam wrote in a note, "Timmy and I would like to have Helen as our 2nd mother cause we both love her very much . . ."

Well, I came close. Helen made seven trips to America while I made three to Ireland.

Then there was the note from Lisa dated Jan. 10, 1972, the fifth anniversary of her mother's death: "Thank you, thank you for bringing Pam, Timmy and me through 5 long yrs. We would never have made it without you. Some of the times have been rough especially on you."

Rough on all of us. But, by pulling together as a family, we'd made it. That's what it was all about.

ಣ

Daddy's Special   *December 7, 1987*

As I hovered over our big wood-burning range on Thanksgiving Day, it occurred to me that this made 20 years in a row I had cooked a holiday meal for my children. No big deal, but it did set me to speculating on the number of meals I'd cranked out before they left home—which I imagine has been the speculation of every preparer of family meals since the first cave woman tossed a leg of brontosaurus onto the fire.

I suppose the main reason I never shoved cooking off onto my children was the fact that I enjoyed it. Now, I'm no gourmet cook—never have been, never will be—but I do like to fool around in the kitchen, throwing things together to see what happens, composing variations on standard themes, retaining the melody but supplying different background instruments.

This happened to me one time, maybe 15 years ago. I've forgotten the circumstances, but I had concocted my own brand of chili and decided to alter its presentation. And to my complete astonishment, my children loved it. Began demanding it. Began calling it "Daddy's Special."

Another strange thing happened. Every time my kids found out that Daddy's Special was on the menu, neighborhood kids began showing up at dinner time—and, naturally, were included at the table.

One such Chesapeake lad, Bobby Garringer, now a grown man, visited us this summer and remarked: "The thing I missed most when you all moved away was Daddy's Special."

I suppose anyone's recipe for chili will do, but, for the sake of neighborhood kids everywhere, here's Daddy's Special.

Put into a large saucepan a couple of pounds of the leanest ground beef you can find (although this is a recipe for a family of four, I am immodest enough to anticipate a demand for seconds), cover and place over low heat. As it browns, pour off liquid (reserve to pour over your dog's dry food) and chop meat with sharp utility spoon. Do this until it is dry and resembles heavy sawdust.

In a large skillet that has a cover, sauté a diced bell pepper and a diced white onion in a small amount of vegetable oil. While this process is taking place, open a couple of quarts of canned tomatoes. Put half into a food processor (a blender will do but won't work as well) with a couple of diced pickled jalapeño peppers. Blend and reserve. This is your sauce.

Dump second half-quart of tomatoes into processor. Add two diced pickled jalapeños, two heaping tablespoonfuls of chili powder, one heaping tablespoon of ground cumin, a tablespoonful of salt, a generous shake of garlic salt. Blend, then add to the sautéed stuff. Blend the remaining quart of tomatoes and add. Then add meat. I usually add a 15 1/2 ounce can of drained red kidney beans, but would just as soon leave them out. Cover and simmer forever (well, the longer, the better), stirring occasionally.

Now you'll need some rice. (I've known kids who flatly refuse to eat rice come back for seconds.) I use the five-minute long-grain kind—it's quicker and fluffier and absorbs better. Anyway, I like the "two cups rice, two cups water" formula. It doesn't strain my brain.

Spread rice over bottom of crockery plates (don't use good china or something will melt). Pour over this a generous portion of grated cheese. (I've tried sharp and mild cheddar, Danish Havarti, Colby and Monterey Jack; it all works, but I prefer the last two.) Place plates under broiler until cheese is thoroughly melted.

Now you're ready for your topping, which you have thoughtfully had your children do while you were doing the hard stuff—shredded lettuce, sliced olives (either ripe or stuffed), sliced spring onions (tops and all), and chopped tomatoes. Each customer fixes his own and experimentally adds the hot sauce.

Bon appetit, and all that sort of thing.

଼ଷ

Lindsay, "The Cannonball"   *July 3, 1989*

. . . If this column seems more disjointed than usual, you can put the blame on Lisa. She decided to make a grandfather out of me while I was smack-dab in the middle of it. So I had to rush to Roanoke.

A girl. Lindsay. And over a month early. Lisa always was an impatient little cuss, but that's ridiculous. Oh, well, Lindsay weighed in at five pounds, four ounces—which isn't bad for a preemie. And registered an "eight" on the APGAR scale—whatever the hell that is.

Although I've been old enough to be a grandfather for some time now, getting used to it is going to take some doing.

For when I hear the word "grandfather," I always visualize Heidi's— a stern, irascible old gray-beard living on his mountain all by himself.

I ain't ready for that implication.

଼ଷ

Olivia

Name: Olivia Hale "Jah-Jah" Chappelear. Whew! Imagine walking around under a load like that. Weight: Seven pounds, twelve ounces. Place: Community Hospital of the Roanoke Valley. Time: Monday, May 17, 8:48 a.m. Mother: Did a fine job. Recovering nicely. Father: Very supportive. Held up well. Grandfather: Survived.

At the hospital, Pam, with Olivia nestled in her arms, related to family members how she had awakened around 2 a.m. with the feeling that events were imminent. So she got up and did a load of laundry (sometimes female logic escapes me). Then she stretched out on the sofa with a watch and pen and paper, and began timing her contractions. Then she made a pot of coffee, called her husband at 4 and they arrived at the hospital at 6.

The Cannonball was delighted with the news that she now has a new cousin. Months ago, she'd predicted that it would be a girl, and had named her "Jah-Jah" (which she has already changed to "Livvy Jah-Jah.")

In recent weeks, her Aunt Pam had let her feel the soft kicking of the fetus. This must have led her to visualize what happens during the birthing process. For when her mother, Lisa, told her that a friend of the family had given birth, she turned to a playmate and exclaimed: "Well, it's about time they stuck the bones in that baby!"

 CB

Eliza

When I got up Tuesday, a call on my recorder from Mike. Said he was calling from the hospital and that Lisa was in labor and probably didn't have much longer to go. Then, maybe a couple of hours later, another call. "This is The Cannonball," the voice said. "I now have a baby sister."

Had a breathing test and when I got back from it, Lisa had put two calls on my machine. I called, and she sounded pretty good. Elizabeth Atwood Quigley was six pounds, 14 ounces, 19 1/4" long. Talked to Lisa tonight and she said she and Mike had had a rough night, but said they were doing okay. Said Pam and Olivia had arrived this evening and had been cooking and helping. Think that's fine.

CB

Pappy Jack with his grandkids. Lindsay "The Cannonball" Meredith (left), 1993, and Eliza Quigley (right), 1999.

Olivia Chappelear in Pappy Jack's garden, 1999.

A deer herd grazes contentedly at the edge of the Kestner garden in this view from Jack's bedroom balcony.

6 ~ Wildlife

We can not remember a time when wildlife was not a part of our lives. Even in suburban Chesapeake, we were the family that always took the injured, lost, or homeless animals in.

Beyond the usual array of cats and dogs, hamsters, turtles, fish, and birds, we took in a multitude of needy creatures. Some of our guests included an injured mallard, Peep-Peep, which resulted in Dad converting a corner of our backyard into marshland, and three possums, Wynken, Blynken, and Nod, who were adopted after their mother was killed. Our mother rescued an orphaned family of rabbits that were given the run of the house.

This appreciation and respect for wild creatures dates back to Dad's childhood spent in the woods around Hayters Gap. Once he returned to the mountain for good, he recognized that he was now living on the wild animals' turf. His philosophy was live and let live—if they didn't disturb us, we didn't disturb them. Certainly the deer that destroyed his garden year after year drove him crazy and he spent countless hours using both traditional and unconventional means to keep them out.

Going even further, he often invited the wildlife indoors, annually looking for blacksnakes to live between our floors to control the mouse population, and always quite amused when one would appear unexpectedly during a dinner party.

As with most things that interested him, Dad spent hours observing and detailing those observations in his journal. Many of these journal entries became subjects for his columns. And his readers responded in kind, calling and writing him with their own experiences.

The first column in this chapter, "Watching Wildlife," marked the start of his weekly column, "A View From the Mountain," in the *Bristol Herald Courier*.

ॐ

Watching Wildlife

I've just finished watching a ruffed grouse, a hen, nervously cross my front lawn from the heavy timber in the west to the thickets on the east, shifting from a hesitant walk to a gliding run and then back to a walk again. No big deal, but it did bring to mind what a bumper year this has been for watching wildlife on this remote farm above Hayters Gap.

Turkeys, for example. They've been around ever since we've been here, but this is the first year that large flocks have foraged the fields below the house. One brood came up to the gravel of our driveway, just a few steps from our front door.

On another day, I saw young turkeys exhibit a trait I'd thought was limited to fledgling grouse and quail—an unquestioning obedience. Twelve half-grown youngsters and three hens were fanned out on the lawn above the garden, foraging for insects, when one of the hens apparently issued a warning command. Instantly, all 12 zoomed through the grass in single file with necks outstretched—like a long arrow shot from a bow—and entered the woods.

The turkeys left my garden alone, but deer just about wiped it out. Broccoli is their favorite vegetable. It's also one of mine, for it freezes well and is quickly prepared. Normally, I put up around 200 servings per season. This year? Zilch.

Someone told me that deer dislike the smell of mothballs, so I put a couple under each of my 70 broccoli plants. The next morning, I happened to glance down at the garden shortly after daybreak, and saw three deer headed up the field in that direction. The buck in the lead walked straight to the broccoli. I grabbed my binoculars for a closer look. The buck dropped his head and sniffed the mothballs curiously—then calmly proceeded to devour the plant! Does anyone need a stock of mothballs?

Broccoli isn't all. For the first time in ten years, they've developed a fondness for tomatoes. Passing the garden one day, I noticed there were enough ripe ones for a picking. But when I went down the next day, they had mysteriously disappeared—although deer tracks were abundant.

A few nights ago, I returned to the mountain shortly before midnight. As I rounded the last curve and passed our root cellar, my headlights picked up an eight-point buck munching apples at the base of a tree a few feet from our living room window. No wonder I've never found any on the ground.

So, come deer hunting season, I will put those apples and broccoli and tomatoes into my freezer via venison steaks, right? No, wrong. Some of my more pleasant boyhood memories of this mountain involve roaming its woods and fields with a gun on my shoulder. I enjoyed hunting, and do not think I was morally or ethically injured therefrom. To the contrary, hunting was interwoven with my initial love of nature and the out-of-doors.

But hunting was a stage I passed through. And the simple fact is I do not enjoy killing anything anymore. Not that I sit in judgment on the hunter. To me, it's a matter of individual sensitivity, of individual choice. Killing a deer and putting it in the freezer offends me no more than buying a steak and putting it in the freezer. The butcher is the surrogate hunter. But any "sportsman" who kills simply for the pleasure of killing has my abiding contempt.

I think Thoreau had it about right when he wrote in a chapter on "Higher Laws" in Walden: "We cannot but pity the boy who has never fired a gun; he is no more humane, while his education has been sadly neglected."

But then he added: "No humane being, past the thoughtless age of boyhood, will wantonly murder any creature which holds its life by the same tenure that he does. The hare in its extremity cries like a child."

The way I enjoy deer is when I'm sitting on our pavilion as the shadows deepen and the setting sun paints the high ridge of Little Mountain across the valley. Somehow, their frolicking in the field below the garden blends in naturally.

Apples and broccoli are a small price to pay.

☓

Animal Kinship   *May 16, 1988*

Returning from dinner with friends in Bristol later than I had planned, I found Duke sitting in our front yard with a dead possum. Possibly it was his way of saying, "Well, maybe next time you'll feed me before you go out."

I decided to postpone burial rites until daylight, so I tossed the possum into the pavilion trash can. As I did, I was suddenly seized by a sense of déjà vu. The same thing had happened nearly 25 years earlier. In Chesapeake. Our dog at the time was a dachshund by the name of Tykie. Late one evening, his barks and snarls indicated he was tangling with something in the hedges outside our kitchen door. I investigated and found he'd killed a possum.

It was too dark for digging, so I tossed it into one of our trash cans.

When I got home from work the next day, I dug a hole in the garden, dumped the carcass into it, and was about to shovel in dirt when I saw the possum give a twitch. Or thought I did. Which didn't make sense, for it had been stiff as a board when I carried it to the hole.

I hauled it out to make sure. Again, there came a twitch. Looking closer, I saw that it came from the marsupial pouch of that old sow possum. I opened the pouch and found three miniature possums inside. All three together wouldn't have filled a thimble. They were pink and mostly hairless and had their eyes closed. Otherwise they looked okay. I called my wife, and she immediately suggested that we try to raise them.

"On what?" I asked. "You got any possum milk? They'll have to have milk for weeks."

"I'll find something," she said. And she did. Pam and Tim were still on formula at the time, so she tried that. And it worked. At least, the babies accepted it from a medicine dropper.

Wynken, Blynken, and Nod, the children dubbed them, and delightedly looked forward to their frequent feedings. They could afford to be delighted. They didn't have to get up at all hours of the night. I can recall many 4 a.m.'s in our kitchen, trying to focus my bleary eyes and hit those ridiculously small mouths with the end of a medicine dropper. Asking myself: What in the hell am I doing here?

After all, this was an animal that had survived without assistance for several million years. Had, in fact, come down to its present state in almost unaltered form. An animal so prolific and adaptable it would undoubtedly go on surviving no matter what. So, what possible difference could it make in the grand scheme of things if these mites survived or died?

The logical answer, of course, was "no difference." However, we continued the feeding schedule. Continued until one weekend when we all went shopping and carelessly left the kitchen door ajar. The feral instinct of the dachshund was just as strong as the survival instinct of the possums. Tykie nosed the door open and made short work of the brood. We found their carcasses scattered on the floor.

It saddened the children, and my wife even more. She subsequently adopted a pair of rabbits whose nest neighborhood workmen had unearthed. She raised them in a little alcove under the stairway. I can recall dinner guests who would suddenly stop chewing when they happened to glance down into our living room and spot a pair of wild rabbits frisking around under the soft glow of a table lamp.

Little wonder that our kids turned out as they did. Even today, they'll stop their cars to remove tortoises from the road.

116

I've frequently mused over the reaction of individuals to lesser forms of life. Some seem to feel an instinctive bonding, a kinship. Others are left cold. I've finally concluded it's largely due to parental attitudes, parental examples.

If our dad hadn't let my brother, Bill, and me adopt a blacksnake we caught one summer, then I probably wouldn't have agreed to Tim's request for a five-foot boa on his 7th birthday. And he'll probably pass this on to his children.

And that, I suppose, could eventually become imprinted on the family genes. It's a sobering thought.

CΒ

Sounds of Spring   *March 27, 1989*

The first phoebe arrived March 11. I was sitting at my desk and caught a flash of movement in the maple just outside the window. And there he was. Flicking his tail up and down and uttering his immodest call, "Phoeee-beee. Phoebe pretty!"

At least, that's what it sounds like to me. But then, I have the same tin ear for bird calls that I have for music. Maybe the "he" was a "she." Males and females look alike. Whatever the sex, they're a much more reliable sign of spring than a robin. In fact, the very next day, I hitched up the disk to the tractor and went down and pulverized half my garden.

This year, as if to reinforce the phoebes' proclamation of spring, the frog choir down at the beaver pond got together for their first rehearsal. If I had to pick one sound that typifies spring more than any other, I'd have to say frogs. "Spring peepers" go back to boyhood.

The first sunny afternoons of March would find me, after school, over in Anderson Woods just south of King College. There was a small, marshy area below the Huff home that was a favorite breeding ground for peepers (which are true tree frogs, not chorus frogs, although they frequently sing in the same choir). The sound of my approaching footsteps would put a damper on their serenade, but I'd lie face down by a pool and keep still.

Before long, a tiny snout would break the surface near a stick or water plant, followed soon by the whole body—the whole one-inch of him. Then his throat would swell and he would deliver his ode to spring— a peep with a trill on the end, delivered at one-second intervals. I enjoyed his song so much that, one year, I gathered a mass of gelatinous eggs and

117

took them home and put them in a makeshift aquarium.

I made it out of a gallon vinegar bottle—wrapping a string soaked in gasoline around the top, setting it on fire, then tapping the neck until the top part broke off. Kind of crude, but it worked. And I had the pleasure of watching the embryos develop slowly into incredibly small tadpoles, and the tadpoles into frogs. I added a section of window screen for a lid, and caught house flies for my guests.

I can still remember waking up at night and listening to their chorus coming from the top of the bookcase next to the fireplace—a bit of spring brought indoors.

附

A Mystery   *June 18, 1990*

It's a good thing I don't have any close neighbors. Anybody watching me would have decided I'd flipped out for sure. There I was, walking back and forth through the thick woods adjacent to our house stopping every now and then to cup my ears with my hands and turn in a circle. Then I'd switch on a cassette recorder while I turned in another circle.

What I was trying to do was locate and record a mysterious sound. What kind of sound? Well, even after days of listening, I still find it hard to describe. I suppose I could say it's a sort of trilling, flowing sound, swelling and fading, obviously coming from several sources, almost like a chorus singing counterpoint.

Well, I walked all over those woods and never did pinpoint it, or even find a member of the choir. I'd move to the point where the sound seemed to be coming from, stop and cup my ears, then turn in a circle to try to get a fix. No soap. The sound had shifted to another spot. So, I'd move there and repeat the procedure—only to find it coming from yet another direction.

Vaguely, in the back of my mind, I recalled being puzzled by a mysterious, shifting sound up here once before. The more I thought about it the surer I became that it had happened several years ago during the incredible visitation of the 17-year-locusts.

So, when I returned to the house, I dug out my journal and flipped back through it. And there it was—under May 28, 1986. However, the two events were quite different. Back then, the sound had been so loud, so raucous and repetitive, the thought had crossed my mind it might even be a congregation of crows—speaking in tongues, maybe, for it didn't sound like crows.

Anyway, when a friend came up to visit for the day, we walked down the tree line to see if we could sneak up on whatever it was. When we arrived at what we thought was the point of origin, my journal notes, "it stopped down there and reappeared toward the pond in the southeast. Then the northwest. Then another group in the northeast." Finally, we just shook our heads and gave up.

During this period, the 17-year-locusts (periodical cicadas) were beginning to appear by the thousands. Our roadway leading down past the garden looked like a colander where they had bored back up through the surface after spending 17 subterranean years feeding on roots. Every shrub and bush was decorated with their translucent exoskeletons—left behind where they broke out to emerge as adults.

Males would begin vibrating a membrane on their abdomens to produce the resonant mating call that female cicadas find so irresistible. (Well, if you'd spent 17 years by yourself in a hole in the ground, any old screech might sound irresistible.)

When thousands of males vibrate simultaneously, the din is simply deafening. Overwhelming. Unbelievable. It nearly drove some visitors crazy. The sound even penetrated the house. And it went on for weeks. My last cicada entry was dated June 17.

Of all the strange occurrences we've witnessed since coming to the mountain, without hesitation I'd rate the cicadas Number 1.

But, back to the present: Could the sound be coming from cicadas? Answer: No, not unless something weird was happening. To my knowledge, there's no record of periodical cicadas breaking their established patterns. They only re-emerge in any given locality every 17 years (or 13 years for some species). Anyway, the two sounds aren't the same. While even a modest breeze through the leaves will block out the current chorus, nothing could muffle those cicadas. Moreover, there are no exit holes or exoskeletons.

When I'm baffled by some aspect of Mother Nature, I generally call Doug Ogle, science professor at Virginia Highlands Community College. So I called. Doug generously drove up here and we took a stroll in the woods. And listened.

"Gray treefrogs," he said. "I'm pretty sure they're gray treefrogs. But I have a recording at home I'll listen to and give you a verification call." He did—and confirmed it as *hyla versicolor*, one of two species of the little two-inch tree climber.

Doug also said a Virginia herpetological survey has revealed only 11 spots in Southwest Virginia where it has been identified: three in Lee County; one each in Scott, Grayson, Smyth, and Wythe; two in Dickenson;

and two here in Washington County (one near Yellow Springs, the other near Mendota).

And now there's a 12th spot—up here on the mountain. Well whadda you know, some day Hayters Gap might get on the map after all!

ℭ

Ladybugs and Other Visitors   *April 12, 1999*

Insects baffle me. For instance, the "ladybird beetle," or "ladybug," as it is commonly known. Since last fall, this house has been thronging with them. Whenever it looks like they've finally started to thin out, along comes another influx.

For years, we've had an occasional hatch during the winter months, mostly coming down from the light fixture in the living room, but they've always disappeared. Not this year. I've had reports of the same thing happening at other houses in the county. In fact, a Pulaski couple who came visiting last month, Mary Clare and Bill Wohlford, reported they'd visited a similarly afflicted household out in their county.

Which means that these infestations extend several miles northward. How far, and in what other directions, I don't know. Oh, well, if a house is going to be overrun with bugs, you'd have to go a long way to find a more beneficial one. It's strictly carnivorous, eating harmful aphids and scale. In fact, according to the Funk & Wagnalls Encyclopedia, that's how the bug got its name:

"Because of the help ladybird beetles rendered farmers in destroying agricultural pests, the beetles were popularly regarded in the Middle Ages as instruments of benevolent intervention by the Virgin Mary, whence the common name . . . ."

I can believe it. Several years ago, aphids were literally destroying our tobacco crop. Then, miraculously, ladybugs arrived. And the crop was saved.

There are many species of ladybugs scattered throughout temperate and tropical regions of the world. The "vedalia" in Australia has been imported by California citrus growers to fight the cottony cushion scale insect.

Another species, the "convergent," swarms on western mountain tops where they are collected by agricultural firms and distributed to farmers for aphid control. Hey, guys, I've got a few for sale. Cheap.

For the uninitiated, the ladybug resembles a pea cut in half. Legs unbelievably short and slender, with a head so small it's hardly visible.

120

The two sheaths under which its flying wings are folded vary in color and decoration. My guests measure a quarter-inch in diameter and are dark orange in color with a multitude of dark dots.

I'm inclined to think they're *coccinella novemnotata*, although the only species listed by Funk & Wagnalls that "often hibernate in houses during winter" is the *adalia bipunctata*. But the *adalia* has only one spot on each sheath, so that eliminates it as the local resident. I'm having as much trouble with the exact identity of this beetle as I did with the identity of tiny flies that invaded the house five or six years ago.

During that episode, I walked into my bedroom one night and discovered a cloud of insects hovering around the fluorescent light above my desk. I didn't like the idea of working at my computer with that mob overhead, so I fetched a can of insect spray. A multitude of bodies descended, covering my desk and everything on it. After removing the corpses, I began working—only to look up a few minutes later to discover another cloud had taken its place. Holy cow, the house had sprung a leak!

I got up and looked at the window screen. Under it, a vast army was pouring into the room. It took the rest of the spray to halt them. Just to make sure, I sealed the bottom of the screen with duct tape. Even that didn't work. They kept finding their way inside. I hung a couple of sticky fly tapes at either end of the light above my desk and attached the ends to each other, like a hammock.

Believe it or not, in less than an hour it was covered. In fact, they began accumulating in clumps. Every now and then, a sticky wad would detach itself and land on my desk. Yuk! Down in the kitchen, the plastic cover below the fluorescent light was black with them. When I emptied it, it filled a quart container.

In desperation, I even bought an electronic bug zapper and hung it out on the sun deck to try to thin their ranks before they got inside. Its mesh was covered so fast it had to be cleaned every few hours.

What kind of insect were they? I have no idea, other than they resembled tiny flies. I couldn't pinpoint them in any of my reference books. A hard rain finally wiped them out. I tell you, life on the mountain is never boring. If it's not Mother Nature, or the dogs, it's something else.

Like, the other morning I added the usual Clinch Mountain Cream (spiced rum) to my first cup of coffee. I'd discovered long ago that this not only markedly improves its flavor but also helps get my emphysema-addled engine turning over. Before I had my first sip, I had to leave the kitchen and go outside for something, I've forgotten what. Returning, I found my coffee lukewarm. So I took it into the laundry room, stuck it into the microwave, and stepped back into the kitchen to fix my usual bowl of shredded wheat.

All of a sudden, it sounded like a stick of dynamite had gone off in the laundry room. I rushed in—to find the door of the microwave blown open and coffee everywhere. Apparently, alcohol in the spiced rum had vaporized and filled the microwave. When it reached electrical wiring— whoof!

03

Tobacco-Chewin' Rats   *November 6, 1989*

The old farmhouse had been standing vacant for 16 years before we moved in, so naturally critters seeking shelter had utilized it. Including rats. Apparently, they'd been long-established in the loft of the nearby woodshed, and in an area above the kitchen—a windowless space we didn't try to utilize since it had no flooring.

As boarders, those rats were surprisingly unobtrusive. While field mice scampered all over the house, the rats kept strictly to their homesteaded area. There was a large walnut tree between the house and the woodshed, and its nuts provided their winter larder.

On many a night, we were awakened by the sound of walnuts being rolled around like bowling balls on the kitchen ceiling. ("Set 'em up in the other alley, Zeke!") Other than this minor annoyance, we were seldom aware of their presence. Live and let live, we said, and didn't bother setting traps.

It was several years after we'd moved up here on the ridge before we discovered they'd followed us. We'd raised a crop of sorghum for molasses one year, and had saved the heads for seed. We'd put the heads in a burlap sack and hung it by a cord from a rafter in our attached woodshed.

We were thinking mice, not rats, so it came as a shock when the sack was discovered half-empty, with several ragged rips in its fabric. Within a few days, the heads had disappeared. Then we began catching glimpses of the rats themselves—usually just flashes around the eaves or stud braces. That was one thing about those rats—I never saw one on the ground. They like high places.

Tim mentioned our uninvited guests to an area exterminator, and was told they were probably "roof rats" that could climb and jump like squirrels. Which came as no news to us. Since I had several boxes of junk (but junk I wanted to save) stored on shelves in the woodshed, I started trapping. Forget it. I couldn't catch a one.

I did manage to blow one away with my pistol when I saw him peeking over the eaves, but he was the only casualty. Then, a couple of weeks or so ago, Tim and I were out back working on the bush hog when we heard the sound of gnawing and tearing coming from the storage loft of the tractor shed. Obviously, a rat preparing its nest.

I fetched my pistol and climbed the ladder to the loft. But he was operating in an area just under the slope of the roof and I couldn't get to him without moving a dozen boxes. So I decided to treat it like any other problem. I put it off.

Then I began finding papers lying on the ground beneath the loft. Stuff I'd stored up there in boxes. It was too late in the season to find a blacksnake to stick up there. Instead, I bought a new set of traps and baited them with cheese. Days passed, with nary a nibble.

Then one day I climbed into the Subaru, which we also park in the shed, and made a discovery I found hard to believe. I'd left a foil package of Lancaster chawin' tobacco on the passenger seat. Now all that remained were a few shreds of foil. Every speck of tobacco was missing. Mixed with the shreds were numerous large rat droppings, so there was little doubt about what had happened. A tobacco-chewin' rat?

I related the incident to a friend. She scoffed, and wanted to know if they spit out the window as they drove down the road. Several days later, I climbed into the Subaru again—and again found a package of Lancaster ripped to shreds and the rat droppings. You don't believe me? This time I fetched my CamCorder and preserved the evidence on film.

There are only two ways those rats could have gotten into the car: dropped down from the loft onto its roof, and thence through the open window; or else leaped some four feet from an adjacent ledge. That same day, I climbed up to the loft to check the traps.

I found that finally, finally, I'd caught one of those things. She measured 13 inches from the tip of her nose to the tip of her tail. Then it struck me: Since those rodents were obviously addicted to nicotine, why not use tobacco for bait?

It sounded like a preposterous idea, but, then, the idea of a tobacco-chewin' rat was preposterous. So I baited three traps with Lancaster late that afternoon. The next morning, I went out to check. Even before I climbed up into the loft, I saw a long, scaly tail hanging down through a crack in the boards. This one measured 14 1/2 inches—and had his mouth full of chawin' tobacco.

I've encountered some strange events up here on the mountain, but this one takes the cake.

೮ೞ

Roof Rats

I was here in my room when I heard what sounded like someone chopping wood nearby. A muffled, rhythmic, "thump. . . thump. . . thump." I stepped out on the deck to see what direction it was coming from. When I did, the sound faded, but when I came back inside, it increased. The thought that it could be coming from somewhere in the house gave me an eerie feeling.

It suddenly stopped. However, when I was downstairs later in the day, it began again. No doubt about it, it was coming from directly overhead, between the floors. Which made no sense. Although we'd had roof rats scampering around between the floors for years, I couldn't picture one with an ax. Again, it stopped, so I shrugged and forgot about it—my usual response to phenomena beyond my comprehension.

Over the next few days, though, it reoccurred several times. Happily, on one such occasion, Tim was present and heard it, too. Which was a relief, for I didn't think that both of us would be going nuts simultaneously.

Tim took a trip away from the mountain. While he was gone, the thumping began again. That did it. I fetched a crowbar and pried off a section of paneling in the stairwell so I could look between the floors. Now I had access to their playground—a house-wide, 16-inch-high area between floor and ceiling, crisscrossed with supporting 2x4's. Directing the spotlight toward the rear of the house, I saw that a whole section of insulation had been ripped off the wall and now lay in a pile, probably their nest.

I also sighted a big roof rat. Trouble was, he didn't have an ax in his hand. This didn't solve the mystery of the chopping noise. That came the following day after I heard a series of scamperings, obviously made by two rats, and followed by that curious thumping. Rushing upstairs, I got the spotlight and returned to the opening. When its beam picked up a rat, I couldn't believe my eyes. It was using its hind quarters to thump on the plywood ceiling. Never, never, had I heard of a rat thumping like a rabbit, but there it was.

Since I'd been unable to locate my rat traps, I went up to my room and got my Hi-Standard .22 pistol. Returning, I located one of the rats and fixed the spotlight on it. I'm not sure whether the beam held the same fascination as it does for a spotlighted-deer, but that rat scampered over and stopped within four or five feet of me. I carefully raised the pistol and blasted her (it turned out to be a female).

The other rat didn't appear scared, so I fixed the beam on him. He, too, seemed fascinated, or else had a death wish, for he approached the opening. Unhappily, he stopped adjacent to an electric wire. I think I must have unconsciously raised my aim away from the wire, for I missed.

When Tim learned that I was firing a high-velocity slug amid our wiring, pipes and tanks, he shook his head and went out and bought a box of shot-shells. Instead of a lead slug, these contain 165 tiny pellets. They work, too. The next day, I lured the remaining rat with the spotlight—and shot him dead. A male. Obviously, a pair.

In past years, I've tried to find a blacksnake to slip between floors to take care of mice. Well, when I came down the steps the day after removing the paneling, a large blacksnake had his head poked out of the opening. I figured he was the one I'd discovered weeks earlier when I stepped out onto the deck one night to check hummer feeders. He'd slithered over the side— back to the ground, I assumed. Instead, he'd found an entrance into the area.

Why hadn't he taken care of the rats? Apparently, they were too large to swallow, but I imagine he'd ingested whatever offspring they'd produced. He'd been an occupant for a while, for his shed skin lay near the opening.

Like I say, life here on the mountain is never dull.

CƷ

Blacksnake? *June 27, 1988*

Coming through Lindell on my way home from Meadowview, Tim came off Route 700 just ahead of me. He pulled over and flagged me down. I could tell he was a bit excited when he walked back to the car.

"I've just had the weirdest snake experience!" he said, and began relating it.

After passing a snake coiled in the road a half-mile back, he looked in his rearview mirror and saw that the snake hadn't moved. Thinking it had been injured by another car, he backed up to get it off the road.

"I pulled alongside and flicked my jacket out the window to shoo him off the road," Tim said. "But he didn't shoo, he struck at the jacket. And when I pulled the jacket inside, he began striking at the side of the car. Time after time." Another car came by, so Tim pulled up to let it pass, then backed up and tried the jacket-out-the-window routine again.

"This time, his fangs came right through the jacket and he got stuck," Tim said. "He was writhing around, so I lowered him down to the road to free himself, and he did. But he struck again—higher up on the jacket—and got stuck again."

Tim said he didn't feel like letting go of the jacket, since the snake didn't need it in hot weather. But he didn't feel like getting out and arguing about it, either.

"So I drove slowly down the road, almost to Lindell, shaking that snake," he said. "Some guy was watering flowers in front of his house and he just stood there, staring. He must have thought I was nuts."

The snake, which Tim estimated at something over three feet, finally freed himself and slithered off the road. We examined the jacket for venom, but found nothing. We agreed it couldn't be a blacksnake, for only venomous snakes have fangs. But Tim insisted it looked like a blacksnake.

Returning home, I began making phone calls to try to find a herpetologist. Over the years, I'd been told that blacksnakes occasionally mate with copperheads, and the result is a venomous blacksnake. I'd scoffed at the idea, for it made no more sense than, say, a groundhog mating with a beaver. Both are rodents, and look alike in many respects, but the genetic predisposition is simply lacking. Still, I wanted to find out if it was possible.

I finally contacted Doug Ogle, who has a strong interest in reptiles. Doug said, No, forget about the cross-mating. He suspected that people reporting such a phenomenon had simply seen two species denning together during the winter—which they frequently do.

"I tell my students that, just because they sleep together all winter doesn't mean they are fooling around," he said. Doug then gave a solid clue to the snake's identity.

"Our timber rattler has a black phase during which he looks very much like a blacksnake," he said.

I consulted my handbook on snakes—Peterson's <u>Field</u> <u>Guide</u> <u>to</u> <u>Reptiles</u> <u>and</u> <u>Amphibians</u>. It said of the timber rattler (the only one of three species of North American rattlesnakes common to this area) that "completely black specimens are not unusual in uplands of the Northeast."

The clincher came later. Tim had used his girlfriend's camera to take a couple of snapshots of the snake from the car window. He had the roll developed and brought the prints to the mountain.

We compared them to the color plate of the black phase of the timber rattler in Peterson's guide. They were identical—the lower half black-brown, the upper-half much thicker and striped in an irregular pattern.

"Looking at the photos, I don't know how I mistook that thing for a blacksnake," Tim said.

Strange, during nearly 11 years of living here on the mountain, not once have we seen a rattlesnake. Yet Tim meets this most venomous of our area's reptiles (its Latin Name is *horridus horridus*) in the middle of a well-traveled highway—and plays with it for ten minutes.

Residents of the Lindell area, be advised: If you run across a timber rattler, he may have a toothache from being dangled along your road. He's also likely to have a sour disposition.

☙

Serpentine Sex   *June 17, 2002*

Walking into my kitchen a few afternoons back, my attention was immediately drawn to a throw rug in front of the sink. On it, locked in conjugal embrace, were two copperheads—mating.

Now, I have nothing against sex but it seems to me there was plenty of room outdoors for that sort of thing. The rug was a gift from a friend. The next time I saw her I asked if she knew it could also be used for serpentine sex. She found the story incredible.

After the initial shock of seeing two venomous reptiles making whoopee in my kitchen, the thing that struck me most was the difference in their sizes. One was about twice as long as the other. I don't know whether it was a tall man with a short woman, or a tall woman with a short man. And I wasn't about to try and find out.

By the time I had fetched a hoe from the tractor shed, they'd slithered into the narrow passage between the refrigerator and sink cabinets. The small one disappeared into the wall through a narrow slit at the baseboard while the large one vanished underneath the fridge.

I called Tim, over in the next holler, and explained the situation. I told him I was going to try to shoot the one under the fridge but I needed someone to hold my spotlight. He came up immediately. As soon as we removed the drip pan, there it was in plain sight. I blasted away with a pistol loaded with fine pellets. Bull's eye.

I pulled it out and we measured it. A little over three feet long. I don't know how long the other one was. In all probability, that will remain a mystery for it hasn't reappeared. I wasn't particularly worried about the possibility of a venomous snake in the house since copperheads are definitely non-aggressive. They don't even coil unless they feel threatened. However, if I were a copperhead and somebody stepped on me, I'd consider it an act of aggression. So, I began turning on lights when I went downstairs at night.

Tim carried off the snake for disposal. A few days later he told me that he'd pried its mouth open and couldn't find any fangs. He believed it could be a corn snake. I quickly consulted my reptile reference book. Sure enough, the color and markings of a corn snake are strikingly similar to those of a northern copperhead, the variety we have here.

If I killed a corn snake, I'm truly sorry. As rodent exterminators, they're extremely beneficial. In fact, I'd rank them with blacksnakes. Had I been sure it was a corn snake, it would have been welcome to stay.

CS

Beaver Construction   *November 2, 1987*

Early one evening, I was rushing off the mountain to keep a dinner date when I was forced to come to a halt below the pond. Stretched full length across the road was one of our larger apple trees.

"Well, what in the world?" I muttered to myself as I climbed out of the car. Then a suspicion dawned—and was immediately confirmed. The beavers. One of them had chawed through that tree like a rotating buzz saw.

I was already late. The tree meant I'd have to go back to the house and cut down through the fields and exit below our old farmhouse. Irritated, but at the same time amused, I began backing and looking for a place to turn around.

Beavers have proved an interesting and sometimes exasperating addition to the assorted wildlife of this mountain farm. They arrived some three years ago. Soon they began building their lodge against the pond's dam a few feet above the waterline, extending it downward to provide the underwater entrance demanded by their building code—or, at least, their genetic code.

Since beavers are largely nocturnal, I began spending quite a few evenings down at the pond just after sunset, watching them munch on roots and grasses, admiring their splendid tail-slapping surface dives.

Then I began seeing only one. Rumor reached us that someone had slipped in and shot its mate. Tim checked with the game warden at Tumbling Creek concerning a replacement, and was told not to worry: another beaver would probably just wander in.

Not long afterward, I had to go out one night. Rounding the curve below the house, my headlights picked up an animal sitting upright in the middle of the road. It looked like a king-size groundhog, but since groundhogs aren't usually nocturnal, I figured it was our remaining beaver.

But what was he doing nearly half a mile above the pond? Was he looking for his mate?

I braked to a halt a few yards above him. He didn't move. Leaving the engine running and headlights on, I got out and walked over and squatted down within touching distance. I told him I knew he was lonely, but that if he proceeded a couple of hundred yards up the road, there was a 92-pound Doberman running loose who would happily take him limb from limb. He kept sitting there until I stopped talking, then dropped down on all fours and ambled off in the direction of the pond.

One day, I discovered the main body of our dam had been extended across the 30-foot runoff area. This extension was an intricately woven structure of branches and mud and sticks and rocks standing about 18 inches high.

I didn't mind—until several weeks later when I noticed the water level had risen until it was oozing over the east end of our clay-core dam. Only a couple of inches, but a heavy rain could start a rivulet that might endanger the whole structure.

That night, I went down and tore out a ten-foot section of the extension—almost getting washed away in the sudden runoff. But when I passed by the next day, it had been completely restored. And with what incredible engineering skill! It couldn't have been done more precisely if a surveyor with a transit had been calling out level marks from the opposite end of the dam. Construction had occurred in utter darkness in a rushing torrent of water, with building material cut and ferried, and with only mouth and claws for tools. Yet the water had been raised to its exact former level.

That night, I returned and renewed my demolition. Suddenly there came a loud smack from out on the pond, followed immediately by another smack. Two surface dives? I grabbed my flashlight and directed its beam out on the pond. It reflected from not one but two pairs of eyes. The beaver had found a mate! I started to wade in and finish the job, but something held me back.

Well, I told myself, if the whole dam washes away, it'll just have to go. Even a beaver shouldn't have to work on his honeymoon.

129

Ice crystals glisten on the trees in December, 1998. Photo by Mike Quigley.

7 ~ Seasons

There was some part of every season that Dad loved. He marveled at the beauty of the fog rolling in, capturing perfectly the effect it had on the senses. He called himself the "Rain Man" because it was "his kind of weather." And he taught us to appreciate what others saw only as a nuisance. Like rain and fog and snow and cold.

High up on his mountain he lived with the consequences of the changing seasons daily. He spent as much time out-of-doors as possible, happily watching the poplars on Little Mountain green up in the spring and watching wistfully each year as they lost their leaves in early fall.

Dad kept detailed notes on the weather and the changes each new season brought. Most of his daily journal entries began with a report on the current temperature, other notable weather conditions, and, often, a description of the changing view looking down into the valley and far beyond.

Rain Man

It was my kind of June! Cool, rainy, lush. The exact opposite of last June, which was hot, dry and—whatever the opposite of lush is. Teetotaler, maybe? Except for the final days, the temperature up here didn't climb above 75 degrees. Fact is, with the exception of one day, we had 13 straight when it was in the 60s or below.

My kind of June! No need to mention rain, right? Well, I'll mention it anyway, for I am a rain man. I like the smell and feel of it in the air, and on the window screen. I like the roar it makes in the woods, and on the tin roofs of our shed and pavilion. I like the metronome drip of it from the eaves. I even like to walk in it. This said, we did get a bit much in one hunk, didn't we?

Even that had its plus side. Our Christmas trees, for example. Their annual growth spurt came on early, so Tim and I got a start on the annual shaping while the weather was still cool.

I'd hoped that, by this year, Christmas trees would have been removed from the agenda of my life. Not so. Although we did unload a batch last December, there are still 533 of the little beauties flourishing in the fields. And I do mean flourishing. It's been a growth explosion that's resulted in the frequent use of a stepladder.

Hornets and yellow jackets still favor the white pine as a habitat. One of the latter crawled down between the top of my pants and my T-shirt. He must have braced himself against my belt to get good stabbing leverage, for I think his stinger would have come out my back if I hadn't had a solid breakfast.

Incidentally, if you ever get stung by wasp or bee when you are out in the woods, simply reach down, get a bit of earth, put it in your palm, moisten it and apply the mud to the sting. If no water is available, use spit. Inelegant, perhaps, but it works. The kids and I have been using mud (preferably clay) for years, and have found it just as effective as any standard medication we've tried.

But, back to rain. My garden looks like it's on steroids. Fact is, I can't remember a year when potato plants have grown so thick and tall. How tall? Well, I put a row of tomatoes four feet below the last row of potatoes. When the potato plants fell over (as they do on approaching maturity) several were leaning on tomato plants. The tomatoes, of course, had burgeoned themselves. I'd tied them up three times by the third week of June. Possibly they've sucked up a bit too much water, for some of the early fruit are exhibiting cracks.

But you can't give a potato plant too much water—provided the ground is well-drained. I dug up a few around the middle of June to see how they were doing. Believe it or not, they had already equaled in size what I dug last year at the end of the season.

Let's see, what else can I credit to the rain? Well, the beaver pond, for one thing. First June I can recall when it's stayed full. And this in the face of a leak I still haven't been able to pinpoint.

Although I doubt that it's connected to rain, mourning doves have been calling in the dead of night. Maybe the whippoorwill wakes them and they just get into the act. During the day, doves come whistling in from nowhere, like grey rockets, and land on the driveway in front of the house. For a while, I figured they came to eat the fine gravel. Birds that live on seed and grain, like doves, have well-developed gizzards and need gravel.

Then I happened to remember my daughter Pam's wedding in May, and the birdseed that was thrown as they departed in their getaway car. That must have been it.

⚃

The Raised-Leg Forecast   November 15, 1993

What a strange end to the leaf season. Even after several frosts and freezes, an astonishingly large number are still hanging on. In September, I didn't think it was going to be a good year for color. Dogwoods, one of the first indicators, weren't particularly brilliant. Although the season was certainly no match for splendiferous '88, it was still above average and has made up in duration whatever it lacked in brilliance. Early snowfall, late leaf departure. A strange combination.

To me, the curtain comes down when I look out across the valley at the top ridge of Little Mountain and see nothing but a filigree of bare trees. This generally happens during the last week of October. Although they've thinned out quite a bit, at the time of this writing there's still a lot of leaves up there. Also, the tree line dropping away in front of our house is still thick with leaves. Mostly browns and ochres, but leaves nevertheless.

But the most puzzling thing has been the retention of greenness, particularly among the oaks. The green, of course, is chlorophyll, and chlorophyll is the tree's timecard. They punch in with it to signify they're in a manufacturing mode. Yet, even after those first frosts and freezes, there were still trees that were basically green. In November, yet.

Could it be that the seemingly endless drought of last summer interrupted the manufacturing process to the point where they kept trying to fill their quota? I have no scientific data to back up such speculation, but at least it would follow the pattern of my garden.

On Oct. 28, I went down to strip peppers and whatever else was left, and discovered summer squash in bloom. I can't remember that ever happening before. Why, I even picked my last "sugar baby" watermelon. But I was in a bit of a rush so I didn't get to the turnips.

Well, three days later I put on my long-johns (the earliest I've done that) and went down and dug them out of three inches of snow. Yes sir, an interesting finale to an interesting season.

Staff writer Anne Grundon of this newspaper called the other day and left a message on my recorder asking if I knew anyone in the area who makes weather predictions based on woolly worms or the like. I didn't, but I passed along the name of a woman down in the valley who might.

Ah, me, once again come the annual winter weather predictions based on the woolly worm and the thickness of squirrel fur and the date which birds leave on their migration and the bountifulness of acorn mast and . . . well, you name it.

Anne didn't ask if I made such predictions, so I didn't volunteer. As a matter of fact, I do. And I use a method based on science instead of superstition—although I admit I came across it purely by chance.

Now, everyone knows that all adult male dogs cock a leg when relieving themselves. Well, last fall I noticed an interesting phenomenon with Buck and Leroy. They were alternating in what seemed like a pattern. On some days, Buck would hike right. And so would Leroy. Maybe for two or three days in a row. Then they'd switch and hike left. But why?

Some of you may recall Prof. Alain Frobischer's "Theory of Alternates," which caused such a stir in the scientific community when it was published a few years ago. Well, I read through it again until I found what I was looking for—correlates for the canine behavior. By extrapolating Monsieur Frobischer's multiples into rotational weather patterns, I was able to come up with a clear-cut picture, week by week, of the winter weather.

I made notes, and you know what? Those dogs were right on the money. Well, they did miss the blizzard of last March, but I think that was because Buck didn't keep his mind on his business.

So, what's this winter going to be like? Be of good cheer, three or four days of true Indian Summer are still scheduled for later this month with blue skies and temps above normal. Prepare for outdoor activity.

But look out—beginning in the second week in December, a period of atrocious weather. Cold, with snow, pushing into the Christmas holidays with only a sprinkling of days of relief. However, the year will end on a mild note.

January. Sorry, folks, those mutts are calling for eight days of measurable snowfall and below average temps. This will continue into February, but with a pronounced break of several mild days in mid-month.

March. Greenup will come late but with a vengeance. Flowers will bloom before the last snowfall at the end of the month.

So, there you have it. Just clip this column and stick it on your refrigerator door and check things off as they occur. Forget the woolly worm, this is the Buck & Leroy Raised Leg Method.

You can trust those dogs. You know I do.

ɞ

Prognosticating   *September 19, 2004*

What's the prognosis for leaf color this fall? Well, not very good. The early-turners here on the mountain are saying it will be a moderate-to-poor year. By early-turners, I'm talking about dogwood, sumac and Virginia creeper. Over the years, I've found them to be extremely accurate. I can recall only one instance when they were wrong.

Excuse me, I should say when my interpretation of them was wrong. I'd read them to mean a poor year but it turned out pretty much fair to middlin'.

Leaves began coming down in my mile-long driveway during the first week of September. Mostly poplar. Not a bit of color among them. On the other hand, I have a poplar just east of this house whose leaves show a pretty good grade of gold, not the dull brown of those in my driveway. So?

Admittedly, there's an inconsistency among trees. That became clear September 4 when some visitors and I were sitting out on the pavilion. All of a sudden, something struck its tin roof with a sharp clang. We looked at each other. "Did anybody throw a rock?" I asked, looking around. Nope, everyone was seated on the pavilion.

A few minutes later, the same thing happened again.

"Could it be acorns from that tree?" one guy asked, indicated an oak that was overhanging the roof.

I shook my head. "We've never had acorns from it," I said.

True enough, but a scan of adjacent ground provided proof that we were sure getting them this year. And they're still coming down. Lots of big ones. But why did that tree wait over 20 years?

Old timers are wont to shake their heads over an unusually heavy mast of acorns and solemnly predict a severe winter. Their theorizing is that Mother Nature is providing it for her forest-dwellers to help them make it through the bad months until spring.

Old timers also have a bunch of other indicators they rely on. If leaves fall early, the winter will be mild. If they hang on until late fall and are denser, it will be harsh.

Also, an abundance of woolly worms indicates a bad winter. If they have markings on them it means severe weather at the beginning and end.

If hornets build their nests high in the trees, it indicates a mild winter. Close to the ground, a bad one.

All this may sound a little far-fetched, but who am I to sneer when I use the dogwood, sumac and Virginia creeper as prognosticators of color? I only wish there was a good solid indicator in the spring of how hot the summer will be. It might eliminate the need for setting up my air conditioner in one of the hall windows.

Early in the summer, my son-in-law Mike was visiting and suggested that he install it so it would be ready in the event of a sudden hot spell. I agreed. I've never argued against cheap labor. So Mike installed it. And there it sat all summer, unused. I never once turned it on—the first summer in memory when it hasn't been in use.

The turn-on point in the past has been 80 degrees. Once it reaches that mark, on it goes. This year, it never got beyond the 70s. I'm not sure how it was for the rest of you folks, but here on the mountain we had a mild summer.

It would have been a great one for working in the garden. Unhappily, gardening is now beyond me. My son, Tim, planted and cultivated four rows of potatoes. And it's a good average crop.

My only effort in that direction was to set out four tomato plants in two big pots out on the deck. I watered and weeded them regularly, even drove a couple of stakes for support. Result—splendid plants but only half a dozen golf-ball-size tomatoes.

CB

A Glorious Fall

What can you say about a season that's been 90 percent Indian Summer? More! More! More!

I still can't believe the number of perfect days we've had. When I failed to take advantage of one, I felt guilty, like I'd won the lottery and failed to collect my prize. Normally, I'd have spent a lot of those days out in the woods gathering firewood, but bursitis in my left shoulder rendered that verboten. So, except for the small stuff, Tim had to do it all, with the help of a couple of his friends.

And he did a good job. Some seven or eight truckloads. The best part about it was that it was all dry. There've been years we've gotten a late start and would cut a standing dead tree only to discover it was soaked to the core. I now face this winter—which I'm afraid will be a bad one—with a full woodshed.

My big regret is that I didn't put out a fall garden this year. First time I've missed in 17 years. Why, I could have been eating fresh greens and turnips and lettuce and stuff all the time. I missed the standard Aug. 10 planting date, then one thing after another happened until September when I decided, well, what the heck, I'll just do without one this year—the best year for fall gardens I've seen.

Although hard frosts have been reported in many places, we still haven't had one up here, thanks to the phenomenon known as "thermal displacement." Thermal displacement results from a flow of heavy, cold air down the side of the mountain after dark. This slides under the lighter, warmer air that has accumulated down in the valley during the day and lifts it up to our level. Which is fine with me. I'll trade frosts for mild air any old day.

Even my woodpile has been affected. Since our house faces south and bakes in the sun all day, I've had to build a fire only three times in my bedroom—and probably wouldn't have been uncomfortable without one even then since 68 was as cold as it got inside.

Those clear, sunny days with their low humidity produced another delightful effect. The air was so clear it seemed like you could see forever, plus ten miles. A couple of Saturday afternoons ago, I was returning from a tailgate party at Emory when I rounded a curve and the whole south side of Clinch Mountain hove into view. I simply had to pull over to the side of the road and stare, for never had I seen it defined more clearly.

My mountain. At least, that's the way I've viewed it for well over half a century. I could pretty much trace the old mountain road that I used to follow as a youth hiking from my grandparents' farm down in the valley to the fire tower.

I could see the break in the top ridge where a couple of cabins are located now and where I used to take a shortcut to the tower—shorter and rougher. I liked to go that way because it followed the ridge and led by the "Aberdeen," a huge outcropping of sandstone that was visible even from my car out near Midway.

Below the Aberdeen was "Chimney Rock," a tower of sandstone. After my wife died and I began bringing my children here for long hikes, we built a fire beneath a hemlock at its base one snowy day. Heat from the fire dislodged a bower of snow that landed on the fire and put it out—exactly as in Jack London's story, *To Build a Fire*.

The tower itself thrust up from Hayters Knob like a thin pencil. When I was a lookout there back in '55, I climbed up and down its angling flights of steps several times a day.

A half-mile below the tower I could see the scooped-out head of White Rock Cove, another favorite hiking spot for me and the kids. I could also see the break in the ridge that dropped down to the head of Little Brumley Creek.

On a snowy day back in the '30s, I started out from my grandparents' farm and hiked to the tower, accompanied by my cousin's collie-shepherd, Laddie. When we got there, I decided to climb the tower and look at the scenery.

As I stood there a hundred feet above the ground, Laddie must have thought I was going to step off onto a cloud and leave him, for he climbed every one of those steps to the top. Then he looked down—and melted into a quivering heap. You know, I had to inch my way down those icy steps clutching the rail with one hand with that fool dog tucked under my other arm.

We walked down Little Brumley to Big Brumley to the road and on in to Hayters Gap—over 20 miles of rough walking through the snow. Today, what with old age and emphysema, I'd have a hard time just climbing the steps of the tower.

Oh, well, the dogs and I have enjoyed our meager walks through the woods on the glorious days of this fall. It's good to be alive on such a day whether you're old or young, dog or human.

෴

Fog settles against the slopes of Little Mountain and beyond to the south. Courtesy of Mike Quigley.

Fog Theater   *February 20, 1989*

Living up here on the mountain is fog theater. Not only do we have lots of fogs to watch, but center aisle seat, too. Little Mountain across the valley is the backdrop against which they perform, shifting scenery around like drunken stage hands.

On one recent afternoon, the whole mountain moved in and out of visibility. At times, fog would creep up its lower slopes, and at other times, shed itself against the trees of the ridge. Once when I glanced out the window, I found the slopes dotted with tufts of white—like we used to dot our Christmas trees with cotton to imitate snow.

On another morning, I looked out of my bedroom window and found fog filling the valley and stretching eastward to what must have been Allison's Gap above Saltville. Ten miles of fog!

Earlier this month, between our unbelievable January and a return to cooler weather, an unstable weather system stalled out overhead and we had three days of fog. I'd been embarrassed to tell you the hours I spent watching it.

Although fogs generally perform down in the valley, there are times when they mount assaults against our slopes—slipping through the trees like the ghosts of Indian warriors long dead, determined now to capture our fort.

A spiderweb glistens in the morning sun. Courtesy of Lindsay Meredith.

As a boy staying at my grandparents' house down in the valley, I recall those fogs. The trouble was, I couldn't see the fog for the fog. Being in it, there was no perspective. Except on those September mornings when I went squirrel hunting.

One of my favorite hunting grounds was a bench of hickories on the lower ridge of Little Mountain. I would take my grandfather's old 12-gauge duck gun and go down to the Zack Hole and begin the ascent of the ridge. The climb would lift me through a white, silent world. The only sound was the drip of moisture from the leaves of the trees overhead. Spider webs were bejeweled with it.

As I moved up that ridge trail, at some point I would push above the fog—and find myself staring out across a valley that resembled the top of a frosted cake. It looked solid enough to walk on. Little did I know that over half a century later I would be living on the mountain on the opposite side of the valley, staring out over an identical layer of fog.

To me, there's something strangely soothing about a fog—although I'll readily admit I don't like driving in one. Maybe it's the dampening effect it has on sound, a lowering of the ambient decibel level. Or maybe it's just the security of being wrapped in a fleecy blanket.

Fog can come from several conditions of the air, but it results from only one thing: condensing moisture from a zillion tiny droplets. Actually, fog is just another name for a cloud created near the surface of earth or a body of water.

It can happen when warm, moist air moves across a cold surface. We get it up here when a warm spell moves in while snow is still on the ground. The sudden chill condenses the moisture.

Or it can form on a cold night when air near the ground loses warmth through radiation. That's when we get the layered fog down in the valley.

It can even form when the temperature of the air remains the same, but its moisture content increases. Example: When a warm front and a cold front collide, and rain from the overriding warm air falls through the cold air beneath it.

Here on the farm, a cold snap in the fall will produce a phenomenon on the beaver pond called "steam fog." Cold air above the pond is warmed by the sun-heated water until its moisture reaches the saturation point— "dew point"—and turns to steam.

Not long after their mother died, I took our children in a rented camper to Hidden Valley Lake—a wilderness area cupped on top of this mountain some 12 miles due west. On one night, there was a full moon. Since we were the only humans on the lake, the whole basin was wrapped in unearthly stillness. And steam fog was rising in the moonlight. It was a scene of transcendent beauty, one that lingers in my mind to this day.

Something over 30 years ago, I served briefly as a lookout at Hayters Knob fire tower. The tower straddles the Washington County/Russell County line some four miles back of this house on the highest peak of the mountain. On my first night in the tiny cabin at the foot of the tower, I awoke after midnight to find the door had blown open and snow was covering my blankets—in mid-April!

But even more vivid in memory is the fact that clouds had descended and were driving past that little shack. The beam of my flashlight couldn't penetrate ten feet outside the door. As I hastily built a fire in the stove, this somehow had a comforting—even an exhilarating—effect.

Yep, I like fog. So, if you have any extra, you can send it up here. It's welcome.

෪

Spring Firsts   *March 22, 1999*

If the seasons have gender, then spring is a female—a flighty debutante who arrives at her cotillion just any old time she feels like it. Sometimes early, sometimes late, but always welcomed warmly.

I've welcomed her in several columns during the past 12 years, and even before then in my ill-kept journal. Our first spring here on the mountain has an entry dated "9:20 p.m. Sat. March 11, 1978." It begins:

This has been a week of firsts:

First time this year that the thermometer has edged above 60. Sixty! Can you imagine?

First time the pond has been without ice since Dec. 28. It began melting yesterday on the western side and by this afternoon was clear.

First time this year we haven't had a fire in the living room fireplace.

First time this year we've slept in our own beds in our own bedrooms instead of sleeping bags on cots in front of the fireplace.

First time we've made maple syrup. It ain't worth the effort. We got less than a pint from four gallons of sap. Incredibly sweet, though. A second batch of six gallons is currently steaming away on the big wood range.

First time we've had a salesman knock on our door. This last event occurred this afternoon. Tim and I were gleaning firewood from the brush pile created when trees were cut to clear space for the new house. Pam came walking up the trail from the old farmhouse, grinning from ear to ear.

"You'll never guess who just came driving up!" she said. "An Electrolux salesman! I didn't know who it was when he got out. He said he had a thing about mountain roads and decided to explore ours.

"He asked if he could demonstrate his machine. When I told him our house didn't have electricity, he just stared for a moment and said, 'Well, I don't guess you can use one'." It must be spring. Civilization has begun to encroach.

That's how it was in the spring of '78. As other springs came and went, we became more sophisticated, paying closer attention to the subtle shifts of the season. In a column celebrating her advent a decade later, I wrote:

Spring is folding a load of laundry and not finding a single pair of long-johns in the lot.

Spring is the first collection of moths on the kitchen door at night, attracted by the light. No matter how hard you try to flatten yourself and slip through a crack in the door, they somehow manage to get inside.

Spring is Duke (our first Doberman) unwrapping himself from his personal heater and taking the first of his long walks down through the fields and across by the old farmhouse and back up the road. Checking to see if anyone has made off with a couple of acres during his hibernation, I reckon.

Spring is glancing out the kitchen window and seeing a phoebe inspecting the spaces above the porch logs, looking for a nesting site.

Spring is the first buds of maples, the first shoots of pokeweed thrusting up through the rotting leaves, the first fiddleheads on the ferns.

Spring is walking down to the garden where the tiller has been resting under its No. 3 washtub all winter, and giving the engine a crank to see how it sounds.

Spring is the spicy smell of a mess of creasy greens, cooking up with fatback.

Spring is stepping out the door and being greeted by the pervasive undertone of running water. The accumulated inches of winter rainfall can almost be measured by the decibel level of the streams.

Spring is the frog choir down at the beaver pond tuning up after its long layoff. Actually, we hear these "spring peepers" down in the valley several days before they organize their choral group at the pond. The mountain warms up more slowly.

Spring is a little brown bat, tilting above the lawn in early twilight. On second thought, the little brown bat is not to be relied on. We had an experience with one during a false spring in early March ten years ago.

I'd been standing on the porch of the old farmhouse when it drew my attention by cavorting in the bright afternoon sunshine, a fact almost as strange as its erratic flight. Now, a bat's normal flight is erratic but beautifully controlled. This one was literally tumbling all over the sky. He came bumping along toward the house and landed at the base of the big pecan tree.

I walked over and took a look. He appeared to be in a semi-comatose state—eyes shut tight, mouth open, gasping for breath. It struck me that bats have a high incidence of rabies. Tim and I killed it, nudged it into a mayonnaise jar, and delivered it to the State Health Department office in Abingdon for examination.

Happily, it came back negative. We subsequently learned that a bat emerging from hibernation while the weather is still cold can go into shock. It simply can't handle the sudden transition.

Spring doesn't cause me to go into shock, but, after a harsh winter, which this one wasn't, I find it hard to believe.

The thing that finally convinces me is the smell and feel of fresh earth down in the garden as I cover a row of onion sets. It's the smell and feel of life after the long death of winter.

ॐ

It's time to grade Buck and Leroy as long range weather forecasters. Remember, I wrote a column last November recording their weather predictions for the next five months. It was their "Raised Leg Forecast."

I decided to take weather notes and award the pooches 20 points for every month they predicted things correctly, while docking them proportionately for what they got wrong.

For November they predicted: "Three or four days of true Indian Summer are still scheduled for later this month, with blue skies and temps above normal." Well, chalk up 20 points. My journal entry on Thanksgiving Day noted that we'd just had, "Four unbelievable days of Indian Summer, but it's now coming to an end."

Their December prediction: "Beginning in the second week, a period of atrocious weather. Cold, with snow, pushing into the Christmas holidays with only a sprinkling of days of relief. However, the year will end on a mild note." On the morning of Dec. 8, I awoke to snow. It didn't last long, but my entry of Dec. 15 noted: "Rain last night, turning to snow. Ground covered. Five inches in Wytheville. Intermittent cold rain today."

On Dec. 21, I noted: "The first day of winter—and it's here, big time! Rain turned to snow yesterday afternoon. Three and a half inches on the sun deck. Have had to break ice in the dogs' water bowl several times today."

Did it extend into the Christmas holidays? You'd better believe it! Tim and I spent Christmas Day in Roanoke. We drove back that evening through a howling blizzard. I wrote that traffic "was slowed at times to 30 mph. Snow turning to ice on pavement. Wrecker crews and snowplows everywhere."

But did the month end on a mild note? Well, yes and no. Dec. 31 was warmer than the proceeding three days but it was also a degree below normal. I pointed this out to the dogs and told them I was going to dock them for it. They were outraged. Hot and cold, they said, was always a matter of comparison. The 31st had been milder than the proceeding days so the month had ended on a mild note. I remained unconvinced and subtracted ten percent—two points—from their score. Talk about snarling!

Their prediction for January and February was dire. Two of those eight snows came on the 3rd and 4th of January—so deep I had to cancel a doctor's appointment in Bristol. The third snow came two days later, on Friday. And the fourth the following Friday. It was four degrees when I drove into Abingdon the next afternoon—and five below zero a couple of nights later.

The fifth snow came the following Monday. I woke up to the sixth on Friday, the 21st. But then the temps moderated. It was dreary, with rain, but where were the seventh and eighth snows? Chuckling, I pointed this out to the dogs. They just smiled and said, wait and see, wait and see. And they were right. On the morning of the 30th and again on the 31st, the sun deck was white with snow.

Did the bad weather extend into February? Indeed, it did. More snow on the 1st. But what about that "pronounced break of several mild days in mid-month"? It began on the 14th. The 15th was five degrees above normal, the 16th 10 degrees above, the 17th was 15 degrees above, and Friday, the 18th, 19 degrees above normal—the warmest since November!

But the dogs goofed in March. Well, they say I goofed, and maybe they're right, for I wrote: "Greenup will come late but with a vengeance. Flowers will bloom before the last snowfall at the end of the month."

As I have noted in this column before, it's "greenup" when I look across the valley and see the first tender green of poplars on Little Mountain. And that doesn't come in March but in April, usually between the 10th and 20th. As for flowers blooming before the last snowfall, there was snow on the 29th—and we had molten mounds of forsythia and vivid jonquils long before then.

The dogs were right much upset when I told them I was going to dock them 50 percent for March. Still, I think they did rather well. Twenty points for November, 18 for December, 20 each for January and February, and 10 for March.

An 88 percent accuracy rate for a five-month forecast! Why, not even Dave Dierks or Scott Fisher could do that.

Remember, last Nov. 20, the National Weather Service issued a three-month long range forecast which called for a milder than average winter. Ha!

Those weather people would save us taxpayers money if they'd stop buying computers for forecasting. Buck and Leroy are for rent. Cheap.

Above, the newer Ford tractor parked at the edge of the garden. Below, Tim in the Christmas trees, 1988.

8 ~ Farming

Once we settled into the new house on the mountain, much of Dad's time and energy went to raising gardens and tending the land. A lot had changed in terms of methods and farm equipment since last he participated in "serious" farming as a boy. But, as was his usual fashion, he took to it with enthusiasm and eagerness.

He learned the inner workings of our old 1949 8N tractor. He pursued untold methods of ridding his gardens of deer. And eagerly ventured into the rather painful enterprise of Christmas tree farming with Tim.

Many of these farming chores were not without their hazards—some with comical results, some downright frightening. Two such incidents that prompted an "Oh, my God, Dad . . . " response from us involved perilously close brushes with death atop the tractor while bush hogging. But he thrived on the work and it was heartbreaking to see him have to give more and more of it up with his advancing emphysema.

He would often talk about the pleasure he found in the rhythmic nature of these jobs: the annual planting and harvesting of his garden, the patterns the bush hog left in the fields, and the crack of the ax against a dead tree.

ଔ

The Tractor

Coming to the mountain meant getting used to a lot of strange equipment. Although my boyhood had been pretty much divided between Bristol and Hayters Gap, the equipment on my grandparents' farms had been mule-oriented.

But the world had changed, and our introduction to its mechanization was a 1949 Ford 8N tractor. It provided our first tentative contact with the land.

In the beginning, I thought of the tractor as a toy, a step up from the "Stanley Steamer" with pump-pedals I found under the Christmas tree one glorious morning. The night after the tractor's arrival, Tim and I decided to take it on a joy ride from the old farmhouse to the site of our new house, high on a ridge overlooking the valley.

Its headlights didn't work, so Tim perched on a fender, Ray-O-Vac in hand, and lit the trail recently gouged into the side of the mountain. Duke provided escort service. There wasn't a moon, but the night was clear and full of stars. They seemed to pop out as we left the overhanging trees at the top of the grade.

For a long while, Tim and I sat there on the tractor, enjoying the stillness broken only by katydids, and a little screech owl whickering down in the holler. Mist filled the valley below and crimped itself against the side of Little Mountain. Starlight revealed ridge after ridge falling away before fading against the sky.

A rare moment, one I guess I needed to resolve lingering doubts about our move to the mountain. And I did have doubts. Doubts about giving up a job I thoroughly enjoyed, selling a comfortable home and uprooting a family, trading it all for primitive living and dubious financial survival.

At those times, when I'd question my sanity, I'd sit down and read a bit of Thoreau—"Let the noon find thee by other lakes, and the night overtake thee everywhere at home."

Other than joy riding, a tractor had three functions: it pulls, it lifts, and it operates machinery—sometimes all three at once. That old 8N had four cylinders. A couple of years ago, I bought a Ford 2000 with only three, yet it's heavier and much more powerful due to cylinder capacity and gear ratio. Upper and lower gear ranges give eight forward speeds and two reverses.

We have many of the usual accoutrements for a small farm—plows, disk, bush hog, lift-boom, cultivator, even a blade. The blade isn't for farming, but, up here, it's essential. Our mile of private road is mostly winding and steep, so gravel washes with every heavy rain.

I grew fond of that tractor by working with the blade—experimenting with adjustments in the "top-link" of the three-point hitch, checking different angles and elevations as it smoothed the surface.

Because of the lightness of the old 8N (it wasn't designed for heavy equipment), the bush hog proved the most challenging attachment. Still, I enjoy bush hogging. Somehow, it goes with a crisp autumn day and a high blue sky.

I like the patterns it leaves on the bosom of a field, the contours that follow the fence lines. My last bush hogging in the fall is the long field dropping away below the house. That way, its contours will please the eye until green-up in the spring.

It's good to sit on a growling tractor when leaves are beginning to turn and distant ridges are etchings in purple. Sun warm on arms and face as you cut one swath, then warm on neck and back during your return. Grasshoppers jump and flutter, and thistledown floats in the air like an invading army of ants had just made a parachute jump.

And over the whole field, the big blades spread the smell of fallen leaves and fresh-cut grass.

os

Bush Hogging   *September 4, 2000*

I bush hogged our big field below the garden last week, the penultimate mowing of the season. There'll be a final one in October when weeds and grass have pretty much stopped growing.

Symmetrical lines are pleasing to the eye. That's why baseball diamonds are mowed in patterns. That big field is the foreground for our view from the mountain. I'm not sure how many acres are in it but it takes a little over five minutes for me to circle the perimeter on my first mowing swath.

Bush hogging. I'd never even heard of a bush hog until we moved to the mountain 23 years ago. (As a matter of fact, we arrived 23 years ago last Thursday. Longest I've ever lived in one place.)

For you city slickers, a bush hog is simply a squat, metal box hitched to a tractor. It houses a pair of heavy swinging blades which cut a five-foot swath and can handle saplings half the thickness of your wrist.

I wondered how long the bush hog had been around and went to the internet to find out. No luck. But I did discover a company called "Bush Hog" in Selma, Alabama, established in 1951, so they're probably around a half-century old.

In looking for the history of the bush hog, I came across a lengthy article, written by a farmer, called "Choosing, Mounting and Using a Bush Hog Type Mower." I wish it had been available when I first started using the thing.

He wrote: "The bush hog type mower is one of the most dangerous pieces of farm equipment in production today. Another hazard is the fact you are often driving nearly blind in tall grass, weeds and brush, often on very rough terrain with hills and ditches that can cause an overturn."

I learned the truth of that statement the hard way. There have been three occasions in the past 23 years when I came perilously close to sudden death or, at the very least, serious injury. Two of those involved bush hogging.

The first incident occurred some 20 years ago when I was mowing the side of a steep hill near the old farmhouse. Noticing a large tree limb ahead, I reached down and pulled up the control arm of the hydraulic lift so that the bush hog would clear it.

Instantly, gravity swung that monster (it probably weighed close to 500 pounds) down hill. The little 8N didn't stand a chance of controlling such a force, and began to roll. Instinctively, I bailed out on the upper side. Both bush hog and tractor rolled over, making a complete turn over a nearby bank. They both landed right side up in the road below. No damage, except to my dignity. However, if my foot had gotten caught beneath one of the pedals I might not be sitting here writing this.

My foot did get caught in the second incident, which happened several years later when I was bush hogging high weeds in the barnyard not 50 yards from the site of my first mishap. One of the 8N's front wheels ran over a large object hidden by the weeds. The wheel came down with such an impact I was bounced into the air. I landed half on, half off the tractor.

Unhappily, my left foot came down on the ground directly in front of the big rear tire. It rolled over my foot and started climbing my leg. I knocked the tractor out of gear, but that still left me in a rather awkward position. My right foot was caught under the brake pedal and the weight of the tractor on that sloping ground prevented my wiggling free. I was, quite literally, being torn apart.

Now, I don't have one of those cool heads to think through an emergency situation. Instinctively, I pushed down the clutch pedal with my left hand and knocked the gear shift into reverse with my right. Instantly, the governors opened up and the tractor backed off my leg.

The entire incident lasted no more than a few seconds. The pain could have lasted for hours until someone arrived. I walked around on crutches for a few days but that was a small price to pay in view of what could have happened.

I still enjoy bush hogging. I imagine some farmers view it as monotonous but I've never found it that way. The dogs think it's boring. Well, Buck and Leroy do. Little Girl uses it as an excuse to go tearing down through the fields, ending with a dip in the pond.

⚃

The Broccoli Bed   *March 27, 1989*

I began bedding broccoli after our Clinch Mountain deer developed a gourmet taste for it. By having a bed to reset from, I didn't have to keep going back to the nursery for more plants.

When we first arrived on the mountain, I used to burn the broccoli bed, not gas it. I recall a March evening 11 years ago when I burned the bed under the light of a full moon. Stretched out on the ground just above those glowing coals, hands locked beneath my head, watching tufts of cumulus brushing the face of the moon, I seemed to feel the mountain communicate itself through my back.

Getting acquainted with a new place comes in slow, sometimes faltering steps. Like human relationships, I suppose. Maybe it was just the warmth of the fire, or the solid thrust of the mountain, or even the full moon—which always triggers a sort of madness—but, anyway, for the first time since our arrival, I felt a strong sense of belonging.

Which is a feeling hard to get when you kill the weed seeds of a plant bed by sticking a sheet of plastic over a can of methyl bromide. But a herbicide's easier than a bonfire. And I've gotten lazy in my old age.

Last year, even a bed didn't work. The deer ate the bed. As a result, for the first time in a decade, I bought broccoli at the supermarket.

⚃

Potatoes and Tomatoes   *October 16, 1989*

Generally, I wait until October to dig potatoes. Not just from procrastination. It's cooler then, and the bugs aren't so bad. I also try to make the occasion coincide with a visit by one or more of my offspring. No point in letting free labor go to waste.

Consequently, when Lisa decided to bring the Cannonball down for a visit (the Cannonball being my four-month-old granddaughter, Lindsay), I decided that potato time had arrived.

I'd been laboriously "gravelling" a few at a time all summer, so I was looking forward to doing it the easy way—astride a tractor while they boiled up around a plow behind me. However, when I went down to bush hog the patch to get it ready, I discovered smartweed had taken off like wildfire during all the rain and was covering the patch like a blanket.

Now, smartweed supposedly gets its name from its juice, but I think it comes from the fact it's smart enough to hug the ground and dodge a bush hog. I sure couldn't remove it. As if smartweed wasn't enough, we found the soil still saturated from rain—more so than any October I could remember. As a result, we had to stop every few feet and shove and tug at the earth and smartweed caked on the plow.

Tim and I finally gave up. We decided (groan!) to do the remaining patch (something over 500 feet) by hand. Fortunately, it was a perfect potato day, with the first leaves of autumn sifting down through clean-washed air, and White Top and Iron Mountain rearing purple in the distance.

The Cannonball sat in her "bounce chair" in the shade of the Blazer and supervised. At least, she made supervisory cooing sounds. (I maintain it's never too early to start making a "Mountain Mama" out of a little girl.)

We were almost through the first row when the viscous earth proved too much for the spade, and the handle snapped. We threw up our hands and quit.

Four days later, Pam came visiting with her husband, Don. More free labor. So we gave it another whack. Although the earth was still loaded with moisture, four days of sunshine had helped. By slathering old crankcase oil on the plow, we found we only had to make two or three stops per row to pull off the mat of earth and smartweed.

As a result, we now have around 500 pounds of splendid Kennebecs in our root cellar—about as fine as we've grown. Quite a contrast with last year when we ran out halfway through the winter.

A friend down in the valley didn't get his potatoes planted until June. Normally, missing spring rains would be a guarantee of a poor crop. But it rained all summer—and his potatoes are as large as I've seen anywhere this year.

A great year from the garden. The only failure I had was fall turnips. Something must have been wrong with the three ounces of seed I planted, for it produced nothing but tops. Not a turnip.

The thing I miss most when the garden goes to sleep for the winter are the tomatoes. Like the country song says, "There're only two things that money can't buy—true love, and home-grown tomatoes."

If I didn't like tomatoes so much, I'd refuse to buy them in the supermarket. They simply don't taste like tomatoes. Columnist Lowry Bowman once described that taste succinctly. "Like Kleenex," he wrote. Exactly.

Speaking of tomatoes, earlier this year, Hunt came out with a special tomato sauce which included peppers, onions, and celery. I tried it, and found it several cuts above regular sauce. For I'm a lazy cook. Always looking for short cuts. And this, to me, was a short cut.

I can't think of a dish in my meager culinary repertoire in which I use canned tomatoes by themselves. I always add peppers and onions, and sometimes celery (which is bland, and adds more to the tactile qualities of a dish than its taste).

So when canning season rolled around this year, I chopped the tomatoes and added finely chopped onions and bell peppers and hot bananas out of the garden, plus a couple of stalks of celery. It works great!

Now, all I have to do when I open a can is add the seasoning that varies with the dish—chili, spaghetti sauce, soups, casseroles, shrimp creole, chicken cacciatore, or what have you.

Thank you, Mr. Hunt.

CB

Eliza and Leroy wait on dinner.

The Christmas Tree Business   *December 24, 2001*

When we moved here and found several vacant fields, we asked ourselves, why not plant them in Christmas trees? Although I'd never ventured into the world of entrepreneurs, I knew that every year people bought Christmas trees.

So, around 20 years ago, Tim and I planted several hundred white pines. I foolishly thought that planting would be it—that afterwards I could just sit up here, happily mildewing, while the things matured like investments in CDs.

Instead, I discovered that years of hard labor lay ahead—bush hogging around them three times a year, shaping them mid-summer by swinging big chef's knives under a blazing sun, wiping sweat out of our eyes while fighting off bugs. And even after seven years it wasn't over. For now we were faced with getting those trees into area living rooms.

The logical thing would have been to sell them wholesale to retailers in late summer. But, thanks to my usual procrastination, we found ourselves shoved against the Christmas season with trees still in the ground. Reluctantly, I had to face the fact that my contentedly slothful life was going to be shattered by a stint as a Christmas tree merchant.

Friends steered us to a vacant filling station in downtown Abingdon owned by an Abingdon attorney. When contacted, he not only agreed to its use, he generously declined payment. A flying start! Well, not really flying. More like a walk. The attorney had been negotiating the sale of the property and now had trouble contacting the prospective buyer who had the key. The upshot was that a week later we had to have a locksmith come up from Bristol to pick the lock.

On a Sunday afternoon in early December, a friend and I took a bunch of price tags down to the pine trees. We'd decided on a top price of $20 for the largest and best-shaped ones. The best bargain in this area, we smugly believed. Those trees really ought to move!

Setting prices for the other trees was a bit difficult. It involved walking around a tree, mentally comparing it to the $20 paradigm, subtracting points for size and aberrations, then coming up with an arbitrary figure. At my friend's suggestion, I tagged a few stunted trees at $5, although I doubted that anyone would be interested. I was amazed when they turned out to be our best sellers.

The next day, Tim and I rented a truck and brought it to the mountain. I chainsawed trees while Tim loaded. The next day, we made a second run. Total: 61 trees.

Tim, who lived in Abingdon at the time, agreed to open the stand at 11 a.m. and work it until mid-afternoon. One of his friends, Allen, would then take over and stay until business grew slack in the evening. I generously agreed to open on Saturdays and hold the fort until mid-afternoon.

Well, our sales during that first week didn't exactly knock us off our feet. Through Saturday, we sold 30, roughly half the business I thought we'd have. And only three of those were $20 jobs. By Thursday, most of the cheaper trees were gone, so Tim arranged for another friend, Eddie, to bring his pickup to the mountain. We cut and hauled another 31 small ones. No, we hauled 27. Four blew off and were lost en route.

By the following weekend, it became clear that the trees just weren't moving out. We thought about turning to Congress for tax relief but instead set the top price at $15 and reduced others proportionately. Sales still dragged. On Monday, we knocked the top price down to $8. Result: three were sold.

In desperation, on our final day I painted a sign that read: "Name Your Price—And Take a Tree!"

So, how did we do financially? Well, here's the record:

Expenses: license from the Town of Abingdon, $20; truck rental, $64.80; sign painting, $54; radio ad, $35; locksmith, $32.50; office supplies, $8.97; stands, $66.68; kerosene for heater, $9; Allen's salary, $226; electricity, estimated $30.

Profit: we sold 70 trees for $758.50. Subtracting $517.95 expenses, we were left a net of $240.55, or $3.44 per tree.

Even so, it was better than the following year when we went into the hole. No sooner had we opened a stand out on Highway 11 than we got freezing rain, followed by snow. Result: 10 trees sold, with expenses close to $200.

The third and final year, I simply advertised for people to drive up and cut their own. I've lost the record of how many we sold but I sure did meet a lot of nice people. Some came from as far away as Blountville and Clintwood just to get a tree here on the mountain.

Now, if any of you have postponed buying one, you can come up today and cut one of those 20-foot babies. Be my guest.

Anyway, a Merry Christmas and a prosperous New Year to all of you. To achieve the latter, I suggest you stay out of the Christmas tree business.

СЗ

Ironically, I spent a large hunk of the Fourth of July down among our Christmas trees, giving them their annual shaping. I say "ironically" because there's something a bit incongruous about celebrating Independence Day in the forced company of a bunch of stupid pine trees. I feel like I've been their slave forever.

Unhappily, the Fourth of July falls within the narrow parameters of their shaping "window." You do it then or not at all. After the sales fiasco of our trees during the past couple of seasons, I swore I was through bothering with them. Finis. Kaput.

But I hate waste. So it was back to that big, heavy chef's knife again, swinging away. Tim and I have been partners in this loathsome venture for a decade. He's usually down there in the fields with me at shaping time. This year, however, he was working unbelievable hours helping get a new gourmet restaurant (The Courtyard Cafe) off the ground in Marion. As a result, no Tim in the pines.

Since I couldn't find other help, I was stuck with shaping 500 trees by myself. So, to keep from being bored to death, I turned to music. I took the Subaru (instead of the Blazer) with its four-speaker stereo system. I also took a dozen cassettes I'd made from LPs, some dating back many, many years.

Now, my taste in music is a bit like Duke's taste in food: If he can swallow it, he thinks it's delicious. So these tapes were inclusive rather than selective. First, I tried the Big Band sound I loved to dance to 150 years ago—Glenn Miller, Benny Goodman, Woody Herman, Tommy Dorsey.

No good. A great beat but mostly too fast. It wrecked my rhythmic 30-strokes-a-minute. Tex Beneke or Gene Krupa can wear your arm plumb out.

Next I tried country. Although I've never been what you'd call a country music buff, there're some vocalists I like simply because of the way they sing and what they sing. The late Jim Reeves is one. His big, easy baritone settled in among those pine trees like it belonged there. And Sammi Smith, my all-time favorite female vocalist. Big in the '60s but whatever happened to her?

Sammi began singing in Oklahoma honkytonks at the age of 12 and the huskiness of cigarette smoke and stale beer and that special sadness of youth is still in her voice. There must have been a dozen vocalists who recorded the Kristofferson classics, "Sunday Morning Coming Down" and "Help Me Make It Through The Night," but nobody had Sammi's special phrasing and delivery. Nobody.

I had a feeling that another '60s artist, Acker Bilk, would fit in with those pine trees. And he did. (My generation will scream "heresy!" but Acker plays a better clarinet than Benny.)

Trouble was, songs like his haunting "Only You" slowed me down. I had to take time out to reminisce about dinners featuring slow, easy talk and sparkling wine glasses and a face framed in candlelight across the table.

Oddly enough, it was a current composer, Ray Lynch, whom I played over and over. Lynch, a guitarist and keyboardist, both writes and records. His stuff has been labeled "New Age," but that doesn't mean diddley, for he combines classic with pop. It's even danceable. Last summer, a friend and I were listening to his "Celestial Soda Pop" in the kitchen, and were so moved we went out front and jitterbugged barefoot in the grass. In the moonlight. Kinda nice.

About the only music I didn't listen to was rock. Well, I did turn it on once after I stumbled into a yellow jackets' nest and got stung. I drove the Subaru as close as I could get, found a rock station on the radio, turned it up full blast, then walked to the opposite end of the patch and worked there for a while.

Well, sir, when I returned every one of those yellow jackets was dead. And every one had died with an expression of indescribable agony on its face.

Music didn't remove the bugs or sweat of monotony from tree-shaping, but it did help. And part of that help came from the evocation of faces and relationships and experiences—the magical assembly of the scattered fragments of life.

Standing on a mountain farm my grandfather owned a hundred years ago, listening to songs going back half a century, getting ready for tree sales next Christmas. A strange continuity.

Sibelius' "Finlandia" settles among the pines as gently as the gathering dusk. Rays from the setting sun glide up the side of Little Mountain across the valley, then rise to a distant, high-floating cloud, then disappear. The moon comes up. I watch it while I dangle my sore right arm, thinking, "I bet it'll take two hands to hold my Bacardi and tonic tonight."

But I also think, "You're a lucky man. You're a lucky man!"

CB

157

Jack and Duke. Photo by Earl Neikirk. Courtesy of the Bristol Herald Courier.

9 ~ The Dogs of Clinch Mountain

Dad's columns on his dogs were, without question, the most popular columns he wrote. Perhaps it was the pure love he had for them that his readers could feel, or maybe they connected with his sorrow when he would lose one of them, or they shared in his amusement and laughter over their antics.

Dad admired and loved Duke, our first Doberman, beyond all others. Duke was as much a part of the mountain as any of us. His death in 1990 was devastating to Dad and he compared his grief to the intensity he felt when our mother and his parents died. This biting grief was probably due in a large part to the fact that Duke was Dad's most enduring companion through the years, and after we left home, he filled those empty spaces.

He used his columns to educate as well. He routinely encouraged his readers to spay and neuter their pets. He often wrote about the two animal welfare organizations that he publicly supported: the Margaret B. Mitchell Spay/Neuter Clinic of Washington County and the Animal Defense League of Washington County.

He also wrote many scathing columns about people who dumped dogs along the roadsides. No one made Dad angrier than those who mistreated animals. Anytime he would suspect abuse of a dog he would intervene. He might stop to feed and water an obviously neglected dog, or talk with the owner of a chained, unprotected one, or often, would simply buy the dog and bring him home to the mountain.

Duke

Duke is dead.

In his younger days, after another of his gastronomical exploits—such as stealing three pounds of milk chocolate off my pantry shelf and eating the whole thing and then begging for breakfast the next morning—I swore that, sooner or later, that dog would eat himself to death.

Then he became afflicted with "wobbler syndrome" and I had to revise my thinking and conclude that paralysis would eventually do him in. But he fooled us all.

Duke's final meal was a breakfast. We shared it on the front porch where we could enjoy the scenery and each other's company. Instead of my customary bowl of cereal, I'd decided to have a plate of ham and eggs and toast—much to Duke's delight.

As usual, he stood with his forefeet on the bench, head at my shoulder—obviously resenting every mouthful I took for this meant one mouthful less for him. When I finally put the plate on the floor, he went through his share in no time flat.

It was afternoon before I saw him again. And he was a changed dog. He'd drink water, then just stand there, staring at the bowl. He was humped up. And panting. Once he vomited a clear fluid.

I'd seen those same symptoms five years earlier after he'd stolen some corn on the cob and eaten it. Since Duke didn't believe in wasting anything he could swallow, he'd eaten cob and all. Result: an emergency operation to remove a section of cob that had blocked his intestines.

I called the vet who had performed the operation, Dr. Peggy Rucker over in Lebanon, and gave her the symptoms. She said to bring him in that afternoon. However, by the time I got ready to go, he seemed much better. So I called and postponed the appointment until morning.

But that evening he grew worse. I was up and down with him all night, letting him outside and watching while he vainly tried to relieve himself. I'd lie down with him and pet him and talk to him for he was in obvious pain. He kept puffing out his cheeks when he breathed.

Radiographs the next morning showed a huge mass blocking his lower abdomen. It was his prostate gland, Dr. Rucker said. Because of its size, there was a high probability of malignancy. If so, she said, the veterinarian schools at Virginia Tech and UT had the only vets in the region who did prostatectomies, thanks to the complicated urethral involvement in canines.

"No way will I put him through that!" I said. "Not with his age and condition. But can you perform an exploratory operation just to confirm your diagnosis?" She could and did—and found the rampaging cancer had already spread to the surrounding lymph nodes.

So, less than two months from his 14th birthday, Duke was put to sleep.

In our 13 years on the mountain, there have been two permanent fixtures—Duke, and our beat-up old Blazer. They arrived together, and thereafter Duke claimed it as his personal vehicle.

Duke also became a part of everything we did. Wood-gathering, farming, gardening, construction projects, long hikes, or just long evenings in front of the fire—whatever was going on, he was an eager participant.

Patterns are hard to break. So there was a sudden emptiness when I went downstairs in the morning and found no Duke at the foot of the steps—deep, intelligent eyes crinkled in a warm welcome, that stub of a tail going a mile a minute.

I still catch myself saving part of my bowl of cereal for him, or a hunk of sandwich. And that good, rich, familiar Duke smell still lingers in the house.

But you can't live in yesterday. So, five days after his death, I found another Doberman, a miniature of Duke, and brought him home with me. He's ten weeks old and his name is Buck.

Why Buck? Well, one of the first books that Mother read to my brother and me was Jack London's The Call of the Wild. Buck was the canine hero, and he probably had something to do with my lifelong love of dogs.

If my Buck grows up to the size of his feet, he'll probably be even larger than Duke. But he has some big shoes to fill. The Dukes of the world are special.

Why do people who have loved and lost a dog go out and buy another one, knowing they'll probably have to go through the same pain all over again? The answer is simple: The relationship between human and dog is unique, transcending in some aspects the depth of friendship between human beings.

Certainly, my own life was richer because of Duke.

"Dog Days" are so named because the dog star, Sirius, rises at the same time as the sun between July 3 and August 11. It generally coincides with a sultry slice of weather, but here on the mountain, real dog events seem to happen then, too.

Duke, the greatest dog I've ever owned, died July 31, six years ago. A week later, another Doberman, Buck, arrived on the scene, and precisely five years later, another part-Doberman took up residence.

Duke had been an integral part of our life on the mountain. When the children and I decided on the move, we knew we'd be living remote from other human habitation, so a guard dog would be appropriate. Pursuing a newspaper ad of a Doberman for sale, I found a bony, malnourished, worm-infested animal on the end of a chain. Two months later, he was a sleek, strong, happy, free-running dog.

Duke and my daughter's collie-shepherd, Brette, got along famously. One of their favorite stunts was to turn over a rain barrel and race it down the side of a hill, barking all the way. It was a great life for a dog who had known nothing but a short chain. Maybe that's why he clung to it so tenaciously following incidents that would have taken a weaker dog away.

One day, he went to sleep under the Blazer while Tim and I were cutting wood in a drizzling rain. When we climbed in to leave, I drifted off and ran across his abdomen, rupturing the urethra. His abdominal cavity filled with urine. Peritonitis should have killed him. Instead, the late Dr. Jackie Hewitt opened him up from stem to stern, flushed the cavity and swabbed internal organs. Somehow, he pulled through.

Another time, he was struck by a visitor's car and pinned beneath its intensely hot oil pan. By the time he was freed, one side had been literally cooked. Over the next few days, flesh fell off until his rib cage was exposed. Daily immersion in an antibiotic bath saved him, although he had to wear a steel plate for months on a fractured foreleg.

When Brette was put to sleep because of a non-treatable respiratory condition, Duke grew lonely and began journeying down into the valley to romp with a pair of chow dogs. Returning one evening, he was bounced by a pack of wild dogs. Although ripped up considerably, his strength and speed somehow saved him.

Then he developed "cervical wobble," a critical condition of the spine. But he endured even this until prostate cancer took him off.

My sense of loss during those first days of August was the greatest of my life. So much so that, a week after his death, I went up to Wytheville and bought a three-month-old Doberman pup. Buck couldn't erase the memory, but at least he occupied my time just keeping him out of mischief. A year later, he was still at it, so a veterinarian friend in Roanoke came down for my birthday and brought Lady the Rottweiler as a distraction for Buck. It didn't work, but the Lady Bug is still aboard.

Leroy the Mutt wandered in one winter midnight from no telling where, liked the accommodations and stayed.

A couple more pooches subsequently took up residence. I picked up both Liza Jane and Suzannah at roadside where, apparently, they had been left by dog-dumpers. Liza Jane established herself as Queen of the Mountain. She kept the other dogs in what she considered their proper places. Even Buck was intimidated.

Not long after Suzannah arrived, she, too, began giving herself airs. But she didn't live long enough to become the established queen. One day when I was leaving the mountain, she darted directly in front of my car. Death came almost instantly.

Then, one Sunday, all four dogs left for a stroll but only three came back. We hunted for days, and still haven't the faintest idea what happened.

All those dogs had personalities of their own, all interesting. But none began to approach Duke in the traits of character that I remembered and cherished.

Then, on the 6th of August last year, I encountered Lucas—a skeleton of a dog on the end of a chain. Starving, not a drop of water. I bought him, not with the thought of keeping him, but simply to remove him from his misery. In a week, he put on over ten pounds, and began showing signs of developing into an unusually handsome dog. Although his Doberman genes were dominant, his coat and markings were unique. So was his carriage and walk. Was I at last to have a dog that measured up to Duke? I began to wonder.

It wasn't to be. Last April 6, he disappeared following a fight with Buck that severely injured a forepaw. In spite of a two-month search, that was the last I saw of a dog that showed great promise.

Sometimes I have to wonder if dogs are really worthwhile. But then I have to ask myself what I would do without them.

ଓଷ

Buck's Puppy Stage   *January 21, 1991*

"Is there such a thing as a hyperactive dog?" I asked the dog trainer. "Yes," she replied, "and you have one."

163

Buck, as a puppy. Photo by Don Chappelear.

So maybe that explains why Buck didn't graduate *magna cum laude*. Oh, he graduated all right. Even got a diploma. But I was hoping he'd come back from two weeks at obedience school a changed dog.

And to a limited degree, he did. He now heels on a lead pretty well, and will sit and stay on command. When he feels like it. But his most egregious habit remains firmly imbedded in his character—i.e., he still views himself as a guided missile to be launched indiscriminately at any target of opportunity, friend and foe alike.

The day after he returned from obedience school, we had three visitors. Each one left the mountain in a sour mood and muddy clothes.

Of course, I now know what to do: Give him a "sit" command while stepping backward, then reaching forward, I grasp his collar. And he sits there—for about five seconds. Then, to show his appreciation for such a delightful game, he twists that powerful Doberman neck and clamps his mouth around my wrist. Not hard. Just appreciatively. And when I walk away from him, I get over 80 pounds of exuberant puppy in the middle of my back.

"He was difficult," the trainer admitted, "and I'm afraid you're going to find him difficult, too. I've known people with hyperactive dogs who simply couldn't tolerate their behavior, but who were so attached they couldn't let them go. So they put them on tranquilizers."

I didn't have any valium on hand so I offered Buck a rum and tonic. He declined. Said it violated his moral principles. At least, I've found something he won't put in his mouth. You wouldn't believe the stuff he's transferred from various shed shelves to the front of the house. Here's an actual list:

Mason jars, a length of logging chain, newspapers (I think he likes to keep up with current events), an old inner tube I'd saved for homemade washers, the forked pole that propped up our clothes line (he chewed off the fork), two pairs of my best work gloves, a beer mug in which I stored paint brushes (I don't know what happened to the paint brushes), a tire gauge, a couple of heavy plastic buckets (now demolished), a bag of clothespins, assorted hand tools, several sections of wire mesh gutter-guards, and an impressive array of firewood. I wouldn't mind him transferring the firewood to the front porch if he'd only learn to stack it neatly.

One day, I looked out the window and saw he'd brought around a large cardboard box we use to store stove wood. Before he had a chance to rip it to pieces, I went out and brought it in. While there, I looked around to see what else he'd added to his collection—and saw yellow powder and the remnants of a brown bag around the yard. From somewhere, he'd managed to get down a bag of Manzate insecticide.

I felt confident he hadn't eaten any of that yucky stuff, but, in order to rip up the bag, he must have gotten some in his mouth. And it becomes toxic on contact with liquid. So I went in and called the Blue Ridge Poison Center at the University of Virginia. The obliging woman who answered quickly researched the chemical and told me the symptoms to watch for. He exhibited none. In fact, the only change I noted was that he seemed hungrier than usual that night.

Buy him his own toys, you say? That dog must have gone through at least $20 worth of rawhide chews. Even the largest ones last less than an hour with him. One day, I saw him offer one of his chews to our cat, the Count. He took it out on the driveway and dropped it at the cat's feet. But the Count wasn't having any—not for consumption and not for play. Long ago, he learned that playing with a Doberman pup was about as safe as playing with a steamroller.

Fact is, the two weeks that Buck was away at boarding school were obviously the happiest days the Count has had since last summer. He became friendlier, ate better, put on weight, lost the haunted look in his eyes, and started sleeping on the foot of my bed.

Buck still can't understand why the cat gets to spend so much time inside and he doesn't (answer: He wrecks the house). So he stands outside the kitchen window on top of the picnic table, staring in dejectedly, trying to make me feel bad.

His trainer did have one word of encouragement: He will probably outgrow his hyperactivity the way a child does.

"He should be over it by the age of three," she says.

Three! He's only seven and a half months! Duke, I miss you.

The Count

Cancer has claimed another longtime resident of the mountain. The Count, our black ex-tomcat. Eight years old. Relatively young, as cats go. Invasive squamous cell carcinoma of the upper left jaw. Terminal and inoperable. No real option except euthanasia.

Even so, deciding when to put him to death was difficult. An animal can't confide how much it's suffering. You can only observe and weigh quality of remaining days against quantity.

First, he lost vision in his left eye, then gradually the ability to eat. He'd rub against my legs and beg for food, but when I gave him some he could only sniff hungrily and sit looking at it. The hinges of his jaw must have been affected. I even opened a can of fancy crab meat. But the most he could do was give its liquid a few laps. That's when I made my decision.

The malignancy had probably been there for months before it was detected. It had slipped in like a thief in the night. Back in early summer, I'd noticed a watery discharge from his left eye. Even though it didn't seem to bother him, I got a tube of tetracycline ointment and started treating it.

No results. Then, not long afterward, his appetite began fading— although he remained an active, healthy-looking cat. I took him to a veterinarian who pointed out a slight swelling beneath his left eye. A swab up his left nostril emerged spotted with blood. Further examination revealed an upper tooth so loose that the vet pulled it out with his fingers. Then X-rays showed an advanced, irregular growth. And a biopsy told the rest.

The Count. Although I'm not what you'd call a cat man, over the years I came to like and respect the little guy. He had character. Pam got him as a kitten to replace Kitters, a white Persian who had mysteriously disappeared one night—probably via a Great Horned Owl.

Duke was delighted with this new addition. While instantly challenging any dog his own size, Duke liked all manner of small critters. Also, as the only four-legged member of our family, he must have been getting a bit lonely. So, he took the Count under his wing and brought him up right.

They became a regular team, exploring the surrounding woods together, mouse-hunting the field below the house, sleeping on the carpet in front of the fireplace on long winter evenings. Yep, they were quite a pair. I don't think I've ever seen a dog and cat more attached to each other.

Occasionally, the Count would go off on a jaunt of his own for two or three days. When he returned, Duke was always delighted. He'd nuzzle him, while the Count rubbed around his legs.

One day, I came downstairs and found Duke stretched out on the floor. The Count was stretched out, too—on his back across Duke's forelegs. Almost comical.

Then Duke died, and the Count became a changed cat. He'd always been independent, showing affection for humans only sporadically, but now he actively sought my company, even sleeping on the foot of my bed. I'm not sure whether he sensed my loss or was simply expressing his own. Then along came Buck, and the Count's life changed again. Forever.

He tried to make friends with Buck, but instead of finding another companion he found a bully.

He'd always been an outdoor cat. Unless there was snow on the ground, mousing was his pastime and delight. It was a rare day when I didn't look out my bedroom window and see a small, solitary, black figure down in the field, sitting intent and watchful for hours on end. But that pleasure was denied him during the final year of his life. Buck made him an indoor cat out of him.

Strange, on his last night here, instead of going to one of his usual resting places—the foot of my bed, or a window sill—he went to the exact spot on the living room floor where Duke had spent his final night when he was dying of cancer.

At the vet's the next day, I gave him a final pat and told him he had been a good cat and handed him over.

I buried the Count up on the ridge beside his old buddy, Duke. I think they both would have wanted it that way.

∝

Leroy   *December 30, 1991*

As if two dogs weren't enough, now I've got a third one. Leroy.

Leroy wandered in shortly after midnight a few nights ago, from whence or why I have no idea. Uninvited and unannounced. Well, Buck announced him. I was upstairs working when I heard Buck give his "there's an animal out here" bark—short, repetitive, monosyllabic.

I switched on the floods and went outside, expecting to find a possum. Buck was standing below the pavilion, barking up at something in the

Leroy

shadows under a bench. When I walked over, I saw a tail start wagging. Oh, no, I said to myself, not another dog! But it was. A handsome little dog, about half the size of a mature German shepherd. And the same type of coat, only darker. Friendly. He came down the steps to greet me.

And Buck immediately attacked him. The dog rolled over, feet in the air, showing total submission. I scolded Buck and petted the newcomer. He had on a collar but no tag. And he felt well-fed. Probably under a year old. Where in the world had he come from at this time of night? Hounds wander in occasionally but this was no hunting dog. And it didn't make sense that someone would dump an animal that had been well cared for.

The dog got to his feet. And, tail wagging, began bouncing around Buck, inviting him to romp. Buck agreed, although he obviously was more interested in establishing dominance.

I decided to treat the situation like any other problem—ignore it, and maybe it will go away. So I went back upstairs. I could hear them romping outside, but there also came occasional yips of pain.

Buck is a bully. Bullies, I have observed, tend to be big and strong and stupid, with an overbearing disposition—a description that fits Buck like a glove. Generally speaking, he and Lady have gotten along rather well. Every morning they take long walks together—sometimes down through the fields, sometimes into the woods. But, early on, when their romps turned into arguments, I began noticing her backing down—even though, as a powerfully built Rottweiler, she could probably have held her own.

Unhappily, once Buck established this dominance, he began abusing it. I've seen him attack her for no apparent reason. Which surprises me, for I'd always believed that males decline to attack female dogs. Buck must be some sort of genetic aberration.

Anyway, when I heard Buck abusing our guest, I went downstairs and brought him inside. At least, that would give the stranger a chance to travel on. Before long, I heard noises and went down to investigate.

I discovered that Buck had reared up on the kitchen table and removed a Christmas-wrapped book and ripped off the wrapping. He'd also reared up on the wood range and removed a wicker plate and torn it up. Ditto

168

the thruway where he'd grabbed a glove and destroyed it. Yessir, a fine, indoors dog, that Buck.

I took him outside and snapped him onto the chain nailed to Lady's doghouse (she's never bitten anyone, but she sometimes intimidates strangers, so I keep the chain handy). I'd no sooner re-entered the house when I heard a tremendous noise. When I looked out, I saw Buck yanking that heavy doghouse around like a matchbox. He finally ripped out the nails holding the chain. Then he just stood there, chain attached, rooted

Lady

to the ground like a horse who's been left with its reins dangling.

Fine, I said, just stand there all night. At least your bullying will be handicapped.

The next morning, I fed the stranger and named him Leroy. Why Leroy? Well, why not? I've never known a dog called Leroy. Then I took him down to the old farmhouse Tim is remodeling and put him in one of the outbuildings. Returning home, I began calling around the neighborhood to see if anyone knew who owned him. No luck.

I confined Leroy for a day and a night, then left him outside with the door open so he had access to food and water. My hope was he'd continue his journey to—well, wherever. Several hours passed, and my relief grew. Then a visitor came upstairs and said, "Guess who's outside playing with Buck and Lady?"

So here I am stuck with a third dog. Which really wouldn't be so bad since he's a friendly, handsome little fellow. But Buck continues to bully him, and that's not fair.

So, if any of you out there would like to give a belated Christmas present to someone, Leroy's available. If I offered up Buck for adoption, I'd probably be better off—but I wouldn't wish him on my worst enemy.

ငဒ

Bouncer   *July 23, 1990*

On my way to Abingdon, I was maybe half a mile down Route 700 headed for White's Mill when I spotted a pair of dogs—one black, the other brown—in the grass by the side of the road. The little black dog was lying down, the little brown dog standing beside it.

When I came back that way some four hours later, they were still there—the black dog still lying down, the brown one still standing beside it. I backed up, switched on my caution blinkers and went over to investigate.

When I approached, the brown dog wagged his tail but the black dog simply lifted his head, then dropped it. His eyes were dull with suffering. Apparently, he'd been badly injured by a car. Well, at least the driver had had the decency to stop and take him off the road.

Decency? Leaving an injured dog without food or water or shelter? Yeah, a real Good Samaritan. I had a water jug in the rear of the station wagon, so I poured a cup and offered it to them. The black dog took only a few listless sips, but the brown dog drank the cup dry.

I put the black dog in the back of the wagon, then tried to catch the brown dog. But he was too leery. At the nearest house, a woman, a Mrs. Wolfe, said, no, they weren't her dogs, but "my daughter-in-law came in the other night and said she'd seen somebody in a truck with one headlight dumping a couple of dogs over the hill there."

Which is where I'd found them. Suddenly, the picture became clear. Some slimeball had found the perfect solution to getting rid of unwanted dogs: Just wait till night, then slip down a lonely country road and dump them.

I turned around and headed for a veterinarian on the other side of Abingdon. As I passed the brown dog I stopped and once again tried to catch him. No soap—although he did run after me when I left.

Dr. Gent examined the black dog and shook his head. "Severe nerve impairment," he said. "He'll have to be put to sleep."

Enroute home, a thunderstorm broke and rain came down in buckets. I wondered if the brown dog had found shelter. When I reached the spot where I'd first seen him, there he was. He'd returned to the place he'd last seen his buddy. Maybe it was the rain, or maybe he was simply weak, but, anyway, he let me pick him up.

I brought him back to the mountain, picked up some of Duke's Alpo at the house, a blanket, another jug of water, a couple of containers, and took him down to the corncrib next to our barn. Duke, of course, simply won't tolerate a strange dog. Anyway, the corncrib was airy and dry. It hadn't been used since we converted it into a cote for Pam's doves, Romeo and Juliet, many years ago.

Brown dog was so hungry I had to be careful not to overfeed him. Then I spread out his blanket and left him to recuperate. He bounced back fast. When I went down the next morning, he was not only ready for breakfast but a walk as well.

He's an unusual looking dog. Long, brown hair with a long, feathered tail and long body. But short legs. He looks like a collie that's been raised under a coffee table. Small, pointed face, like a fox's, and with a fox's eyes. Light weight.

He doesn't just walk, he bounces—sometimes up to my chest when he feels affectionate. Which is often. So that's what I've named him: Bouncer.

Trouble is, I can't keep him. For one thing, it wouldn't be fair to Duke. When I return from feeding and walking our guest, Duke sniffs the legs of my jeans and fixes me with a reproachful eye as if to say, "I know you're having an affair with another dog. How could you?"

But the real thing is it's not fair to Bouncer to keep him totally isolated except for a few minutes out of 24 hours. A dog needs company as much as he needs food and water. So I'm putting him up for adoption.

I've had him dipped for ticks and fleas, wormed, and given all of his shots. Dr. Gent thinks he's somewhere between 12 and 18 months old. Intelligent, obedient, housebroken (so help me, he refuses to go to the bathroom in that corncrib!), cheerful and affectionate.

But, most of all, he has character. Any dog who will stick by an injured friend, refusing to leave even when hungry and thirsty himself, certainly has more character than the guy who dumped him.

So, if you'd like to adopt Bouncer, call me. The only thing I ask is that you guarantee a good home, hopefully one with lots of running room. And maybe let me visit once in a while. To tell the truth, I've gotten kind of attached to him.

(Connie Woods, who lived on Boone Lake, adopted Bouncer and they enjoyed many happy hours boating together.)

଼

Lucas   *September 11, 1995*

Something new has been added to the farm, something I needed like another hole in the head. A fourth dog is now in residence.

A month ago, I had business off the mountain. As I drove up a private lane I passed a small dwelling whose front porch light was on. No vehicle nearby. In the yard was a doghouse, and chained to it was a miserable skeleton of a dog. Every rib stuck out. His bony hips, rearing above his

171

back, reminded me of starved dray horses I'd seen as a boy.

On my way out, I stopped and walked over. There was no food pan, no water pan. He was on a chain less than ten feet long. Not a light chain, one with heavy links. Although there was a shade tree some 30 feet up the hill, the doghouse had been set out in the full glare of the sun. And it was the hottest August in 40 years.

The light on the front porch indicated that the dog's owner had been gone for some time or else was planning on being gone. So I went home, fixed up a container of food, found a water pan and a couple of half-gallon jugs.

Returning to the site, I filled the water pan and carried it over to the doghouse. As I started to set it down, water slopped out. Instantly, the dog began licking the ground where the water had spilled. When I set the pan down, he began lapping furiously. He drank a full half-gallon without stopping. I wouldn't have believed it possible if I hadn't seen it with my own eyes. When I filled his food dish he went through that just as ravenously.

On my way home, I began pondering how best to get that dog away from there. As I saw it, I had two choices. First, I could notify one of the county's animal control officers. I hadn't hesitated to do it when I encountered abuse situations in the past, and always with good results.

But this dog looked like he couldn't take much more. I figured that anyone who abuses a dog over a long period of time isn't likely to reform overnight. No, the quickest and easiest solution would be just to buy him. So I did. But when I started to unsnap his chain I discovered it had no snap. His collar had been wired to it. Since the wire itself was rusty, this undoubtedly meant that from the time he first had been attached, the chain had been the limit of his world. Ten feet. And he was six months old.

I was amazed at how light he was when I lifted him into the car. Not over 30 pounds. Although his shape and color and markings were those of a red Doberman, his tall, pointed ears and coarse hair resembled those of

Lucas

172

a German shepherd.

Ah, me. The longer I live the less I understand people. Why anyone would acquire a pup only to torture it with thirst and hunger and heat and a chained existence is utterly beyond me. Evidently they feel that if they own an animal they can treat it any way they please. Not so. Not in a civilized society. Governing bodies wisely pass laws protecting animals just as they protect children.

Anyway, my immediate job was rectifying Lucas' malnutrition. I launched a high protein, high calorie regime: three cups of dry dog food, a cup of lean chicken, a cup of boiled rice, a cup of chicken stock, vitamin supplements and a calcium-magnesium tablet. Twice a day.

This was roughly three times what my 111-pound Doberman, Buck, was getting. Lucas gulped it down and asked for more. Within three days, his washboard ribs began fading. After six days, I took him to a vet for his puppy shots. Naturally, he'd had none of those. Lucas weighed in at 41 1/2 pounds, a gain of at least ten pounds. However, noting the stark evidence of malnutrition, the vet expressed doubt that he would ever "realize his full growth potential".

I'm not so sure. On his 25th day here, he weighed in at 58 pounds. No fat—in fact, he's still skinny—but in less than a month he'd almost doubled his size. Which is a sad commentary on his previous condition.

Twice a day, I'd gone down to the corncrib to feed him and take him for a walk. I wanted to make sure he was strong and healthy before I found a good home for him. After our evening walk, we would sit on the front porch of the nearby old farmhouse. Just socializing and enjoying the peace and quiet.

This was a mistake. I got attached to him. And began wondering if I could work him into my gang of dogs up on the ridge. With some misgivings, I decided it was worth a shot. Tim came up and we built a pen abutting the pavilion. I figured the dogs could get acquainted through the wire while Lucas built up his strength.

It worked. In less than a week, Lucas and Lady and Leroy were romping together on the lawn above the garden. Today, Buck and Leroy still put Lucas in his place when he gets too rambunctious, but that's the puppy in him.

He wasn't a puppy when I found him. He was only an object on the end of a chain.

CB

173

It was five years ago this week when Lucas, the most handsome dog I've ever owned, simply disappeared. I still don't know what happened, but it may well have involved Buck. He and Buck had a guarded relationship at best.

Buck darted in front of my car one day and suffered several cuts and scrapes. A couple of days later, perhaps still hurting from his wounds, Buck attacked him. They had a real set-to. Lucas suffered severe puncture wounds in the pads of a forefoot.

A few days later, Leroy and Lucas both disappeared. Leroy came back but Lucas didn't. It marked the beginning of a lengthy and stressful search. At first, there was a routine combing of this entire area, plus telephone calls to neighbors. I printed up posters with his photograph and description and offered a $200 reward.

Days passed, then weeks. I upped the reward to $500, then $1,000. Tim and I plastered the area, even went as far north as Tazewell County. I did two or three columns on him. Coupled with the reward, they resulted in dozens of phone calls. Many were simply calls of sympathy but others were of sightings; at least the callers believed they had seen him.

And, my, how they were spread out. One woman was positive he had showed up at a picnic at Mountain City. Then there were calls that he had been spotted simultaneously on both sides of Bristol. The largest number, and most credible, came from the North Fork of the Holston. My friend Jerry Thornhill, who lives across the mountain, volunteered to take his canoe from the Hayters Gap bridge down to Holston. I promptly accepted. So, on May 31, we boated down the river. Every hundred yards or so I would call Lucas' name. It was a pleasant trip but resulted in only a sunburn and a rather hoarse voice.

Over two months of almost daily searching, aided by my son and friends. I couldn't begin to estimate the number of hours, or miles traveled. The posters with my $1,000 reward brought an unusual consequence. People who spotted a dog resembling Lucas would call Animal Control to come pick him up, then they'd call me. One such call took me to the Animal Shelter in Smyth County. He was a beautiful animal, mostly German Shepherd, but not Lucas.

He was scheduled for euthanizing. Since I was indirectly responsible for his being there, I felt obligated to save him. Tim and I picked him up and brought him to our corncrib, a temporary home for a number of animals.

I bonded immediately with Brownie. We'd take walks, and sit together on the porch of the old farmhouse. Obviously, he'd been starved for affection. I would have tried working him into my pack but, recalling what had happened with Lucas, I decided against it. Brownie was eventually adopted by a family in Bristol. Although they cherished him, he died from some ailment within a year.

Topper, a Great Dane I picked up after she'd been dumped on top of this mountain, was adopted by a Russell County family but died from heat exhaustion.

And then there was Batman, a puppy I picked up in the final stages of malnutrition who doubled his weight in 24 days before I found him a good home.

Two dumped dogs that Tim picked up, Homer and Jethro, were eventually taken in by a veterinary friend in Roanoke, who placed them both.

Little Girl, the dumped pup I picked up at roadside three years ago, has proved to be a real treasure. Intelligent and affectionate, she follows me up and down stairs and into whatever room I go into.

Little Girl

But, that's not surprising. It's been my experience that dumped dogs are a cut above the average canine.

Dogs. Maybe I ought to write a book and call it, "The Dogs of Clinch Mountain."

ℂ𝒮

Farewell, Buck   *March 4, 2002*

The big Buck is dead. Nerves leading to his hind quarters that had been badly damaged by a stroke in July '98 kept degenerating until there was no choice but euthanasia. A wrenching decision, as everyone who has gone through it knows. My only consolation was the knowledge that his life here on the mountain was one that most dogs would give their

Jack and Buck

right forepaws to lead.

When my first Doberman, Duke, died of prostate cancer in August 1990, I was totally devastated. I had been closer to that dog than any human I'd ever known.

Realizing this, a veterinarian friend in Roanoke thought it would speed my recovery to get another one. Fast. So she steered me to a Doberman puppy in Wytheville.

That's how it all began. Thereafter, except for my occasional absences from the mountain, we were together 24 hours a day. Buck went to sleep when I did, got up when I did, and was usually part of everything I did.

Buck was an "inside dog," sleeping upstairs in my bedroom. The others were "outside dogs." Over the past dozen years, there've been plenty of those, including Lady the Rottweiler. Lady died peacefully in her sleep in Sept. '99, a grand old gal.

There have also been a variety of dumped dogs, including Little Girl, who I picked up at roadside. She is still with me, as is old man Leroy, a little mutt who wandered in here one midnight over ten years ago and refused to leave.

When Buck had his stroke, we didn't know what was happening. He hunched down and refused to move and was obviously in great pain. After a battery of non-definitive tests at Virginia Tech's veterinary college, including a spinal operation, Pam picked him up and delivered him to my veterinarian friend in Roanoke to see if she and her staff could do anything for his paralysis.

It was a slow process. Every day for 75 days, he had physiotherapy. There were injections, even acupuncture. Gradually, he responded.

When he came home, Buck was overjoyed. Little by little, he improved, becoming more sure-footed. His big frustration was not being able to climb the stairs to my room, but by Christmas I was beginning to hope for a complete recovery.

Then, in January, he had another stroke. It was back to Roanoke.

This time, he experienced what the veterinarian termed a miraculous recovery. He was back home in two weeks. Although he never lost the looseness in his hind quarters, he improved to the point where we went on long walks. This lasted until last summer when he and Leroy had a horrendous fight, which I'm confident Buck instigated. Buck had his faults just like we humans.

By last month, nerve deterioration had reached the point where hind legs were getting tangled and he was falling frequently. Getting to his feet was a painful struggle. His walk was a stagger, and at times the hips came out of socket. He'd lost excretory control months earlier.

There was no overt pain. This was neurological. But clearly he'd reached the point for euthanizing. Still, I decided to give him one last chance. Tim took him to Roanoke for a final evaluation. His tests revealed a total loss of deep reflexes (nerve function) in his rear legs. So, Tim brought him back to the mountain. Veterinarian Dr. Fred Gent kindly agreed to come up the following day and administer the lethal dose.

For his final meal, Buck had a big steak (medium rare) and shared my asparagus and Hollandaise sauce. Through it all, he'd never lost his appetite. In fact, food and affection were the two main things in his life—in that order.

I decided that an appropriate spot to put him down was the bank in front of the house. There, he'd spent countless days sunning himself while gazing out across fields he viewed as his own.

Buck struggled against the needle. I'm sure he knew exactly what was about to happen. But he went down easily and quietly. I kept petting him until he crossed over.

I'm also convinced that Leroy knew exactly what was happening, too. In the past, he's always greeted every strange vehicle, but when Dr. Gent drove up he remained in the leaves behind the woodshed. A few minutes later, when we carried Buck up the ridge to his grave, Leroy remained there, although he'd always followed our truck.

Buck and Leroy had some horrendous set-to's, but, for the most part, they'd been buddies. In fact, before Buck's stroke they'd frequently romped together.

That same evening, Leroy provided further evidence he knew what had happened. Breaking a habit of many years, he stretched out on the cold kitchen floor instead of going into the living room to snooze. And there he remained. Even since Buck's stroke, the living room had been his room. Was Leroy's abrupt shunning of it an act of respect or an act of grief?

The next evening, Leroy didn't show up for his dinner. I looked

177

everywhere around the house. No Leroy. Tim wanted to know if I'd looked up at Buck's grave. I hadn't, so I took a flashlight and started walking up there. Tim was right. As I approached our pet cemetery, Leroy met me. He followed me back to the house but refused to eat his dinner.

Dogs. The longer I'm around them the more I'm mystified by their sensitivity and strange gifts.

෴

Casey
June 14, 2004

Tim, who lives over in the next holler, got up a few mornings ago and discovered that his golden retriever, Casey, was missing. By noon, Casey still hadn't showed up, which was most unusual.

Tim had to go into town for something. As he drove up a hill on his way out he was forced to stop. There, in the middle of the road, was a new-born fawn. And there, lying beside it, was Casey.

The fact that Casey was protecting it wasn't as much a surprise as the fawn itself. It was an albino, completely white except for a dash of brown on top of its head and a few dots of brown over the rest of its body.

Knowing that the fawn's mom wouldn't come back as long as Casey was there, Tim walked him back to the house and put him inside. Then he walked back to his vehicle. He found the fawn standing up, but not in a normal stance. It was standing on its four ankles, feet curved underneath.

Tim drove around it and on into town. When he returned a couple of hours later, it was lying beside the road. Tim proceeded on down to his house, still hopeful that the mom would collect her infant.

Later that afternoon, he fed Casey and his black lab, Sally. Casey only ate half of his bowl, then took off. There wasn't any doubt in Tim's mind where he had gone. Sure enough, on his way up here to work in our potato patch, he discovered the fawn had moved over the bank and was lying against a log. Casey was guarding it. So he took Casey back home.

After Tim finished the potatoes, I grabbed my digital camera and we went down to the fawn. I got some good shots of a cute and highly unusual little mite.

Tim called Dennis Austin, our local game warden, and explained the situation. Austin said to leave the dogs inside, that this was the only hope for the mom to return and collect it.

When the dogs were let out the next morning, Casey immediately took off. On his way to work, Tim found fawn and Casey together. When he approached, the fawn stood up—on its ankles. Casey licked its forehead, and the fawn nuzzled his side like it wanted to nurse.

That morning, Tim called Dr. Alanna Dingus, a wildlife specialist at Southwest Virginia Veterinary Services in Russell County. She told him that if the fawn's mother hadn't returned she probably wasn't going to. Best he bring it across the mountain for treatment.

That's what he planned to do. But when he returned to the mountain that afternoon, the fawn was dead. Casey was still guarding it. Dr. Dingus had commented that albinos are frequently born with severe deformities. Was that the reason the mother didn't return, did she somehow sense that her new-born wasn't going to make it? Who knows? Actually, that would be no more remarkable than Casey's protective instinct.

This wasn't the first time he'd displayed it. Four years ago this month, Tim heard him barking one evening below his house. It was a short, repetitive bark that most dog owners have come to recognize: "Come here! You need to come here!"

When Tim investigated, he found Casey standing, tail wagging, beside a new-born fawn. Although the dog clearly wasn't going to harm it, Tim thought it best to take him back to the house so its mom would have a chance to rejoin it.

Once inside, though, Casey insisted on going back out. Tim finally relented and Casey dashed back to the fawn. There he spent the night lying by its side.

Several times during the next three days, the fawn would bleat and Casey would come running. Whenever Tim's other dogs attempted to follow, Casey would threaten them so fiercely that they'd turn back to the house.

Each of those nights he spent lying beside the fawn. Now, here's a dog who happily kills every groundhog he can catch. Plus rabbits and squirrels. But, somehow, he's able to differentiate between fair game and a helpless fawn needing protection.

Some people insist that dogs are incapable of human emotions. Like compassion. Well, how else can you explain Casey's behavior?

CB

Lucy   *February 2, 2004*

This is the story of Lucy, a feral dog who probably won more hearts than any other dog I've known. Which is strange, for no one was able to touch her, much less pet her.

Lucy arrived in the vicinity of Lowe's at Exit 7 around two years ago. No one can remember the exact date, or whether she was dumped or just wandered in. She was probably half-grown at the time. Lucy appeared to be a border collie—head and ears, body and tail. She was black with white legs and chest, and a white ring around her neck. But her most unique quality was her total skittishness around humans. Even those who fed her weren't permitted to get too close. These included women employees at Lowe's, one of whom had fed Lucy for over a year. Others came from all over the area.

One day, three couples in separate cars arrived by chance at almost the same time. They all swapped stories about how they'd met her and become attached and began feeding her.

Another little mutt showed up at Lowe's in roughly the same time frame. Smaller than Lucy but showing border collie blood. The two dogs began hanging out together. Naturally, he was given the name Ricky. And, naturally, the inevitable happened. Lucy came into heat and they mated.

Unlike Lucy, Ricky loved to be petted. One Lowe's employee took advantage of this, grabbed him and took him in for neutering, shots and an anti-flea dip. He was then foisted off onto me. A worthless little mutt but he seems delighted with life on the mountain.

Capturing Lucy was another matter. I have a cousin in Bristol who, with his wife, last spring began noticing Lucy running around Lowe's. They decided to catch her and give her a home. Ha! Numerous attempts brought only failure.

A Glade Spring woman I've known for nearly 20 years began feeding her daily. Finally, she, too, decided to try to catch her. No, not to give her a home but to have her spayed so she wouldn't get pregnant again.

Most dumped dogs yearn for the protection and associations of a human home. Not Lucy. A true feral, she was happy to be running free. Although pleased to see those who fed her regularly, this didn't include physical contact.

The woman discussed the situation with a veterinarian who gave her a tranquilizing drug. Taking a blanket and heavy gloves, she and her husband went to Lowe's where they fed her canned dog food containing the drug. Lucy got woozy and laid down. But when they tried to sneak up behind her with the blanket, she got to her feet and staggered off. Finally, they gave up. In fact, the woman finally gave up feeding, too.

"I got so involved, Lucy just took me over emotionally," she says.

During the last days of June, Lucy's swollen udder indicated that whelping was approaching rapidly. This deeply concerned her many friends. They began speculating about where she would have her pups.

Lucy was absent for several days. When she showed up it was obvious that she'd whelped. But where were the pups? Well, they didn't show up for several days when four of them followed her out of a nearby ravine. It turned out there were two more. Three of the six were snatched up and adopted. A fourth was eventually grabbed by three of the women at Lowe's who had been Lucy's benefactors. All three were bitten. But you can't blame the pup. It was his first contact with humans.

Strange, the appeal that Lucy had for so many people. Well, maybe not so strange. Some dogs, like some humans, project a sort of magnetic personality. A friend who had begun e-mailing me last May about her encounters with Lucy described their first meeting.

"It was a dark and rainy night. I was sitting in the car while Joe went into Wal-Mart. Along came a dog. She stopped. I rolled down the window and talked to her. I asked her if she was lost, was she cold, where her owner was. She stayed for a little and then went walking through the parking lot, dripping wet."

I imagine there are a lot of people out there who remember their first encounter, and who now wonder how and why she suddenly vanished three months ago.

CB

Lucy

Hummer sipping from the sun deck feeder.
Photo by Kathy Shearer.

10 ~ Hummers

Dad loved his hummingbirds. Interestingly, they were a relatively late discovery for him. It wasn't until 1993 that he hung his first feeder. And with the introduction of Sweet Pea to his life, he developed a personal relationship with them.

The hummers were perfect companions for Dad. They provided interesting and entertaining subjects for his curiosity. During peak periods he would hang five to six feeders outside his bedroom windows and deck doors, another three or four along the front porch so he could watch them from the kitchen, and two or more on the pavilion.

When we were visiting on the mountain, the feeders were often so swarming with the little birds that they would wake us in the morning with their low, buzzing hum.

During the hummer season he would meticulously record their comings and goings, their daily consumption, and their behavior patterns. As with any subject that interested him, and always the reporter, he found out as much as he could about them. He read books and contacted leading authorities, until he became somewhat of a local authority himself.

Dad developed lasting friendships with many local people based on their shared fascination. They would call or email back and forth throughout the season, noting the locations of sightings (often competing on who saw the first bird each season), sugar consumption, and other interesting observations.

The hummers entered Dad's life at the right time—his days were quieter now and looking up from his computer he could watch endlessly their aggressive competition and playful antics.

Enticing the Hummers

Until this year, I'd never had a feeder for hummingbirds, mainly because I'd seen so few I figured it wouldn't be worth the effort. But then I recalled the advice in *Field of Dreams*: "Build it, and they will come." So I bought a quart-size feeder equipped with six plastic floret apertures and little plastic perches in front of each.

A hummingbird is strictly a bird of flight, having feet so tiny and legs so short he's capable only of perching. His boots weren't made for walking. Therefore, when he takes a sip of nectar from a flower, he hovers on a blur of tiny wings while he probes with his long, needlelike bill.

The bill houses an even longer tongue, with two grooves running down its length. This permits the edges to roll up into minuscule tubes whenever he sticks his tongue into a flower—or so I've read. There he hovers, sipping through twin drinking straws—like he was a seated customer at a soda fountain. The perches on the feeder let him rest while sipping—which I'm sure fills him with gratitude.

I mixed water and sugar, added some red food coloring, attached a bent coat hanger for a hook, and took the contraption up on the roof. I hung it from the gutter directly in front of one of my windows. It's about five feet from where I'm now sitting and provides a maximum of monitoring.

Well, sir, I was amazed. I saw more hummingbirds that first day than I'd seen in all the years I'd been up here. These exquisite little birds are continually aggressive. Or playful. Or both. They chase each other all over the place, sometimes doing elaborate head-to-head dances in mid-air. They zoom by my window so often it's beginning to sound like warm-up time at Bristol International Raceway.

The Ruby-throated is the only hummingbird we have in the East, but since none of the ones I've seen have ruby throats, this means all are female, or immature. Why no males? I'm not sure—unless the male migrates to Florida ahead of his family. Eventually, though, they all begin their incredible 500 mile flight across the Gulf to the Yucatan or Central America.

Watching them, I was suddenly seized with an inspiration. It came when I noted the striking resemblance between the colored sugar water in the feeder and my last batch of blackberry wine. Why not get another feeder, fill it with wine, and see whether they prefer soda pop or the hard stuff?

Although hummingbirds are the most agile of aerialists, I'd never seen one flying around bombed out of his mind. Maybe I could record it on video. Maybe I could get some film of one flying backwards around the house. That would make ornithological history.

So I bought an identical feeder, loaded it with wine, and hung it beside the first one. Within minutes, a customer landed and took a sip. Instantly, he rared back and shook his head. His expression plainly said, "Well, what in the world . . . !"

He tried the next floret. Same result. So he flipped over to the soda pop dispenser. Occasionally, one would try all six florets before giving up. One of these, after switching to the sugar water, tilted back his head and appeared to be gargling—like he was trying to get the taste out of his mouth.

So, what conclusion can we draw from this? Apparently, they reject Paul's admonition in his epistle to Timothy: "Drink no longer water, but use a little wine for thy stomach's sake."

CS

Sweet Pea

August 16, 1993

Jason Garrett, 16, of Bristol, recently saw something that looked like a large bug crawling in the street. Investigating, he discovered a baby hummingbird, presumably the victim of an overhanging nest accident. He called his mother, Diane, and asked if he could bring it home. Avid animal lover that she is, she said yes.

Now, mother hummingbirds feed their young by inserting their long bills directly down their throats and regurgitating partially digested insects. Which presented a problem for Diane.

"When Jason first brought him in, I thought he was dead," she recalls. "But I got some sugar water and put it on my finger and turned him over, and he just raised his bill and licked out his tongue and ate it."

She says she was up and down most of that night feeding him. The next day he appeared stronger, and before long began sitting on her finger to eat. And then, "Sweet Pea," as she'd named him, began flapping his wings while he held onto her finger—a phenomenon common to most fledglings before they leave the nest. But he's got a lot of flapping and eating and growing to do before he hits the trail south in the fall.

August 23, 1993

Diane asked if I would start taking care of Sweet Pea. "I'm away from home so many hours every day, I'm afraid it'll get out of its box and my dogs will eat it," she said.

"Well," I said, "I think I've got an old bird cage stored down in the woodshed. I'll go look." I found it resting on a board thrust across two rafters—right where we'd put it when we brought all of our junk here from Chesapeake 16 years ago. Covered with rust. I can't recall it being in use since it was occupied by the children's budgee, "Pretty Bird."

I hosed it down, rasped off what rust I could, put some paper toweling in for a floor mat—and Sweet Pea's new domicile was all ready.

When she arrived (I say "she" because of the white tips of her three outer tail feathers) I couldn't believe that anything that small could actually be a living bird. Much less than half the size of a mature Ruby-throated. Only one apparent injury: Feathers were missing from her throat area, exposing a swelling like a tiny, pink goiter.

No one knows how Sweet Pea happened to end up in the street. However, if I had to venture a guess, I'd say she could have been the victim of a blue jay. Jays are notorious nest robbers. It's quite possible that one could have grabbed her by the throat while her mother was away from the nest foraging, and was flying off with her when something caused him to let go.

But the "goiter" doesn't appear to bother her. At least, it doesn't prevent swallowing. Which is important, since nutrition will determine her rate of growth, and therefore the number of days before I am released from parental duties. I've heard mature hummingbirds require an enormous intake of food. Up to half of their weight daily, thanks to being almost constantly on the wing. But I could find nothing in the literature on infant intake.

Diane had bought a jug of commercial hummingbird feed, which supposedly meets the nutritional needs of adults. Plus a small floor-feeder to put it in. But Sweet Pea doesn't seem inclined to sip from it. So I hold her in one hand while I hold her food in the other. She lets herself be picked up, although she sometimes fusses in a tiny, rasping way.

I place the liquid in a plastic cap from a soft drink bottle and offer it to her. Instantly, she shoots out that incredibly long tongue and begins inhaling it. When she stops sipping from the cap, I dip the tip of a finger in it and hold it above her head—which is how Diane first fed her. Instantly, that tongue shoots out again. In fact, that seems to be her favorite method of eating—which isn't surprising, since the overhead approach was how she was fed in the nest.

I decided maybe insects were necessary to complete her nutritional needs. The commercial food's label shows only 0.1 percent protein. So I caught some small field crickets, chopped them up fine, scraped them into a small bowl, poured a teaspoon of water over them, and, using the butt end of a socket wrench as a pestle, ground them up. Then I let this delicious mélange of assorted body parts marinate while it cooled. I offered it to Sweet Pea in a bottle cap. She inserted her tongue one time—and then politely declined.

Thinking about nutrition, it struck me that the closest thing to flower nectar was honey, which is simply nectar processed by bees. So I filled a cap three-fourths full, added boiling water, stirred it up and let it cool. Man, she went for it hammer and tongs! With other food, she shoots her tongue out only as far as the surface, but with honey she sometimes runs it all the way to the bottom of the cap. The honey's stickiness presents a problem for her tongue. To clean it, she runs it out to its full length and then slowly draws it back in. Several times.

On a couple of days, I've hung her cage out on the sun deck not far from one of my feeders to see if adult hummingbirds would come by and hover and sympathize and maybe offer words of encouragement. "Remember Bataan, remember how many survived! You can make it!"

Nope. No interest whatever. So I'm her only companion.

There are times in the early hours of the morning when, bleary-eyed, I'm presenting a drop of watered honey on the tip of my finger and wonder what possible difference this feathered mite can make in the overall scheme of things. Just what am I doing here?

Maybe Sweet Pea, looking through the bars of her cage, thinks the same thing.

August 30, 1993

I never thought this column would degenerate into a running dissertation on hummingbirds, but it seems headed that way. On the other hand, there must be an awful lot of hummer lovers in this area. Following last Monday's column, I received a flood of phone calls. At least six came from people advising me not to feed Sweet Pea honey. Which I appreciated—although by chance I'd been given the same advice earlier by a veterinarian.

I'd called Buck's vet, Dr. Peg Rucker, at Southwest Veterinary Services over in Lebanon, to describe a growth between two of his toes. I casually added that I also needed advice on the care and feeding of a baby hummingbird.

"Then I'll let you talk with Dr. Heintzelman," Dr. Rucker said. "She's our resident expert on birds." Lori Heintzelman, I discovered, was indeed an expert—and began at an early age. As a child, she loved all animals, but birds in particular, so neighborhood kids brought her orphans they'd found, and injured ones.

"I'd nurse them back to health and release them," she recalled.

I was gratified to learn she's even raised injured hummingbirds. Just the person I'd been looking for to tell me what I'd been doing wrong. Quite a few things, it turned out. First, the feeding of honey. It could result in a yeast infection of tongue and craw, Dr. Heintzleman said.

I'd also made another boo-boo. Knowing that all nutrition must include protein, I'd been concerned because Sweet Pea was getting practically none. A friend suggested a little raw egg white. Which made sense to me. I tried it, found that it mixed well, and Sweet Pea didn't seem to mind.

"You're running the risk of salmonella," Dr. Heintzelman said. "Egg, of course, is fine. We have a powered additive that has egg in it—but it's pasteurized."

That's how I got introduced to "Emeraid-II," a dietary supplement formulated specifically for sick birds—18.5 percent protein, 5 percent fat, plus a host of vitamins and minerals. So that's what Sweet Pea is now on.

Dr. Heintzelman also suggested I swap her rusty bird cage for an aquarium since Sweet Pea insisted on trying to squeeze through the bars (she's so tiny, she almost could). This wasn't doing her feathers any good. The next day I bought a ten-gallon aquarium and installed her in it. And I have to admit she looks better.

Dr. Heintzleman also suggested I put a section of over-ripe banana in the bottom. It would attract gnats, she said. That way, Sweet Pea could supplement the Emeraid on her own.

Most of us observe hummers only at their feeders, or sipping nectar from flowers, but a major portion of their diet consists of insects. With their long, sticky tongue, forked at the end, they are anatomically equipped for it. Adults are capable of catching insects in flight, or foraging for them on leaves and bark.

Even their stomach, I've read, has evolved to accommodate this dual diet, with entrance and exit located close together. This permits an easy passage for liquid nectar, while the main body of the stomach serves as a digestive-repository for the exoskeletons of insects.

The piece of banana did attract gnats, but Sweet Pea prefers being fed by hand. What, me work for a living? Well!

I don't mind that she's not potty trained, but I do wish she'd learn to feed herself. Feeding her a couple of times an hour is no big deal while I'm up here on the mountain, but I have to leave occasionally.

Since she refuses to eat from a store-bought floor feeder, I've spent what seems like hours trying to teach her to eat from a jury-rigged contraption consisting of a medicine dropper full of food clipped onto a small branch with a clothes pin.

I'll carefully thrust her needlelike bill into the end and she'll flick out her tongue, eat for a few seconds, withdraw it, then just sit there. Like, "Okay, now what?" I've yet to see her voluntarily eat on her own.

My feeders are drawing increasing numbers of hummers. At first, they paid no attention to Sweet Pea out on the sun deck. Then, a couple of times when I was feeding her, one would zoom in close, poise on a blur of wings, and look us over. It was like they were saying, "Hey, what'd you think you're doing to that kid?" If they're so darned concerned, why don't they take over the feeding?

I've about resigned myself to the fact I'm going to be stuck with Sweet Pea until next spring. At her current rate of progress, she'll never be ready to join the migration south.

That migration has already begun. After nothing but female Ruby-throateds and immatures for two weeks, I've begun to get brilliant males heading south. They leave a full month ahead of the others.

The male leads a pleasant life. He is nothing but a stud. After the female starts nest building, he goes off looking for another relationship. No nest building, nor incubation, nor feeding the kids for him, no, sir. He has his own ideas about family values.

Which gives me an idea. I think I'll leave Sweet Pea here and join the males in Florida.

September 13, 1993

Well, the final chapter in the story of Sweet Pea, the baby hummingbird.

Of the calls that came in following that first column, three asked if I had read a book titled A Hummingbird in My House by Arnette Heidcamp. They said I might find it useful since it was the personal experience of a woman who had a hummingbird as a winter-long guest. One of them, Ann West, in Bristol, said she'd be happy to lend me her copy.

Great! I picked it up to get some quick tips. Arnette Heidcamp had found the little Ruby-throated in her garden "one cold, frostbitten day in late October 1988, long after all the other little hummingbirds had left for their sojourn in more tropical climes."

Knowing that he would die if she didn't do something, she ingeniously lured him into the sunroom of her home by spreading a trail of flowers. It marked the beginning of an incredible seven-month daily relationship.

189

"Squeak," as she named him, turned out to "the experience of a lifetime."

Sweet Pea was also an experience. After being fed by hand for ten days, she suddenly began feeding herself from a small floor feeder, and caught gnats attracted by the old banana skin.

She also became more active, particularly when I placed her aquarium out on the sun deck. Still, it bothered me that she really didn't have space to try to fly. So I transferred her to the floor of a spare bedroom. I cut a small sassafras sapling and placed it on its side to give her freedom of choice as to perching height.

Although able to flutter around on the floor, she still made no attempt at vertical flight—at least, none higher than a few inches. Which didn't seem right, for nothing can match a hummingbird's mastery of the air. He's the helicopter of the bird world. Thinking this might develop into a problem, I telephoned Arnette Heidcamp at her upstate New York home. She agreed.

"I have a feeling it's one of those 'use it or lose it' things, and if not used regularly, the wings may actually atrophy. Breast muscles make up a large portion of its weight."

The hummingbird, in fact, is the only bird that can fly sideways and backwards, thanks to elevator wing muscles (controlling the upstroke) that are extraordinarily developed, thus enabling the 75 strokes a second that we see as a blur.

Arnette suggested I take Sweet Pea outside and encourage her to fly. So I picked her up (a little like picking up a feathered June bug), carried her to the slope in front of the house, opened my hand, and gave her a little toss. She fluttered only a few feet before crash landing on the cushion of grass. But at least it was exercise. So I repeated it several times before taking her back to her bedroom aviary.

The next day, Labor Day, I carried her out again. This time she stretched her downward flight path 15 or 20 feet before landing. Progress! I decided to see if she would try flying by herself, so I let her pick herself up. And she did, fluttering up from the grass before taking off. But she never made it more than a few feet. Finally, she fluttered to the top of a tall stem, hesitated like she was making up her mind about something, then launched herself.

I couldn't believe it. This wasn't fluttering, this was flying. Although she wasn't gaining any altitude, at least she was maintaining a rapid, controlled flight. In fact, just before I lost sight of her (an emerald green bug against emerald green foliage), she veered toward the tree line on the west side of the field.

I rushed down to the spot where she'd disappeared and began looking among the shrubs—only to realize that if I expected to find a green needle in a green haystack I'd need my glasses. So I fetched them from the house.

Why look for her if she can fly, you ask? Wild birds belong in the wild, right? Agreed. But I questioned Sweet Pea's readiness for it. Although there are still plenty of protein-rich insects available, there's a limited supply of nectar-producing flowers, which hummingbirds depend on for their enormous energy needs.

Well, I spent the bulk of Labor Day afternoon looking for that mite. A negative search. Just plain gone.

In retrospect, I'm filled with conflicting thoughts. A part of me said that I did the right thing in trying to develop her flying skills. Another part says I should have been more cautious about it.

But how? And what if flight didn't develop? A hummingbird without flight is really not a hummingbird, it's just a small, caged wild thing.

Although I had Sweet Pea for only a few weeks, I think I know a little of what Arnette Heidcamp felt when she released Squeak the following spring. He simply lifted over her house—and she never saw him again.

"I look for him everywhere, even now," she says.

Cʒ

A Sense of Place   *July 28, 1997*

I have four one-quart feeders which I fill at one time. Two I hang on the sun deck where I can keep an eye on them through my bedroom's patio door. The other two I hang in a cool storeroom to be put up the following day.

The little gluttons had been finishing off the two quarts on the sun deck every day. Yes sir, it looked like there was going to be plenty of birds for the rest of the summer, or at least until the migration south began.

Then, two weeks ago, on July 14, I glanced out my bedroom door and saw both feeders vacant. They'd been in use almost continually. I'd seen as many as a dozen birds at a time.

I waited. And waited and waited. Finally, a single customer came in, had a few sips, and left, leaving the feeders vacant again. The day before, they'd knocked back half a gallon. At this day's end, not much over half a cup.

So, what happened? You tell me. I don't know. It wouldn't make sense to credit this to migration. The middle of July is too late to be migrating northward, and too early to be migrating south.

Have they started a big poker game out in the woods? Are they attending a tent revival somewhere? I spent a lot of time on the internet trying to get some answers, without success. Finally, I telephoned Dr. Paul Johnsgard in the Zoology Department at the University of Nebraska. He's the author of <u>Hummingbirds of North America</u>, the second edition of which came out last week.

I told him I'd been baffled by the sudden disappearance of around 90 percent of my hummers—for no apparent cause.

"That baffles me, too," he replied. "However, we're not always able to recognize the messages they're receiving. Birds may respond to phenomena we're not sensing."

For example, he said, whooping cranes in Nebraska have been known to shift migration patterns because of swings in barometric pressure, although this had not been apparent at first. One thing to bear in mind, he added, was the intelligence of the Ruby-throated. Although its brain is about the size of a pea, it is still capable of some amazing accomplishments.

"I fully believe in the place recognition of the hummingbird," he said.

The first hummer of the year proved it to me. I was sitting here at my computer when my attention was drawn to a movement outside the window in front of me. I glanced up, and there, hovering in the same spot I'd hung a feeder last summer, was a male Ruby-throated. I'd decided not to put the feeder back there this year since it meant climbing up on the roof.

But the hummer remembered—although eight and a half months and thousands of miles had passed. He'd traveled clear to the coast of the Gulf of Mexico and then across it on his 550-mile flight to Yucatan. And then had retraced the same arduous path in the spring.

Lodged in the memory of this feathered mite was not only a remote house high on the side of a mountain, but also the precise spot at the house where he'd had his last swig of sugar water. Incredible!

Have tens of thousands of hummingbird feeders across America changed the feeding habits of these feathered mites, or the pattern of their nutritional intake?

There were no feeders when I was growing up. I'd never even heard of one. However, in the past couple of decades, they've become more commonplace than seed feeders for other birds. Who came up with the idea of sugar water dispensers, anyway?

An account on the internet says the *National Geographic* in 1928 carried a story about hummers being fed from small glass bottles. As a result of the story, Laurence J. Webster, of Boston, designed one for his wife. Webster subsequently had his design replicated by an MIT glassblower.

In 1947, *National Geographic* ran another story featuring photos of hummers at one of these Webster feeders. (Incidentally, the beating wings of the hummers were captured with the help of a new invention, the strobe flash.) National publicity did the trick. In 1950, the Webster feeder was offered for sale by the Audubon Novelty Company of Medina, N.Y.

As far as the possibility of feeders shifting dietary habits is concerned, there've been no studies to that effect. Since genes determine nutritional patterns, it would appear extremely doubtful. Sugar water is not a hummer's primary source of nutrition. It only gives him the energy to go looking for his basic nutrient—soft-bodied insects. These provide essential proteins, minerals, vitamins, and so on.

So, if you're contemplating buying an expensive "complete" hummingbird concoction for your feeder, why bother? Trees and bushes surrounding you are filled with the hummer's favorite bugs.

Have you ever wondered who worked out the ratio of one part sugar to four parts water? Well, it was Mother Nature. It's roughly the same proportion of sugar (usually sucrose) and water in natural flower nectar. This high calorie intake is critical for hummers. It prepares the little varmints for beddie-bye, and is why you generally see them thronging around feeders as darkness falls.

However, a hummer metabolizes at such an enormous rate that even these nightcaps wouldn't suffice if Mother Nature hadn't added a modification. How? Well, by partially shutting down metabolic functions during sleep. Hummers enter a sort of semi-comatose state. Then, with the first crack of dawn, it's back to the feeders to get pumped up so they can start looking for insects.

How many feeders should you put out? The common answer is, as many as it takes to handle the little gluttons. However, another factor can also enter the picture, a factor I discovered quite by accident. This year I hung my first one on a bent coat hanger from the gutter on our sun deck where I could keep an eye on it, and another one on the porch in front of the kitchen window.

Eureka! The porch feeder instantly became the most popular. So I hung another one down there. As the population increased, I added two more. The one on the sun deck continued to attract only occasional birds.

Last week, I was sitting by my bed when I noticed a male Ruby-throated on one of the sun deck feeder's six perches. Not drinking, just sitting there contemplating his sins. For at least ten minutes.

Then, another hummer arrived and tried to take a seat. Instantly, he shot off his perch and chased it away. When this happened several times during the course of a half-hour, the reason for the lack of other hummers became obvious. Occasionally, he'd leave for a few minutes, only to return. How do I know it was the same male? Because he always took the same seat, and never drank more than an occasional sip.

Several hummer-watchers have reported this phenomenon. Although there's generally a lot of fussing and fighting and bad language around feeders, a solitary bully at a single feeder can keep other birds away. Therefore, if you're unfortunate enough to have a bully, best get another feeder and hang it out of sight.

I'm refilling the four downstairs feeders every other day on average, which means they're consuming a couple of quarts a day—sometimes a little more, sometimes a little less. I frequently have a cloud of ten to 15 hummers swarming around them.

ßß

The Right Feeder   *June 18, 2001*

One advantage to lying in my sick bed recovering from pneumonia has been the clear view it provides of hummingbird feeders hanging out on the deck. Maybe I can't work in the garden or mow the lawn, but I can still keep track of those little demons.

Here on the mountain, the hummer season has differed from those of the past couple of years when the birds disappeared for most of May. They stayed gone until the end of the first week in June when another wave arrived. Not this year. After arriving a week early, the population remained relatively stable. Visits at the feeders continued about the same, as did consumption of sugar water.

Then, on Sunday, June 3, visits at the feeders began increasing sharply. Day after day, the numbers increased. Refilling feeders became an every-other-day project. Lisa drove down from Richmond on June 6 to spend four days in a nursing role. One morning when she went downstairs, she counted 15 hummers swarming around the feeder out on the porch, all fighting for seats at the breakfast table.

Reports from people in the area who put out feeders indicate that (as usual) I have more than my fair share of the little feathered mites. Do I do anything special to attract them? Nope. I'm convinced it's the surrounding habitat: a tangle of woods on three sides where hummers can forage for the main component of their diet, insects. Insects supply protein, minerals, vitamins and so on. Feeders, by contrast, are just handy fonts of quick energy.

Those woods also provide another critical element—cover and protection for nest-building. So, if you're not getting as many hummers as you think you deserve, don't blame yourselves. Most likely, it's the lack of habitat. Although certain flowers are supposed to attract them, I've never planted any and still get hummers in droves.

After driving from Meadowview to Hayters Gap one day, Lisa said she'd never seen so many feeders in peoples' yards. "A few years ago there were hardly any," she said. "Now they're everywhere."

True. As far as bird-watching goes, it's been the fastest growing phenomenon in America during the past couple of decades. You can buy feeders in just about any shape, size and design under the sun. To me, that's a problem, for the bulk of these have been designed to attract buyers, not accommodate hummers.

Around ten years ago when I first started putting out feeders, I was fortunate enough to stumble across a basic design that proved ideal. A one-quart opaque plastic bottle with a two-part feeding attachment at the bottom with six apertures and perches. The one-quart bottle is also ideal when mixing the four-to-one sugar water. I use a half-gallon mixing pitcher which precisely fills two at a time.

Alas, frequent washing and filling results in wear and tear. Last August, at the height of the season when the little gluttons were knocking back a full gallon every day, I went looking for replacements. I couldn't find any of the originals, and most of the alternatives were cutesy little gadgets with lots of gewgaws and decorations that don't mean a thing to hummers.

Finally, I located a hexagonal-shaped feeder with a three-pint capacity. Plenty big enough to minimize refilling. Trouble was, it had only four perches. They were located in front of bright yellow flowers, each with a minuscule hole in the center—a close fit for even a hummer's needlelike bill. They served as backups during peak demand last August, although clearly the hummers weren't too fond of them. I've seen them leave a new one and fly to an old one.

Lisa filled the new ones Saturday, June 9. It took five days for hummers to empty one of them, while the other remained half full. During the same period, I had to refill my four old feeders twice. They're drinking around two quarts a day, which is pretty high considering that the bulk of the season lies ahead. I've already bought 25 pounds of sugar. At dusk, when they come in for nightcaps to help them make it through the night, every seat is filled—at least on the old feeders.

I have to wonder at the design of the new contraption. While increasing sugar water capacity 50 percent (over my old standard feeder), seating capacity was reduced by 50 percent. To me, that's fuzzy math.

A couple of years ago, I set up my camcorder to focus on a feeder, and got some great close-up shots. Even so, it can't compare with the video an Abingdon couple brought up here. Their son had discovered a hummer nest containing a pair of newly-hatched babies in a shrub only a few feet from his front door. Daily, over a two-week period, he filmed the mother returning to the nest and shoving her long bill down their throats to regurgitate nourishment.

You could almost see those little hummers grow. Soon they began climbing to the edge of the nest and exercising their wings. Finally, one ventured out onto a branch, and shortly thereafter launched himself into a neighboring shrub. It took several more feedings before the second fledgling felt secure enough for flight, but he made it, too.

In all these years I've never come across a nest itself. And here this guy finds one at his front door.

☙

Rufous Hummers

December 29, 2003

The saga of winter hummingbirds continues. There's been another report of a Rufous at a feeder, this one from a Bristol woman who first observed it on Sunday, Dec. 14. Several visits then and the next day. By weird coincidence, the Rufous down on the North Fork disappeared two days before this one appeared.

After studying Ruby-throateds for over a decade, I was beginning to think I knew a little about hummers, but the Rufous is a different dimension. However, I've learned quite a bit recently. I called and chatted with Dr. Sidney Gauthreaux, a professor at Clemson University in South Carolina, who has specialized in hummers for many years.

I also went to the internet and read an excerpt by Bob Sargent of the "Hummer/Bird Study Group" at www.hummingbirdsplus.org/rufous.html.

The thing that had puzzled me was why this West Coast bird, which nests as far north as Southern Alaska and winters in Mexico, has been showing up in increasing numbers in the eastern U.S. Sargent recalls that in the late '80s he and his wife would drive 600 or 700 miles to investigate a single report of a "brownish hummer." Ten years later, they were receiving 500 such reports. That's the way the eastern population of the Rufous has exploded.

Why has this happened? Sargent speculates that the Rufous has divided genetically into two separate species. "It would appear to us that a part of the Rufous hummingbird population is composed of birds that are no longer 'tropical' birds," he wrote. "This is supported by 22 individual return birds being recaptured at or near their original winter banding location in the winter of '97/'98. Many of these individuals have returned three, four and even five years in a row."

Sargent says that this phenomenon might suggest that now or in the future these individuals be considered a separate species. "What cannot be denied is that the Rufous that we encounter year after year are not vagrant birds," he wrote. "These hummers that we are now calling non-tropical birds have been generally referred to by the ornithological community and writers as vagrants, wanderers, lost, off course, sick or genetically impaired."

Sargent says it's his belief that even though some Rufous ancestors may have been altered genetically generations ago, the "defective" gene controlling migration is now normal for the U.S. population of Rufous. In short, the "winter hummers" around here aren't birds that have lost their way—or their minds.

"It is, in our opinion, a decision over which these non-tropical Rufous have no control," Sargent says. "They are directed to these wintering sites by the genes of ancestors that have wintered there successfully."

He also speculates that if these Rufous are confined to a particular breeding area where they encounter others with a similar genetic disposition, the prospects for a wintering population of Rufous may be on the verge of an explosive expansion. In fact, he says, "it may have already occurred and we are just beginning to document the fact."

He then muses: "Wouldn't it be neat to know that if you hung out your feeder in winter, Rufous would be as dependable as White-throated Sparrows, Juncos and other winter residents?"

Which brings up the subject of leaving out a feeder beyond the first hard freeze. I've always taken mine in, but Dr. Gauthreaux says this isn't necessary as long as we "take care of them." By this he means to either take them in at night and then put them out early the next day, or else attach a 150-watt bulb to a reflector and position it next to the feeder. Or even wrap the feeder in "heating tape" that some home owners use in winter on exposed water pipes.

Hummers in the winter. Who would have believed it? One way or the other, I'm sure you'll join me in wishing hummers—Rufous, Ruby-throated, or whatever—a Happy New Year!

ℭℨ

Hummer in the Kitchen   *April 26, 2004*

My first Ruby-throated hummingbird arrived on the afternoon of Friday, April 16, two days later than the first one had arrived for the past three years. Maybe I should say that's when I saw my first hummer. One could have arrived earlier when I wasn't looking. Tim, who lives about a mile away over in the next holler, said he'd seen one at his house on the 13th.

Ross McClure in Taylors Valley near Damascus also reported his first one on the 13th. Ross and I have been in competition for several years to see who gets the first bird. This year he beat me by three days. Members of the Bristol Bird Club reported even earlier arrivals—one at Vansant on the 4th and one in Buchanan on the 6th. Both areas are north of Clinch Mountain.

On the day I saw my first one, others residents did too. I received a phone call from Big Stone Gap, an e-mail from Emmett Road near the Weir, and another e-mail from Abingdon, all reporting first sightings that same evening. It's a safe assumption that these widespread and almost simultaneous sightings are proof that the leading edge of the first wave had begun moving through.

In fact, hummer activity on the following day surpassed that of last year. I have a feeder up on my deck and a second one down on the porch. There were times when I saw two at a time at each. Last year, such a build-up didn't occur until later in the month.

The arrival of these birds came as no surprise, but the appearance of another one last Tuesday was a shocker. It happened like this:

I'd had a couple of doctor appointments in Bristol and, as usual, laid in a supply of food items on my way home. After storing the groceries, I began cooking dinner and had stepped into the laundry room to use the microwave when something fell down from the ceiling.

At first, I thought it was a moth. Stepping closer, I saw a long bill. Heavens to Betsy, a hummer! I picked it up and discovered that it was completely entangled in spider webs—feet and legs, wings and bill. I know, I know, I'm a lousy housekeeper.

I carefully pulled them off, a process accompanied by indignant squeaks from the hummer. In places, there was such a mass of webs that I had to use tiny scissors to free them.

The kitchen door had been open for about ten minutes while I carried in groceries and stored them. The door is only a few steps from the downstairs feeder. It was a safe assumption that, for whatever reason, it had come in then. But, I'd also had the door open for a while the preceding day. What if it had come in then and I hadn't noticed? Hummers have such a furious metabolism that almost continuous nourishment is necessary. If that had happened, it would need some calories in a hurry.

Suddenly, I smelled my Salisbury steak burning on the stove. Rushing back into the kitchen, I flipped it over. I think it's safe to say I'm probably the only guy you know who has cooked with a hummingbird in one hand.

I took down the feeder and went back into the laundry room and placed it on top of our big freezer. I then inserted the hummer's bill into one of the food apertures. But he didn't drink. So I placed him on the feeder and quietly slipped back into the kitchen. When I peeked in a few minutes later, he was just sitting there, not drinking. So I decided to release him outside. However, when I walked in, he zoomed up to the ceiling and began knocking himself silly along one edge of the ceiling. After much effort, I finally recaptured him.

Again, he was covered with spider webs. After going through the de-webbing process a second time, amid more squeaks, I took him outside into the yard, held out my hand and opened it. Immediately, he took off for the nearest tree line where he landed on a limb. I watched for several minutes but he didn't move. Probably traumatized by recent events. I hope he made it through the night.

If this season goes as usual, we'll have intermittent activity around our feeders until mid-May. Then this northbound wave will pretty much disappear. It won't be until the first week of June that the main wave comes up from the south.

CB

Hayters Knob fire tower.

11 ~ Hayters Knob

The Hayters Knob fire tower, high atop Clinch Mountain, was an important part of Dad's life. He began hiking up there as a teenager when it was built in 1938. In the late 1950s he returned to the tower for a brief stint as lookout. And the tower provided the background for his second teenage adventure novel, <u>Fire Tower</u>, which was published in 1960.

Dad hoped that we would share his enthusiasm for the tower and early on led strenuous hikes to the mountaintop, to which we responded with moans, groans, and tears, as our young legs weren't quite ready yet. However, we came to appreciate the beauty of the location and the Great Channels over which the tower presides.

In 2002, Dad, along with many other area residents, became gravely concerned with out-of-state land speculators' plans to develop the 5000 acres that included the tower and the Channels.

In 2004, less than a year before Dad's death, the entire parcel was acquired by The Nature Conservancy. He was relieved and overjoyed to know that the mountain he had loved since childhood would be protected forever.

Hayters Knob Tower

Chatting with District Forester Harold Hannah the other day, I learned that Hayters Knob fire tower, located above me on top of Clinch Mountain, is being declared surplus and will probably be sold and moved.

Sad news. That tower's been woven in and out of my life since I was a teenager.

Hannah said that in recent years the Division of Forestry has been spending less on towers and more on air surveillance and citizen reportage of fires. Also, it's hard to find appropriate lookouts to staff towers during the spring and fall "burning seasons," particularly isolated ones like Hayters Knob. Vandalism and its accompanying rise in maintenance costs have also become a very real problem at these remote locations.

Towers at Mendota and Leemaster in Buchanan County are likewise being declared surplus, Hannah says, leaving only half a dozen in the district. Of these, only three "critical" ones will be manned, while the rest will be retained as radio antenna towers to relay district communications.

"Fire control is simply a different ball game than it was a generation ago," Hannah says.

Hayters Knob tower was built in 1938, and it wasn't long after that when I began hiking up there from my grandparents' farms down in the valley—never dreaming that one day I'd take a break from newspapering and return as a lookout. A lookout spends his days in a 7x7 foot glassed-in cab atop the 100 foot tower, and sleeps in a little one-room cabin at the foot. But it was still good duty—getting paid just to look at beautiful scenery all day.

I watched the first greenery of spring show up down in the valley, then move in slow day-by-day steps up the side of the mountain. I watched sunrises and sunsets, and circling hawks, and rainbows I could actually look down on. It was only incidentally that I watched for smoke—not once imagining that in another 20 years I'd build a retirement home on the side of the mountain below the tower.

Actually, if I had to select one fragment of time associated with the tower, it would be a winter night after we'd moved into that home— some eight or nine years ago, before the children left. A cold front had dropped a couple of inches of snow before passing on through. It had dragged clouds along with it, leaving a clear sky and a full moon. The night was so incredibly beautiful I suggested to Lisa (Tim and Pam were out on dates) that we hike to the tower. Deep in a book, she passed. So I put Duke on guard duty—to his intense disgust—and set out.

It's only a four-and-a-half-mile walk, but I found myself stopping again and again simply to enjoy the night. Moonlight was bathing the entire mountain, and every tree, every bush and shrub, was casting its charcoal shadow against the fresh snow.

But the thing I kept marveling at was the clarity of the air. The temperature was in the teens, and the humidity must have been near zero, for there was absolutely no haze. That it was a night among nights became apparent when I reached the switchbacks and began catching glimpses of the surrounding country. I was seeing distances I hadn't seen before.

The higher I climbed, the deeper the snow became. At the foot of the knob, it was almost up to my knees, so I had to slog my way the last few hundred yards to the tower.

But it was worth it. For when I climbed to the first landing and looked around, the view took my breath away. From Chilhowie to Bristol, I could see every street light, every car moving along every road.

Abingdon looked close enough to hit with a rock, but it had one very puzzling aspect—a lighted passenger train seemed to be parked on a curve in the air above the town. Then it suddenly struck me that this had to be a ski slope, which meant it had to be Beech Mountain—over 60 air-miles away!

I would have stood there looking all night—except my blood had begun to congeal.

Yes, a night of rare beauty. In fact, if I were told that every memory of my life would be erased from my brain except one, I think I'd probably pick that one to hold onto.

⋘

A 70ᵗʰ Birthday to Remember   *April 23, 2001*

I'm writing this on Thursday, April 19, anniversary of the FBI's 1993 standoff in Waco, Texas, in which 86 people died, and, two years later, Timothy McVey blowing up the federal building in Oklahoma City, killing 167. But there's another April 19 anniversary I recall more vividly, one involving my father and this mountain. It happened 44 years ago today during a break in my journalistic career.

I'd gone to work as a fire tower lookout at Hayters Knob. I'd been up there a couple of weeks and was running low on supplies when I recalled that my father had mentioned he'd like to visit the tower. Well, here was an opportunity for a visit, with grocery delivery thrown in.

I radioed District Headquarters in Abingdon, told them about my supply situation, and asked that my father be telephoned and given a grocery list. A few minutes later, the radio crackled to life with the news that Dad would be coming up the following day, most likely arriving in early afternoon. By coincidence, the following day was his 70th birthday.

Lookout duty in the little 7x7 cab atop that 100-foot tower fulfilled one of my childhood dreams of entering the forestry service. I loved the great outdoors. This ambition was eventually replaced by a dream of writing books. Little did I realize at the time that one day they'd be linked. I utilized my experience as a lookout to write <u>Fire Tower</u>, a juvenile adventure novel published by Funk & Wagnalls in 1960.

In the book, I borrowed heavily from my experiences, including my first night there when I woke up and found the door of the little one-room shack had blown open and my blankets covered with snow. When I shined a flashlight out into the darkness, I discovered that clouds had descended on the mountaintop, clouds filled with swirling snow.

The era of manning towers during spring and fall burning seasons has passed, replaced by heightened communications. Which I think is a shame, for it was a job I dearly loved. Some would probably consider it boring. There really wasn't much to do except keep an eye out for smoke in all directions. If one showed up, a bearing was taken on it with an alidade mounted on a map table occupying the center of the cab. The bearing was then radioed to district headquarters.

At headquarters, the duty man would stretch a string from the tower's position on a huge wall map. Then he'd request a bearing from another tower. At the point where the strings crossed, there was your fire.

One of the things I enjoyed most was watching spring slowly climb the south side of Clinch Mountain from the 1,500-foot valley floor to the tower's 4,000-foot peaks. It was an advance marked by blooming dogwood and redbud and serviceberry, the leafing out of trees. Spring creeping upward in slow increments.

But, back to that April 19th day 44 years ago. When Dad hadn't arrived by 4 p.m., I radioed headquarters to ask if he had left Bristol. Minutes later, they radioed back to say he had left around noon. That meant he was at least two hours overdue.

There were two ways to drive to the tower in those days, one from Route 80 as it crossed the mountain, the other from the bottom of Brumley Cove. I took the latter so I could park my jeep within a couple of hundred yards of the cabin.

The road from Route 80 ended at a clearing near the beginning of the "switchbacks." This trail zigzagged up the side of the mountain. Back in the '30s, it was the route used by mule teams carrying metal components of the tower. One can only pity those poor mules.

I knew that Dad's car couldn't navigate the rough Brumley route, so I began walking down the switchbacks. I found his car parked at the clearing. Which meant that, somehow, he had managed to wander off the trail. Happily, my eyesight was good in those days, and I was a pretty fair tracker. So, I began following his footprints.

About halfway up, I saw where he had failed to turn with the zigzag but instead had gone straight ahead. A hundred feet or so down this off-shoot trail, I began finding scattered groceries. When Dad suddenly realized he was no longer on the switchbacks, he obviously had panicked and plunged straight ahead, dumping groceries as he went. This was understandable, for he was no outdoorsman.

I called repeatedly but got no response. This also was understandable, for two or three hours had elapsed since he had wandered off the trail. Hurrying back to the tower, I radioed in the situation. Headquarters began alerting people by phone down in the valley.

Around midnight, Dad finally made his way off the mountain and to a telephone. And, boy, did he have a story to tell! He said that when he suddenly found himself "lost" he'd decided to follow a stream bed down to the valley. His choice of direction was probably logical, but his choice of a travel route was terrible. Stream beds in this area are a continuing mass of laurel thickets. Anyone who has tried to penetrate one of these thickets can appreciate what Dad faced. He said he had crawled on hands and knees through most of them, and had the cuts and bruises and torn clothing to prove it.

One thing's for sure, it was a unique way to celebrate a 70th birthday.

∞

Last Visit to the Knob   *October 22, 2001*

Its bottom steps were gone, but otherwise the fire tower looked much the same on a recent afternoon as it did 44 years ago when I served there as a lookout during a break in newspapering. Windows of the cab at the top of the 100-foot steel structure might have a few bullet holes, but you can credit that to vandals. Also vandalized was the nearby one-room cabin I'd lived in.

Charles Kennedy and I walked around to the back of the shattered shack and climbed a boulder perched on the dividing line between Washington and Russell counties. Cut into its top was a station number,

The spectacular view from the fire tower, looking south over the abandonned lookout's cabin. Photo by Kathy Shearer.

probably chiseled by my grandfather, Will Kestner, when he surveyed the line in the spring of 1924. I wonder if Granddad paused in his work to drink in the scenery.

The view from Hayters Knob is spectacular. Mountain ranges fall away in every direction. I never got tired of sitting up in that cab and staring at it. Of course, that was my job description. Looking. And radioing any suspicious smokes to headquarters in Abingdon.

At the time, there were 21 manned towers in District Six. As far as I know, the one on Hayters Knob is the last one standing. It holds a lot of memories.

Charles Kennedy had called and offered a lift up there in his six-wheeler ATV. He knew my hiking days were over, thanks to emphysema, but figured since I'd written a book based on my lookout experiences that I'd like to re-visit the place. He was right. I drove up to his house, built on a knob east of the tower, and we climbed aboard the ATV and made the steep climb the easy way.

The little lookout shack had enough left of its floor for me to pick out where things used to be—where I stored supplies, where the little wood-burning stove had set, where the iron cot rested. That blamed cot had sagged so much I developed a back problem. This led to a rather harrowing experience that brought an untimely end to my brief career as a lookout.

Driving out for supplies in my WWII jeep early one morning, I ran over a ledge and the jolt sent my back into spasm. A total lock-up. In excruciating pain, I opened the door and fell to the ground. And there I lay. Helpless.

In the late afternoon, I heard an approaching thunderstorm. Realizing that if I got soaked I'd probably suffer hypothermia, I reached down and cut a lace from my boot, tied a couple of sticks together to form a hook, and used it to pull the jeep door over until I could reach it. Using only my arms, I pulled myself up and hand-walked around the roof to the rear where I fell inside. And that's where the search party found me around midnight, a party that included District Fire Chief Ray Duncan.

Charles and I went next into the Great Channels, located just south of the tower. I doubt that many Washington County natives have even heard of this geological phenomenon, much less visited it. Imagine acres of sandstone, 15 to 25 feet high, sliced haphazardly into channels ranging in width from large cracks to chambers that you could drop a room into.

During breaks from the tower, I'd partially explored them, but was never sure how they'd been formed. So I called the area's leading geologist, Charles S. Bartlett, Jr. It happened, he said, back in the Silurian Period some 420 million years ago when the top of the mountain was the shore line of an ocean (several of our fireplace rocks, gathered from nearby fields, contain fossilized remains of sea critters).

The upheaval that converted a seashore into a mountain range stretching from Pennsylvania to northern Georgia resulted in a series of fractures in the sandstone. Over eons of time, these weathered and widened.

Bartlett described the Great Channels (a name I remember from the days of my youth) as "one of the most distinctive examples, and largest, of this type of fracturing and weathering." Kennedy had explored quite a bit there, so he led me from one channel to another. Some of them seemed familiar, others looked strange.

On our way back, I said I thought an easier route would be to cut down the side of the mountain and hit the road that leads to Brumley. Ha! I got us thoroughly lost. It was nearly dark when Charles found an entrance back into the Channels and, eventually, we got back to the tower.

It had been an afternoon tinctured with memories. I reinforced them when I got home by digging out a copy of the book I'd written, Fire Tower. The Channels played a key role in its plot. When I'd finished reading it, what amazed me was not how many parts of it I'd forgotten (after 41 years, what can you expect) but, rather, recalling the

The Great Channels, 2004. Photo by Earl Neikirk, Bristol Herald Courier.

circumstances under which it was written. If memory serves, I was coming up on a deadline. If broken, this would mean delaying publication until the publishing cycle the following year. Which, in turn, meant I wouldn't be receiving an advance payment until then.

So, I took my two-week vacation early, rented an off-season house near the beach at Virginia Beach (to avoid the distractions of home life) and began pounding the thing out. I would start at 8 a.m. and work until midnight, taking only meal breaks and an occasional walk with a neighbor's retriever.

In 14 days, it was done. All 214 pages of it. Oh, to have such self-discipline today!

03

Development Threatens *April 8, 2002*

Who owns a mountain?

That question was at the heart of a public hearing last month by the Washington County Board of Supervisors. The answer that emerged was that a property deed isn't carte blanche to do whatever the owner pleases. It brought a sigh of relief from a group of residents concerned about a North Carolina land speculator's plan to subdivide nearly 5,000 acres of Clinch Mountain into tracts for home sites.

Actually, it wasn't the first time a Virginia county has placed a restriction on what happens on private property within its boundaries. A couple of years ago, the Circuit Court in York County ruled that a zoning ordinance limiting clear-cut logging on private property near Williamsburg was legal and enforceable. The Circuit Court ruling was appealed to the Virginia Supreme Court. There it was upheld.

Naturally, no property owner likes to be told what he can or can't do on his own land. But when a dispute arises between the owner and a governing body, the governing body tries to balance property rights with the collective rights of the community. Like it or not, that's the way it is. And, to my mind, that's the way it should be.

I'll admit I speak from prejudice. My farm shares its northern boundary with Edwards Wood Products, Inc., the out-of-state land speculator. When we moved here a quarter-century ago, water was obviously a critical factor. When I approached a well-driller, he said flatly I'd never strike water at a reasonable depth high on this ridge.

So, I asked a dowser to come up and do his thing. He did, and his little forked wand indicated a sizable aquifer entering at my northwest corner and angling down the eastern side of the ridge.

Uneasy about the accuracy of dowsing, and knowing how expensive well-drilling could be, I asked a second dowser to come up—without telling him about the first one. He came. And located the same aquifer.

Figuring the chance of this being a coincidence was about a million to one, I asked my well-digger to start drilling. He went to work after lunch one day and before dinner had brought in an estimated 15 gallons a minute at a depth of 141 feet. Excellent water.

But, what would happen if one of the houses on this proposed development had a septic tank dug directly on top of the aquifer feeding my well? What if coliform bacteria suddenly appeared in my water, who would I turn to for relief?

Although subdivision housing appears to be temporarily blocked, concern for water wasn't the only reason that around a hundred county residents showed up at the public hearing to oppose the subdivision. Their opposition was broader and more basic.

Mountains are special, particularly in a region known as "The Mountain Empire." It would be hard to imagine lifting up our eyes and not seeing them. People travel long distances to enjoy mountains. A couple of years ago, there were 285 million visitors at our national parks. The most popular one? The Great Smoky Mountains.

At stake here is the character and integrity of Clinch Mountain. Once breached, there can be no turning back the clock. The damage will have been done. The mountain as we have known it will be forever gone.

The Planning Commission and Board of Supervisors both voted unanimously not to give the land speculator an exemption to county road-building requirements. So, where does his company go from here?

There's a rumor it is considering mining the vast supply of white sand at the top of the mountain. Some 420 million years ago, that area was the site of an ancient seashore. Core drilling to determine depth and quality of sand has already been done. If mining follows, it will jeopardize one of the most unique rock formations in the entire Appalachian range. Known as "The Great Channels," it is a labyrinth of sandstone canyons occupying several acres at Hayters Knob, one of the highest peaks on the mountain.

However, for mining to be feasible, the land speculator must have access to Route 80 where it crosses the mountain into Russell County. Blocking him is Charles Kennedy, who lives with his wife on 103 acres east of Hayters Knob. As evidence of how critical the right-of-way is viewed, Kennedy cites an offer of $375,000 for his property.

"I was tempted," he admits, "but saving the mountain comes first." He refused, and now a lawsuit has been filed to force him to grant it. Realizing what this could mean, a group of mountain and valley neighbors has established a defense fund.

It's our hope that the timeless peace and beauty of this mountain will eventually be preserved through purchase by an organization like the Nature Conservancy. Or even the Commonwealth itself.

⌇

Preserving the Mountain   *April 5, 2004*

Two years ago, when this mountain was threatened by a land developer, I wrote in a column: "It's our hope that the timeless peace and beauty of this mountain will eventually be preserved through purchase by an organization like The Nature Conservancy."

Incredibly, that's now happened. All 4,836 acres stretching out above me was acquired by the Conservancy for $3.5 million on March 26.

"This acquisition advances our goal of keeping large expanses of forest habitat from being fragmented," Matthew Crum, director of the Conservancy's Clinch Valley Program, said in a news release. Crum said that the ecological value of the property lies primarily in its interior forest habitat, critical for maintaining diversity of wildlife. Over the next several months, studies will be made and plans developed that will include public visitation.

One thing in the release puzzled me, however. Calling it "Brumley Mountain." I was born a couple of miles from where I'm now sitting and have never heard it called anything but Clinch Mountain.

I finally found a map published by the Cumberland Plateau Planning District that does show a "Brumley Mountain" located above the little community of Brumley Gap. It overlooks Hidden Valley Lake and Route 19, which lies some 12 miles west of here.

The only "Clinch Mountain" on the map was up in Tazewell County. Oh, well, as far as I'm concerned, The Nature Conservancy can call it anything they like. I'm just delighted they bought it and will preserve it.

The human history of the mountain goes back to the infancy of this nation. If memory serves, it came into the Stuart family in the form of a land grant. The Stuarts retained it until some time in the '60s when it was sold to former district forester Gene Ohlson. Ohlson and an associate subsequently sold it to Tommy Upchurch, a North Carolina land speculator.

Before Upchurch died, he deeded the property to two nephews. They sold timber rights to a logging company, who, in the '90s, cut all harvestable trees. The mountain was then sold to another North Carolina land-speculating firm, who in turn sold it to a similar outfit. When this firm approached Washington County officials for exemptions to road-building and other developments, they were turned down. Both the Planning Commission and Board of Supervisors voted nay unanimously.

When Charles Kennedy refused to allow the developers to cross his land, the company brought suit. That's when all the friends of the mountain stepped in and began raising funds for attorney Gerry Gray, of Clintwood. Gerry was successful in blocking several legal maneuvers. Then, about a year ago, the firm apparently gave up.

I talked with Gerry last week. He said the Conservancy purchase had taken even him by surprise but that he was "delighted."

And so were we all.

The Great Channels, 2004. Photo by Earl Neikirk, Bristol Herald Courier.

Jack, 1991. Photo courtesy of Mike Pierry, Jr.

12 ~ Religion and Politics

This book would be incomplete without a sampling of Dad's columns on politics and religion.

Often Dad's political commentaries resulted in strong reactions from his readers. Some reacted by leaving angry messages on his answering machine or writing scathing letters to the editorial page. In Dad's typical candid fashion, he once wrote in a column that, "bluntness may irritate the reader if it embodies an opinion differing from his own, but, so what? Nobody holds his nose to that page. He can always flip it over." Other readers were equally vocal in their enthusiastic support.

Dad was particularly disheartened by the war in Iraq and wrote a prophetic column on the potential outcomes and consequences. And, across the board, he was correct—except for the expectation that it would be a quick military victory.

Dad's mother was a deeply religious woman and religion played an important role in his upbringing. He even read the Bible cover to cover as a teen one summer. In later years, though, Dad was saddened by what he saw as a shift in the influence of religion—from a unifying force to a divisive one. He was a spiritual man, though, and the sources of his spirituality could be found in the woods, along the edges of the beaver pond, and in his kinship with animals.

Regardless of what you believed and whether you agreed with him or not, his columns always made you think. And for Dad, that was a job well done.

ଔଓ

Let's Try Tolerance

The flap over Salman Rushdie and his <u>Satanic Verses</u> brought to mind a story I heard in Northern Ireland back in the early '70s when I was over there covering "The Troubles."

It was a story about an Irishman wending his way homeward from a pub late at night. As he passed an alley, an arm snaked out and drew him into the darkness. He felt the blade of a knife against his throat as a voice whispered in his ear.

"Are you Catholic or are you Protestant?"

Well, the poor fellow knew that whichever answer he gave, he had a fifty-fifty chance of getting his throat slit. So, thinking fast, he replied: "I'm neither—I'm a Jew."

Whereon there came a low chuckle: "Well, I've got to be the luckiest Arab in all of Ireland!"

It is the ultimate irony that the one thing that all peoples of the world have in common—other than head colds and in-laws—is a pivotal point of divisiveness: Religion. In a very basic sense, every religion, whatever it's called, does the same thing—provides rules of conduct for life here on earth while giving a promise of life after death. Same goals, different rules.

Now, you'd think that, with shared objectives like these, there'd be a little shared understanding. Not so. Well, at least it occurs only rarely in recorded history.

"Tolerance is a divine law," the philosopher Themistius told the Roman emperor Valens some 17 centuries ago (when that ruler had the bad judgment to choose sides during a fight among warring factions of Christians). "God himself has most clearly demonstrated his desire for a number of different religions," Themistius wrote. "And God alone can judge the methods by which humanity aspires to come to an understanding of the Divine Mystery."

Pretty high-sounding. But, then, what can you expect from a guy with a name like Themistius? Still, he did put in a good word for religious tolerance. And there weren't too many such words in his day—or since.

So few, in fact, that back in the 1920s a historian by the name of Hendrik Wilhelm van Loon wrote a book on the subject. This book, <u>Tolerance</u>, was simply a detailed, through-the-centuries search for the reason behind man's inhumanity to man. Van Loon discovered a recurring theme—persons or groups who believed so avidly in the rightness of their own views they couldn't tolerate opposing ones. He concluded:

"The men who have fought for tolerance, whatever their differences, had all of them one thing in common—their faith was tempered by doubt. They might honestly believe that they themselves were right, but they never reached the point where that suspicion hardened into an absolute conviction."

But back to Rushdie. When the Ayatollah Khomeini put out a hit on him in the form of a multi-million-dollar contract (enough to make any self-respecting Mafia boss turn green with envy), the Christian world drew back aghast. Drew back in part, I am inclined to believe, because not one in a thousand has even a passing acquaintanceship with the Islamic faith.

You'd think that any religion numbering 840 million adherents (second only to Christianity), a religion woven into the political fabric of countries in which we have vital national interests—well, you'd think that would be reason enough to make it a part of our educational curricula. Not so.

I'll confess my own ignorance of Islam. It was only during the embassy hostage crisis in Iran that I got curious about a religion capable of producing a crackpot like the Ayatollah, and checked out a few books. Until then, I knew nothing.

One thing I discovered: The Ayatollah no more represents mainstream Islam than TV evangelists represent mainstream Christianity. In fact, it could be said that they have a great deal in common. For each displays a casual disregard for fundamental tenets of their respective books of religion.

The Koran, like the Bible, instructs its followers to harm no one, to live modestly, and to share with the poor. Both books praise a God who loves all people. Fundamentalist Moslems, like fundamentalist Christians, believe that their book of religion is the inspired word of God. But Moslems take this a step further. They believe that a verbatim copy of the Koran exists in their Moslem heaven. It was on this theologically sensitive point that Salman Rushdie, in the words of our president, stepped in deep doo-doo.

Although I haven't read his book, I have read enough reviews and excerpts to know that he employed his main characters in scenes that could be interpreted as a thinly disguised mockery of the origin of the Koran. Since Rushdie had been reared in the Moslem faith, he should have anticipated the reaction. It was dumb, dumb, dumb!

But does it merit execution? Nah. Hanging by the thumbs should be sufficient punishment for just plain stupidity.

છ

217

Although the shooting of the pup Sgt. Boris was a tragedy, it does have a positive aspect. I can't recall another event that has done more to unite a community through its mutually shared concern and sympathy.

Yet, there were those who disagreed. In letters to the editor, one man wrote that "the attention this dog was given was excessive." Another letter writer said he "was shocked and humiliated to see how much concern the community showed over the death of Sgt. Boris the dog . . . It is a mockery of the human race."

While I don't know either of these gentlemen, based on their letters, I somehow feel I'd have enjoyed Sgt. Boris' company more. On the other hand, columnist Cal Thomas probably would have agreed with them, judging by one of his recent columns.

Thomas utilized the column to sneer at how Secretary of the Interior Bruce Babbitt had returned to the religion of his boyhood, Roman Catholicism. He quoted the secretary as saying he "came to believe, deeply and irrevocably, that the land . . . and all the plants and animals in the natural world are together a direct reflection of divinity, that creation is a plan of God."

To which Thomas responded, "I love my cat, but she is not a reflection of divinity." Well, mercy, mercy, here I've been living under the misapprehension that God created all living things. Mr. Thomas' cat must have just happened.

Putting it bluntly, it's none of Thomas' business how any individual finds and follows his faith. Or anyone else's business. That's something, as Thomas Jefferson noted, "between a man and his God."

Up here on the mountain, if I sense a divine presence more in the Nature that surrounds me than I do in, say, listening to the preachments of Mr. Thomas' former boss, the Rev. Jerry Falwell, then that's none of his business. It continues to amaze me how these right wingers always seem to know what's best for the rest of us, even in personal matters.

Thomas says: "Babbitt's theology comes close to animism . . . It certainly is not mainstream Roman Catholic or Christian doctrine." Then he suggests snidely that "if Babbitt would consult a Gideon Bible the next time he's in a motel room, he would learn of the admonition to worship the Creator and not the things He created."

Where in the quote from Babbitt does it say he "worshipped" plants and animals? What he expressed was a kinship with them. May I suggest to Mr. Thomas (with equal snideness, I hope) that the next time he's in a public library he look up the life of Saint Francis of Assisi.

Thomas would discover that this founder of the Franciscan order shared the same point of view as Babbitt regarding "God's creatures." He called animals his "brothers and sisters." It's the same point of view that prompted Shakespeare to write:

> "And this our life, exempt from public haunt,
> Finds tongues in trees, books in running brooks,
> Sermons in stones, and good in everything."

Of course, Mr. Thomas is so far to the right he'd probably label both of them bleeding heart liberals.

Frankly, I'm disturbed by what I perceive as an increasing mix of politics and religion. This makes the second time in recent months that Thomas has utilized his nationally syndicated column to criticize the religious practice of a public figure. Earlier, he devoted an entire column to sitting in judgment on the church that Sen. Bob Dole and his wife attended (too liberal), although the Doles apparently had been comfortable there for years. Dole meekly transferred his membership. Lordy, lordy, it wouldn't do for me to be a politician, for I would have promptly told Cal Thomas which one of his ears he could stick it in.

Have you ever paused to consider what's going to happen if these right wingers take over the country? Will they make sure that all public figures attend the "right" churches, will they insist that God be approached only along their own narrow road? I can think of no more intimate or personal relationship than that embodied in religion. Yet, Cal Thomas and his ilk obviously want to make it part of the public domain.

Oh, well. Back to my original musing on the community's tribute to Sgt. Boris and its characterization as "a mockery of the human race." I take an opposite view. When our "superior" species sees fit to recognize and reward in a "lower" species the qualities of character we admire in ourselves—fearlessness and devotion to duty—I would label that more an exaltation of the human race than a mockery.

When I wrote a few weeks ago asking readers to share their experiences with pets they considered psychic, I was surprised at the response. I was also impressed by the number of extremely close relationships they revealed.

It's a special sort of love. Duke, my first Doberman, was the best friend I ever had. When he died, my grief was more intense and lingered longer than with the death of my wife, or parents.

Does that make me less of a human being? I think not. When any relationship enriches a life, it makes it more of one.

ଔ

Since arguments about public prayer will most likely go on forever, it would seem prudent or even obligatory for avowed Christians to seek the ultimate authority on that subject—Jesus Christ.

Christ not only had something to say, he said it in clear, unequivocal language. You'll find it in the sixth chapter of Matthew: "Thou shall not be as the hypocrites are, for they love to pray standing in the synagogues and in the corners of the streets that they may be seen of men."

A clear no-no for public prayer. So, how should we pray? "When thou prayest, enter into thy closet, and when thou hast shut thy door, pray to thy Father which is in secret, and thy Father which seeth in secret shall reward thee openly."

That's a terse, no-nonsense guide to what should be the most intimate and personal aspect of religion—direct contact with God. I'm puzzled by Fundamentalists who squinch their eyes tight shut against this clear-cut admonition, yet, at the same time, insist that the Bible is the eternal, unchanging word of God.

Much of Scripture, of course, is open to interpretation. Witness last month's news stories about splits over the role of women in the church in two of the nation's largest denominations. However, if Christ's instruction for praying can be twisted to mean something other than that which it says, then anything in the Bible can be twisted to mean . . . well, whatever religious ideologues want it to mean.

Several years ago, I engaged in a correspondence with a preacher on this subject of prayer. He conceded that everyone should engage in private prayer, but there was also a definite place for group prayer. Finally, I told him that if he'd point out any passage wherein Christ advocates group prayer, why, I'd make a $100 contribution to his church. He must have lost my address for I never heard from him again.

I'm not trying to be a smart-ass. I've had no theological training. On the other hand, you, the reader, haven't needed assistance to get this far into this column, have you? Well, it's written in the same English language as my old King James Version. Is the Bible supposed to be written in some sort of esoteric code that only the priesthood can decipher? I think not.

Of course, there were occasions when Christ indulged in spontaneous praying in a public place—blessing little children, healing, or the like. But none of these instances can be classed as planned, formulated group prayer.

One thing's for sure, nobody will come across a reference to prayer at a ball game. What in the world does football have to do with religion? Is God a sports fan? If so, that must be a passage I missed.

Don't ask, "But what can prayer at a ball game hurt?" Are you suggesting that this nation's highest court base a decision on an answer to that question? Some past Supreme Courts have been criticized for "making law" instead of applying a Constitutional interpretation, which is precisely what they would be doing if they based a ruling on, "What can it hurt?"

Instead, the justices, as a body, rely on what legal eagles call *stare decisis*. This is simply a Latin phrase meaning that, once an issue has been decided, it ought to stay that way unless there is a compelling reason to change it. Incidentally, there was nothing in the ruling to prevent ball players from huddling in a group and praying before a game. Or students, for that matter. That has already been ruled legal.

When I was growing up, I'm not ashamed to admit that every time I heard our National Anthem I got shivers up and down my spine. In those days, the Star Spangled Banner was reserved for patriotic, or, at least, solemn occasions. Today? Today, some deep-cleavaged rock star routinely belts it out over a loud speaker system before a sporting event. In short, what was once the most revered song in our national inventory has now become "Show Biz" and "Sports Time." It has been totally trivialized.

And that, I fear, is the direction prayer is headed. Certainly, there will be those who vehemently disagree with this position. Well, fine. To them I say, if you want prayers at a ball game, make it a private ball game, not one in which others have also paid for their tickets.

And, to school administrators who have no qualms about bringing prayer into the public arena, to them I say, Why don't you have the guts to stand up and tell students, "I know more about the right way to pray than Jesus Christ!"

I'm afraid that much of this ongoing controversy about religious matters, about prayer and Bible reading and so on in public classrooms, has the same bottom line. It's a "we" and "they" situation. We want it, they don't want it, and, by cracky, we'll show 'em!

The best one-paragraph summary I've read on the subject appeared in a column on these pages last Sunday. Syndicated columnist David Broder wrote: "If half the energy devoted to insinuating prayer into schools were devoted to strengthening the practice of religion in home and church, this would be a better nation."

Amen!

CB

When President Bush signed the "Healthy Forest Restoration Act" a couple of weeks ago, he was surrounded by those who had played key roles in assuring its passage. He used the signing as an occasion to wax eloquent.

"Almost 750 million acres of forest stand tall and beautiful across the 50 states," he said. "We have a responsibility to be good stewards of our forests. That's a solemn responsibility. And the legislation I sign today carries forward the ethic of stewardship."

It was a speech long on promises but short on specifics. The devastating western wildfires of last summer that threatened communities and destroyed homes were cited as the main reason for the legislation, but he carefully omitted several significant details.

For example, there was no acknowledgment that it also opens up our National Forests to road-building and logging, even in areas located far from homes or communities. Nor did he acknowledge that it contains major roadblocks to public participation in decisions regarding public lands by limiting their use of injunctions and shortening the time for consideration.

It didn't matter to Bush that over 200 scientists, all specialists in biology and ecology, had signed a letter urging him not to do the very things contained in the legislation. They wrote:

"It is now widely recognized that commercial logging (in national forests) has damaged ecosystem health, clean water, and recreational opportunities—values that are highly appreciated by the American public.

"The Forest Service and independent economists have estimated that timber accounts for only 2.7 percent of the total value of goods and services derived from the National Forests, while recreation and fish and wildlife produce 84.6 percent.

"When the dramatic values of ecological goods and services are taken into account, it is clear that protecting National Forests creates more economic benefits than continued logging."

Unhappily, political contributions don't come from ecologists, they come from timber interests—to the tune of several million annually.

Bush made a point of thanking individuals who had been invited to the signing ceremony. Among them was Mark Rey, who, as Under Secretary of Agriculture, oversees the Forest Service. Rey's former job was as a lobbyist for the American Forest and Paper Association. It's pure coincidence, of course, that several items high on the wish list of the Association are now incorporated in the Healthy Forest Restoration

Act. Talk about the fox guarding the hen house. Oh, my.

But, you say, aren't timber and its by-products critical to our own economy? Absolutely. It's why a balance should be struck between ecology and commerce. Trouble is, Bush hasn't made the slightest move toward balance. In every case involving environment or ecology, he's come down solidly on the side of Big Biz.

Another irony is the amount of timber being exported. Japan alone averages $3.1 billion in timber purchases annually. So, here we have trees belonging to the American public being sent overseas to benefit a comparative handful.

I will readily admit to a profound prejudice when it comes to writing about forests. Much of my boyhood was spent in the woods, and I've continued as an adult. During a break in newspapering in the '50s, I became a lookout in the fire tower located on top of this mountain. I wrote a juvenile adventure novel about the experience which extolled not only the surrounding forest but the role of the Forestry Service in protecting it.

Yes, I'm a "tree-hugger," as timber interests sneeringly put it. I hug them subconsciously every time I look out across the hills in front of this house. "I will lift up mine eyes unto the hills, from whence cometh my help."

Timber interests lift up their eyes and estimate the number of board feet.

છ

Don't Rush to War   *September 16, 2002*

Every time I see George W. Bush in one of his splendidly tailored suits it reminds me of another president, John F. Kennedy. Both charismatic, both spiffy-looking. They also have something else in common—declining the advice of top military commanders.

In 1962, during the Cuban missile crisis, all of the Joint Chiefs of Staff urged Kennedy to launch a ground assault on Cuba. He refused. Information that has come to light only during the past decade has revealed that this probably saved the world from a nuclear Armageddon. Unbeknown to the U.S., the Soviets had supplied Castro with tactical nuclear weapons. Unlike warheads on intercontinental ballistic missiles, these are designed specifically for opposing ground forces. If our ground forces had landed and threatened the survival of Castro, these undoubtedly would have been used. And then the nuclear genie would have been out of the bottle.

Bush, on the other hand, is largely ignoring advice from top military men, both active and retired, who urge him not to rush into a war with Iraq. Of course, the backgrounds of these two presidents are in sharp contrast.

Kennedy was decorated for valor after his PT boat had been sunk in the South Pacific, while Bush dodged the draft and combat duty in Vietnam by ducking into the Texas Air National Guard. Back in those days, only the scions of families of power and position could swing such a deal.

Vietnam veteran Colin Powell, in his 1995 memoir <u>My American Journey</u>, chided the "sons of the powerful" for managing "to wangle slots in Reserve and National Guard units."

While Bush kept his own butt out of combat, he appears eager today to send the sons and daughters of ordinary Americans in harm's way. Bush isn't alone. It's amazing how many hawks in his administration managed to duck Vietnam (they've been labeled "chicken hawks"). These include Vice President Dick Cheney, leader of the "Get Saddam Now!" pack. Cheney used a college deferment excuse for four consecutive years, followed by an "expectant father" deferment.

Retired Gen. Anthony Zinni, special envoy to the Middle East, told the Economic Club of Florida in Tallahassee that those urging caution on Iraq are people who have personally experienced war, including Colin Powell, Brent Scowcroft and Norman Schwarzkopf.

"It's pretty interesting that all the generals see it the same way," Zinni said. "And all the others who have never fired a shot and are hot to go to war see it another way."

Those who are urging a quick attack on Iraq point to Saddam's record, to his ruthlessness in using chemical weapons against Iran and even against his own people, the Kurds. And they're right. His record is important. But they're carefully omitting an integral part of it.

When Saddam launched a series of Scud missiles against Israel during the Gulf War (in an obvious attempt to draw Israel into the conflict and break up the Arab coalition) their warheads contained neither chemical nor biological agents. Why? Possibly because he knew this would bring massive retaliation.

Clearly, Saddam would like to dominate the Middle East and just as clearly is without moral scruples for doing so. This said, he also has another overriding aim. Survival. He wants to remain in power.

So, while there may be doubt about his delivering agents of mass destruction against populations outside Iraq, you can bet your bottom dollar he'll use them (if he has them) to counter a U.S. invasion. Survival comes first.

Of course, the chicken hawks claim that the citizenry of Iraq would rise up and join in Saddam's removal. There are those who would do so, yes, but how many? Where is the proof? Absent from Bush's words last Thursday at the U.N., and in the 20-page document released simultaneously in Washington, was evidence for urgency. Apparently, Bush is going to rely on assumptions concerning Saddam's intentions and capabilities.

Question: What if another crisis is deliberately precipitated by another nation in order to take advantage of the huge diversion of troops and material and financial resources that will follow an incursion in Iraq?

China has been slavering at the mouth for just such an opportunity. The main reason it hasn't taken over Taiwan is the American protective umbrella. Without the means to maintain that commitment, what would we do?

Bush has demonstrated that he doesn't exactly shine at looking down the road and foretelling the future. He assured Americans that his massive $1.35 trillion tax cut would still leave plenty during this decade to take care of pressing domestic needs.

This decade? In just one year, the surplus has disappeared and the deficit grows bigger every day. Our national debt stands at $6.2 trillion, and interest for the month of August alone was over $18.3 billion. So much for Dubya's clairvoyance.

☃

The Price of War *February 24, 2003*

Last week, a friend of mine who travels to Canada frequently, e-mailed me a copy of a column from the Feb. 16 edition of the *Toronto Star.*

"Thought you might be interested in this," he wrote. He was right. It provided another take on the millions of people protesting a war with Iraq. When I heard on CNN that these protests had even extended to Antarctica, I found it hard to believe. So I e-mailed a guy down there who is working in the power plant at McMurdo Station.

"Jack, you heard correctly," Dave Smith replied." About 40 people showed up while 700 stayed in bed. Here's a pic for you." The photo Dave sent showed a group bundled up against the cold, standing on ice and displaying signs that read "Wake up and Stop the War!" "No! No!

225

No!" and so on.

I'll give odds that this was a first for Antarctica. When I was down there 40 years ago, the only communication McMurdo had with the outside world was by official Navy radio. Today, personnel have their own internet connections. Truly, we have stepped into the Information Age.

The *Toronto Star* column by Michele Lansberg presented a Canadian's view. "So you wonder why so many Canadians are opposed to the U.S. plan to attack Iraq?" she began. "It's not that we're weak-kneed wimps of Canuckistan or bleeding-heart pacifists or saps who actually believe Saddam, to repeat some of the more boorish epithets."

"Whatever our other reasons for opposing the war, we're also skeptics, remembering the long history of official lies that have served as a smoke screen for U.S. government adventurism in other places and times." Most of her column was taken up with citing examples, several of which have already become public knowledge, thanks to the Freedom of Information Act.

There was Lyndon Baines Johnson's pursuit of the war in Vietnam, even after the so-called attack by North Vietnamese patrol boats on two U.S. destroyers was revealed as radar "ghost images."

"I needn't remind *Star* readers about the government crimes of the Iran-Contra gun-running scandal, ruthlessly designed to overturn the elected Sandanista government of Nicaragua by organizing and arming the Contra opposition," she wrote.

"Browse the National Security Archives on the internet, and you can eavesdrop directly on these ruthless conspirators as they plotted to use the U.S. media to vilify their enemies and whitewash their chosen henchmen.

"But don't stop there. Go ahead and read the transcript of the meeting at the White House in September 1970. They were all there: Nixon, his vice-president, the heads of the CIA, and the military. Henry Kissinger spelled out how they must 'bring down' Salvador Allende, the newly elected democratic socialist president of Chile . . . Allende, of course, was duly murdered three years later in a coup orchestrated by the CIA, which ushered in the 17-year bloody dictatorship by mass murderer Augusto Pincochet."

I'll say, this lady doesn't mince words. And she deals in facts. But I'm not at all sure this is the underlying cause for disunity among our allies. In addition to viewing Bush as an arrogant cowboy (which, to a degree, I do myself) I'd give more weight to a Washington Post op-ed piece written by Zbigniew Brzezinski, Jimmy Carter's national security adviser.

"Europeans are beginning to believe that the United States, largely under the influence of those policy makers most eager for war, is actually planning a grand strategic realignment," he wrote.

"The Atlantic alliance would be replaced by a coalition of non-European states, such as Russia, India, and Israel, each with a special hostility toward various parts of the Muslim world.

"There is justifiable concern that the preoccupation with Iraq, which does not pose an imminent threat to global security, obscures the need to deal with the more serious and genuinely imminent threat posed by North Korea. An America that decides to act essentially on its own regarding Iraq could, in the meantime, also find itself quite alone in having to cope with the costs and burdens of the war's aftermath, not to mention widespread and rising hostility abroad."

No one knows what will happen in the next few weeks, although war with Iraq appears inevitable. Almost equally inevitable is a quick U.S. victory. But what the price will be, as well as the price of the occupation that follows, is anybody's guess.

There are lots of "ifs." The cost in lives, soaring national debt, spiraling oil prices with an accompanying rise in gasoline and fuel oil, a continued slump in the economy and stock market, Mid-East instability, a flood of world-wide terrorist attacks.

Why do you think so many Democrats have stepped forward to challenge a president whose poll ratings are still high? They are well aware of those "ifs." Dubya is staking everything on one roll of the dice. If it comes up seven, there's not a Democrat in the country who can beat him.

But if it comes up snake eyes . . . well, one of my dogs could make it to the White House.

CB

Jack in his kitchen at Mountainside, 2002.

13 ~ Odds & Ends

We close this book with "Odds & Ends"—a repository of sorts that contains interesting and entertaining columns that cross over a variety of subject areas, many suggested by readers especially for this book.

Dad was a bit of a Renaissance Man. He was interested in everything (with the possible exception of rock music). And with his reporter's eye and curious mind he would dig deeply into the subjects he cared most about, whether they were people, places, or events.

Always intrigued by new technology, Dad acquired his first computer in 1985 at the age of 63 and taught himself to use it that winter while snowbound. He broke three keyboards pounding on them as he had his old Underwood typewriter until a technician urged him to ease up, but he became computer-savvy and enjoyed word processing, surfing the web, and keeping in touch with far-flung friends by e-mail.

Despite his "hermit" reputation, Dad loved people and was fascinated by their stories. He was closely tied to most of the residents of Hayters Gap and wrote columns about many of them—from Hattye Counts, the 100-year-old matriarch of the valley, to Raymon Grace, the healer and dowser who is now known internationally.

Dad admired the dedication of the small community that shook off the closing of the Hayters Gap School and turned it into a vibrant community center that hosts various events and houses Head Start, the Senior Citizens Center, and the Valley Rescue Squad. And, of course, close to his heart was the opening there of the Hayters Gap library, now run by Kathy Musick.

He wrote several columns on his struggle with emphysema. These were not columns lamenting his condition but rather sharing with his readers the strategies and techniques he used to fight the steady erosion of his breathing.

And, finally, Dad spoke to the enjoyment he found in writing his weekly column and the gratitude he felt for his readers as they shared his view from the mountain.

ॐ

The Madam's Bathroom   *January 13, 1992*

Milton Abercrombie recently mailed me a faded but interesting clipping from a December 28, 1958, issue of the *Bristol Herald Courier*. It had an Abingdon dateline and began:

"When workmen started tearing down the old Washington County jail here recently to make way for the new one, they discovered some alterations in the plumbing fixtures that brought to light a not-too-glamorous incident in the city's history."

What the workmen had uncovered were remnants of swanky toilet fixtures installed nearly half a century earlier to accommodate one of Bristol's leading madams. The fixtures had been arranged and paid for by a high-ranking city official of Bristol who, to put it as delicately as possible, had been one of the madam's most ardent admirers.

During the early years of this century, Bristol, Virginia, was pretty much a wide-open town. Saloons and brothels abounded. The brothels were centered in two downtown areas, one along Water Street, the other on Commonwealth just off State Street.

"The houses along Water Street frequently were raided by police who rounded up drunks and issued breach of peace warrants, while similar ones on Commonwealth Avenue operated unmolested," the newspaper story relates. You see, the tonier ones on Commonwealth catered to a higher class clientele. Commercial sex was okay for those with wealth, prestige and high positions in the community.

Okay, that is, until a fire and brimstone Methodist minister entered the picture. He held public rallies that pressured city fathers into passing restrictive ordinances. Madams were given a deadline to take their girls and get out of town.

"Old timers delight in describing the exodus from the red light district," the story notes—although the women simply transferred their talents to "Knoxville and other nearby cities."

But one madam refused to go. While agreeing to give up her profession, she said she'd spent too much money making her establishment "the best furnished of its kind in the area," and she was staying, preacher or no preacher. This offer to compromise was summarily rejected. She was arrested, convicted and handed a jail sentence. Unhappily, Bristol had no facilities to accommodate women prisoners. But Abingdon did, so she was transferred there.

It was at this point that "a chivalrous Bristol city official interceded on behalf of the prisoner. Despite criticism and gossip, the prominent Bristolian secured permission to have the most modern bath ever seen in

230

this area installed in the woman's cell.

"Permission was granted, with the stipulation that the fixtures were to revert to the county upon completion of the woman's term."

The story concluded: "Despite the furor the plush bathroom caused, the story had a happy ending. The woman served her sentence—in apparent comfort—and upon her release married a Bristol man and reared a family." Well, the whole thing read more like a script for a Hollywood movie than a newspaper story. I wanted to learn more.

I found a lead in the statement that, "Records show the firm of Fred Hayes Plumbing and Heating (of Bristol) installed the bathroom fixtures in the cell."

I telephoned the Scott Street firm and talked with Herb Hayes. Herb is a grandson of Fred, the firm's founder, who, in 1888, not only brought water to the city but opened its first plumbing shop. Did Herb know anything about The Case of the Pampered Prostitute? Boy, did he ever! At 75, Herb is as sharp as a tack with a memory as clear as a bell. Not only did he recall events, he knew names of all the major players—including the woman and the "prominent Bristolian and city official" who had seen to her jailhouse needs.

I'd include the names here were it not for the possibility that one of their descendants might come looking for me with a club. Herb also gave me the name of the man the madam married, describing him as "one of the most handsome businessmen in Bristol." They set up housekeeping on Euclid Avenue and the house is still standing.

"My granddaddy not only installed her bathroom in the Abingdon jail, he also installed one in her new Euclid Avenue home. I know, for I helped him put it in. It was the first color bathroom in Bristol." Herb recalls that she lived there contentedly until she died at a ripe old age in the 1970s. And Bristol's first color bathroom is still there. I know for I called its present owner, who said he'd bought the house from a church.

Herb described the woman as "fairly well off financially. She'd gotten religion in her final years, so she left her home and all her money to the church."

The wages of sin may be death, but it could be argued that in the case of The Madam vs. The City of Bristol, it paid off rather handsomely.

231

Who'd have thought there'd be that much interest in a wildflower? A couple of weeks ago, I did a column on the coltsfoot, a dandelion-like flower which appeared up here on Valentine's Day. At least, that's when I first found it in bloom. Trouble was, a reference book described it as a northerner, one that didn't venture farther south than New Jersey.

Well, almost immediately I received a call from a woman in the Big Stone Gap area who reported it could also be found over there near the Kentucky border. That same evening, I got a call from Doug Ogle of Virginia Highlands Community College's Science Department. Doug said the coltsfoot has been reported in every county in Virginia, except Wythe and Lee, and most likely is there, too. Its distribution, he said, is included in the "Atlas of Virginia Flora," published in 1986 by Virginia Botanical Associates.

A couple of days later, I got a letter from Linda Baltimore Morgan, who operates a commercial herb enterprise, the Antique Orchid Herbary, northwest of Abingdon. Linda's letter began: "As I sipped on my coltsfoot flower tea this morning, I read with much interest your column about the Yankee Wildflower."

The coltsfoot, she said, "has been regarded as one of the best herbal remedies for coughs and congestion for more than 2,000 years." Originally a native of Northern Europe, Asia and North Africa, "it has naturalized in North America, primarily from Nova Scotia and Quebec to New Jersey and south to Southwestern Virginia." This, she said, is because the Virginia Highlands are blessed with a northern climate.

"If one looks at a planting zone map of the United States, one will see that a dogleg drops out of New England to encompass the central Appalachian Mountains—which contain peaks higher than those of the White Mountains of New Hampshire. It is not at all unusual here to find flora that is generally found only in far northern habitats."

Linda suggests that anyone who wants to see lots of the stuff should go to White Top. "Ditches about halfway up the mountain are full of coltsfoot," she says. "However, leaves and flowers from roadsides should never be collected (for teas) as they contain toxins released by passing automobiles."

Coltsfoot, she says, is unique in that it forms leaves only after its flowers have gone to seed. "Even the great Roman herbalist Pliny was baffled by it," she wrote. Rodale Press, she says, gives this interesting sidelight:

"Before matches were readily available, people would scrape the thick, felty substance from the underside of coltsfoot leaves, wrap it in rags, soak it in a solution of saltpeter, dry it in the sun, and use it as tinder. "The fuzz produced on the seeded flower was used by Scottish highlanders as pillow stuffing."

She says that "native American Indians and American settlers depended on coltsfoot to fight respiratory ailments, brewed teas for both drinking and for soaking blankets to wrap around the patient." Linda was kind enough to include some attractive packages of both the dried flowers and leaves to be made into teas.

"I find the flowers have a complex flavor—somewhat like a mild and flowery spice cake—and drink a cup of the lovely floral tea whenever I feel the need for an expectorant, or to ease bronchitis or asthma," she wrote.

Well, I don't suffer from bronchitis or asthma. And Lancaster chawin' tobacco is the only expectorant I currently subscribe to. But I thought I'd give the stuff a whack anyway.

I found it—well, interesting. But it'll never put Mr. Lipton out of business. I gave it a shot of spiced rum to see if that would perk it up. It did. Settlers and Indians would have been pleased.

Indigestion aside, the coltsfoot is an unusual wildflower. The dozen or so I stuck into the planter of our fountain table in the living room have not only thrived but provided a continuing study. Most plants are heliotropic (responding to sunlight) to some degree, but this one is incredible. The morning after I set them out, I came downstairs to find all those long, scaly stems stretched out yearningly toward our big picture window. They were leaning at close to 45 degrees. And when the sun began sinking behind the woods to our west, those golden flowers began tucking in their petals—until they were mere knots waiting for another day.

Most of them have now turned to seed—clumps of tiny, downy parachutes, like dandelions. But not enough to stuff a pillow. Not even for Duke.

◌ঃ

Crossing Paths in WWII *May 30, 1994*

D. P. Henderson and Lonnie Kidd were the heavy equipment operators who dug the foundation for our house and built our roads and excavated our pond—D. P. with his backhoe, Lonnie with his front loader. Passing by the pond the other day, I thought about the unusual story they'd told me during a lunch break one day.

After working as a team here in Washington County for 15 years, they discovered that Kidd's military unit had liberated prisoner-of-war Henderson deep inside of Germany during the closing days of World War II. I talked with both men recently to see if I had my facts right for a Memorial Day column. Here's the story:

Henderson, who turned 21 in basic training, landed with the 45th Infantry Division at Anzio Beach below Rome in January, 1943. They fought their way several miles inland before receiving orders to dig in. It was a bad spot for foxholes. The Germans held the high ground and rained down a continuing barrage with their awesome "eighty-eights."

Henderson was in his foxhole with a buddy one night when one of those 88-millimeter shells buried itself within arm's reach. If the shell had exploded, they would have been scattered around the landscape, but it was a dud. Even so, the experience so traumatized Henderson that he lost his voice. For over two months, he couldn't speak above a whisper. A few nights later, his platoon went out on patrol with Henderson as lead scout. When he passed word back that there were Germans ahead, the platoon officer refused to believe him and ordered them on. Within minutes, they were captured—and starvation began.

Guarded by Italian soldiers, they were given no food. Several died. Others ate grass. Henderson says he was visited recently by one of those platoon buddies of 51 years ago, Howard Haverson, of Iowa.

"The first thing he said after we clasped hands out in front of my house was, 'Do you remember how we chased that mouse but were so weak we couldn't catch it? If we had caught it, we would have eaten it.'"

Eventually, the men were herded aboard boxcars and shipped straight up across the vast expanse of Europe. Their journey ended in Stalag 2B in the northeast corner of Germany at Stope near the Baltic Sea. Most POWs were assigned work on a large neighboring farm. When the German overseer saw how well D. P. handled horses (he'd worked with them all his life) he was removed from field work and assigned to the stables.

A lucky break, for one of the German girls working there took a fancy to him. Every day, she would hide a rye-bread-and-margarine sandwich in her apron and surreptitiously slip it into the pocket of his shirt.

"That rye was the most delicious bread I've ever had in my life," he recalls. It was a relief from the Irish potatoes, which was the only food served to prisoners—three times a day."

Henderson's voice gradually returned. A year passed. Then came word that the Russians had broken through the German lines.

"They gathered around 1200 of us in Stope and set us walking west," he recalls. "There were no trains. American bombers had knocked out railroads in every direction."

At the beginning of the war, the Japanese marched 70,000 American prisoners 70 miles to prison camps on the notorious "Bataan Death March." Around 10,000, or one-seventh, died along the way. Henderson says his group was marched 600 kilometers (roughly 310 miles) to the Elbe River. It took eight weeks. Around 400—one-third—died along the way.

"At times the Russian artillery would get so loud behind us that they wouldn't let us stop," he recalls. "I remember on one occasion we were marched all day and all night and all the next day."

For eight weeks, they wore the same clothes. Everyone was infested with body and head lice. Legs oozed blood continuously just from the friction of their unwashed clothing.

Henderson said they were lying in a barnyard near the Elbe, picking off lice, when word came that the Americans were coming. Shortly thereafter heavy shelling began.

"The SS officers wanted to shoot us, but our old guards who had been with us all the way begged them not to," he recalls. "Some of us had dived into a barn to escape the shelling when a tank suddenly rolled down an alley. I tell you, that American flag painted on its side was the prettiest thing I ever saw."

Lonnie Kidd says that when units of his 83rd Infantry encountered the prisoners, "they were coming out of barns and bushes all over the place. Everyone was jumping up and down and waving and shouting. They were just ragged skeletons, just starved to death."

Both Henderson and Kidd recall a Red Cross truck entering the area with doughnuts and candy bars, and that some prisoners gorged so rapidly they died from gastronomic shock. Henderson said he and his comrades were trucked into a nearby town, a town whose citizens a few hours earlier had spat on them as they were marched down its main street.

"The senior American officer told us, 'Boys, this town now belongs to you.' I tell you, we had a ball."

ଔ

Velty and Earl

Seventeen years ago, our family was in the midst of preparations for moving from city life, with its conveniences and amenities and crowded streets, to a lonely farmhouse high on the side of a mountain. No electricity, no telephone no indoor plumbing, no nothin'.

The fact we survived as well as we did can be credited in large part to H. R. "Velty" Davenport. Since Velty died last month at the age of 87, a few comments of appreciation are in order.

I've forgotten just how we lucked into Velty's services, but I believe he volunteered. It would have been like him. And appropriate, too, for he'd been reared in the old farmhouse that would serve as a temporary home until our new house was built on the ridge above it.

Velty and the eldest of his six sons, Clyde, began fixing it up while we were still in Chesapeake—adding a bathroom to take the place of the decaying outhouse, paneling the walls (without insulation, the wind whistled right through), and shoring up the foundations. They also put new foundations under the corncrib and installed a new tin roof, hung an entrance gate that we could shut and lock, and renovated things in general.

Once or twice a month, the children and I would make the long trek from Chesapeake. We'd put up at the Empire Motel in Abingdon and spend the weekend cleaning and painting and doing odd jobs like hanging rods for our clothes. The total absence of closets in the house puzzled me. One day, I asked Velty where they'd hung their clothes.

"On our backs," he replied succinctly. "Those were about all we had."

Velty Davenport could do more work in an hour that any other two men I've ever met in my life. Maybe three. He was 70 years old at the time, and probably didn't weigh more than 130 pounds soaking wet, but he was imbued with amazing strength.

I recall one day we had to move a copper tank we were going to convert into a solar water heater. "Wait a minute, Velty, and I'll get a couple of guys to help you," I said. Velty simply squatted down and picked it up and moved it. Well, I might have been able to lift one end but that would have been all.

Velty was born on this farm and grew up here, so he naturally felt an attachment. One day, he asked a little hesitantly how I'd feel about the Davenports holding a family reunion at the old farm house.

I told him that would be fine, for I knew that his kinsmen would enjoy seeing what a good job he and Clyde had done fixing up the place.

Well, sir, that was some crowd. My children still talk about the tables groaning with food and the gospel singing and all. They couldn't believe that a whole barnyard could fill up with cars from one family.

Another of Velty's son, Wayne, also played a critical role in our move to the mountain. Although we lived (maybe survived is a better word) for 13 months without electricity, there was one thing we couldn't do without —water. Wayne had the gift of "dowsing." He located an underground stream of water and the well which we had drilled on that location produced 15 gallons a minute.

Yes, Velty and his family helped ease us into mountain living. A few days before Velty died, I lost another helper—Earl Poston. Unlike Velty, Earl went fast, only two days in the hospital.

It was Raymon Grace who told me about Earl's mechanical genius. "If it's a gasoline engine and something's wrong with it, Earl can fix it," Raymon said flatly. Which wasn't an exaggeration. In the many years that I used his services (all I had to do was phone his house up the North Fork and he'd tootle up here in his pickup) I can't recall of an instance in which he was stumped.

The amazing thing was that he did it with a congenitally malformed hand. Until I met him, I would have sworn that two good hands were a bedrock requirement for any mechanic. Not so. Although he used one hand mostly as a brace, he could remove and re-install delicate parts of an engine that I wouldn't have thought possible.

Two good men. This area will miss them.

⟪ಐ⟫

Progress at the Gap   *August 22, 1994*

When the school board voted to close Hayters Gap Elementary School a couple of years ago, I figured that, well, there goes the institution that holds this community together.

But, surprise, surprise, the school has burgeoned into even more of a community center than before, thanks to a dedicated mélange of volunteers and county officials. In addition to Head Start during the regular school year, it's now the site for everything from wedding showers and family reunions to regular weekly luncheons of Senior Citizens and fund-raising fish suppers. And, most incredible to me, has seen the introduction of a first rate little library whose first Summer Reading Program was attended by over 100 children. The program was fun for the kids. In addition to an emphasis on reading, librarian Debbie Ledbetter arranged a variety of special events—storytelling, clowns, a ventriloquist.

Each child was required to keep a reading log. If they weren't old enough to read on their own they got credit for having a family member read to them. Top reader for the summer was third grader Christina Reynolds with 90 books. Ninety! Just imagine.

When area geologist Dr. Charles Bartlett gave a program on Indian artifacts, 12-year-old Robbie Milhorne became so enthused he went out on a dig the next weekend and then became a member of the Wolf Hills Archaeological Society.

Washington County Library Director Charlotte Lewis has thrown a lot of resources into the Hayters Gap library, and it shows. There's not only an impressive array of periodicals and juvenile and adult books, but also a copier, a fax, and a computer connected with the main library. The computer hookup makes available books from anywhere in the system. On top of all this, the community's own adult literacy program is about to be launched under coordinator Rita Roper.

None of this would have been possible without volunteers, for no county funds are available for regular maintenance of building and grounds. The head honcho here has been Melvin Snodgrass. During the past year, he's donated over a thousand hours of his own time as plumber/electrician/groundskeeper, assisted by Lee and Cannie Caudell and Joe Wilson. They've built an impressive picnic pavilion (open to the community) and are now beginning the layout of a softball diamond.

With progress like that, I've been hard pressed to keep up with it here on the mountain. But I'm trying. My deadline for last week's column caught me and my son frustrated in an attempt to install a new RCA DSS 18-inch satellite dish, so let me bring that saga to a close:

After three days of off-and-on work, we still couldn't get a signal. Although a voltmeter reading had indicated equipment failure, we decided we'd better borrow another meter since ours had been in storage for years. A wise decision. The borrowed one showed good voltage. But where to go from there? We'd checked and re-checked levels on the dish's foot and arm, plus cable connections, angle of elevation, azimuth, and so on.

The dish (the size of a dish-pan) had been installed on the side of the house below a two-foot overhang. Although our calculations showed a clear shot to the satellite, the overhang had a metal gutter. Could this metal somehow be affecting the incoming signal? We called the 800 number in Indianapolis and asked.

"No," the electronics engineer said, "but the overhang itself might —even if you have a clear shot. The signal doesn't travel in a straight line from satellite to dish, it assumes a more vertical angle in the earth's atmosphere."

"How could that be? Is it bent in the ionosphere?"

"I really don't remember. But I'd suggest you drop the dish down a few feet."

We did—and instantly the graphic on the TV screen showed a signal strength of over 50 percent! This shot up to 90 percent after Tim made minute adjustments. Our calculations, both vertical and horizontal, had been surprisingly accurate—only a couple of degrees out.

Failure to mention "vertical descent" in either the installation manual or video had resulted in two unnecessary days of bafflement. But I suppose a few bugs are to be expected when a revolutionary new product hits the market. And it is revolutionary. RCA has reported the largest volume of sales in its test areas for DSS than for any electronic item in history—including the introduction of VCRs.

I can recall evenings as a kid back in the '30s sitting around the big Philco radio in my grandfather's house down in the valley, a radio powered by an automobile-size battery that had to be recharged every few weeks. We'd sit rapt, listening to static-filled music coming all the way from WOPI 35 miles away.

Today, I sit propped on my bed, an RCA clicker in hand, bringing in two dozen TV channels of unbelievable clarity from around the globe. Or, I can select a recent Hollywood movie from a menu on the screen, click on it, and instantly watch that movie.

All this in the space of one lifetime. What an age of electronic miracles we live in!

ɞ

Rural Emergency Services   May 15, 1995

The Cannonball has broadened her lifetime experiences (of nearly six years) with a fish fry at Hayters Gap Community Center. She opted for a hotdog instead of fish, and vigorously applauded the gospel singers. Still, it was the swings and slides of the playground she liked most. That's the way granddaughters are.

There was a large crowd, as there usually is at fund-raisers for the Clinch Mountain Volunteer Fire Department. The "sense of community," which is said to be missing in many spots around the nation, is in abundant supply here.

Fact is, the two teams—fire department and life saving—have fostered it. Volunteers are scattered throughout the community. Several are cross-trained and serve on each team. It was a decade ago they took up residence in the station house down in the valley, and not long afterwards I had to call on the fire department.

After several weeks of mild spring weather, an onslaught of blackberry winter caused me to build a fire in my bedroom fireplace. And suddenly it sounded like a freight train was barreling through the house. I rushed outside. The chimney was belching large quantities of oily black smoke, flames, and tatters of burning creosote.

It was, of course, the phenomenon known as a chimney fire. Generally, this is confined to creosote in the flue liner and does no damage (other than to the householder's nerves). Still, it was comforting to have the Clinch Mountain volunteers up here in about five minutes. They went up on the roof to inspect for damage, crawled up in the attic to make sure no fire had gotten out through a liner joint, and advised what to do the next time it happened.

I've also used Valley Rescue, the life saving crew, a couple of times. The first was two or three years ago when a Senior Citizens group came up from Bristol for an outing. Buck, my Doberman, was on a chain but I was persuaded to release him. He promptly showed his friendliness by rearing up on an elderly woman standing on the edge of our front bank. She fell, breaking her hip. The team was on the scene in a matter of minutes. They examined her, splinted her, and transported her to the emergency room at Johnston Memorial in Abingdon.

I was happy to recall their professionalism when I had to summons them again last month. For myself. That afternoon, I'd been experiencing curious pains in my chest—along the top of my rib cage and down my sternum. I didn't think it was my heart for . . . well, it just didn't feel like it. It was a respiration-associated pain. But, by 8:30 or 9, it had reached the point where I was having difficulty breathing. The oxygen I use at night for emphysema didn't help. So, since Tim hadn't returned from a trip to Abingdon, I called a physician. "To be on the safe side, I'd go to the emergency room," he advised.

I dialed 911. The dispatcher had me enumerate my symptoms, after which he called Valley Rescue. He then insisted I stay on the line and keep talking until somebody arrived—which I assumed was precautionary routine. Joe Wilson, chief of the fire department who lives near the station house, had monitored the call. He volunteered to come up and stay with me until the life saving crew arrived. Which he did.

Joe was followed a few minutes later by Ken Davenport, volunteer fireman who lives down in the valley. And, on the way up, he picked up my nearest neighbor. And then the team itself arrived with their monitoring equipment.

They were Juanita Duff and Troy Thompson, both cardiac-trained, and Steve Kestner who drove the emergency vehicle. I hadn't had that many people in the house since my last party. I felt like I should be serving hors d'oeuvres or something.

Juanita began the cardiac monitoring. She also gave me a nitroglycerin pill to put under my tongue—another precautionary measure. "This will do two things," she said. "Burn—and give you a headache." It did both—but it didn't do anything for the chest pain.

Down in the valley, Tony Worley, cardiac-trained team captain, met us at the church and exchanged places with Troy, who had to go to his regular job. In addition to en route monitoring, they also hooked up a precautionary IV. This would provide a quick venous entrance on my arrival in the emergency room—if such were needed.

Although ER chest x-rays were normal, the duty physician decided to admit me to the hospital's Critical Care unit as a precautionary measure. I must say that that unit, too, has a competent staff. And what a hospital room! I didn't know any like it were available in this area. Why, my bed alone had as many electronic peripheral gadgets as this computer. Oh, yes, there was also a computer monitor hanging over my bed, recording my life functions. Just about every part of my anatomy was hooked up to it except my big toe.

All in all, an interesting experience. And a comforting one. In my remote location, living alone, it's nice to know that fast, efficient help is only a phone call away.

Cଷ

Raymon Grace   *May 12, 1997*

An area man recently flew back from Fairbanks, Alaska, where he had lectured and conducted seminars. It was the latest in a series of similar engagements covering more than a decade and a dozen states. A Ph.D. from a local college, right? Wrong. Raymon Grace has lectured at several colleges, but he's never attended one. Fact is, he's only a high school graduate.

Raymon—stonemason, lecturer, healer, devotee of Native American therapy—has been the subject of previous columns. But since the last one was several years ago, let's play catch-up.

Although I'd met him in early 1977 when we were looking for a

241

stonemason to help build our new house, it was on Good Friday that year that I was introduced to his unusual capabilities.

The children and I were spending Easter weekend here on the mountain, preparing an old farmhouse for temporary living, when Pam suffered a deep gash in one hand. En route to the emergency room, we stopped off at Raymon's to return a chainsaw I'd borrowed. When he learned of Pam's injury, he asked if he could try to help her.

I had no idea what he had in mind, but, since he was obviously sincere, I agreed—provided it didn't take too long. Raymon placed one of his hands a couple of inches above the cut. His wife, Nancy, placed one of hers on top of his, and they just stood there.

Pam started giggling. I didn't blame her, for I was raising an inward eyebrow. She told me later that the cut started tingling and drawing— "you know, like magnets attract each other."

The whole thing lasted only a couple of minutes. I re-wrapped her hand and we took off for the hospital. As we passed by the Empire Motor Lodge where we were staying, I asked the kids if anyone needed to go to the bathroom since there was no telling how long we'd be at the hospital. They said no, so I asked Pam, seated in back, how her cut was doing.

A moment later, she stuck her hand up front, "Look, Daddy!" she said. I looked. The sides of the wound had drawn together and sealed. I braked to a stop and turned the car around. They'd have laughed at us at the hospital if we'd suggested suturing.

Later I rationalized that a lucky wrapping of the towel had drawn the sides together. I'd always rejected phenomena that fell outside the scope of scientific verification, and this mumbo-jumbo was about as far removed from science as anything I'd encountered. I remained dubious even when the wound healed without leaving a scar. But then I got to know Raymon better, and personally witnessed his effectiveness in treating other people.

How does it work? "After 23 years, I still don't know," Raymon says. "I have some theories but I simply can't say for sure."

Of course, healing techniques can be taught to anyone, even though there's a wide disparity in success rate. Raymon had his first instruction back in '73 at a Silva course in Georgia where he was working on a construction project. His first patient was the project superintendent. "When I worked on him and his headache suddenly disappeared, it scared him—but he wasn't half as scared as I was," Raymon recalls.

Since then, literally hundreds of people have approached him with one complaint or another. He has been credited with cures in some cases, improvements in others. Again, Raymon says he simply can't account for this disparity. In the beginning, he used exclusively the techniques of

Jose Silva (aimed at utilizing dormant capabilities of the mind), but has since blended other techniques with them.

One of the most significant blends began in '81 after he attended a Virginia Beach symposium featuring Rolling Thunder, a Native American medicine man from Nevada.

Raymon remembers it as the opening of a door into a centuries-old system of viewing Man and his relationship with nature. It was a revelation that prompted him to go west and study under Rolling Thunder. This study was continued under another medicine man, Chief Two Trees, a Cherokee living near Asheville.

As far as his personal lectures and classes go, it all began back in '84 when he was invited to address a group in Johnson City. Riding down there with him, I asked what he was going to talk about. "I'm not sure, but I'll think of something," he replied.

He did. And while this was his first stint at public speaking, he held the group's attention for the better part of an hour. That was the beginning. Today, his speaking and teaching have reached the point where one invitation sometimes conflicts with another. Recently, he had to turn down an invitation to speak at the national convention of the North American Dowsing Society in Vermont since he'll be in the Northwest Territories of Canada for another engagement.

Raymon Grace is undoubtedly the most independent person I've ever met. He goes striding through life, along whatever byways give promise of new and exciting adventures, always listening to his own drummer.

CR

Hattye Counts

January 26, 1998

Hattye Counts, the matriarch of Hayters Gap and Washington County, will reach the 100-year mark a week from today. A whole century of living. How in the world does a person accomplish that? Are there rules to follow?

In addition to being a hard-working, non-smoking, non-drinker, she does have one rule aimed at making the years more pleasant if not more plentiful: "Live for today. Forget about yesterday and its troubles, enjoy today—and hope for a good tomorrow."

Her life as a school teacher was punctuated with bearing six children, all at home, not in the hospital, and in each case she "was back scrubbing floors within a week."

Although Hattye seems to have enjoyed the whole journey, there's also a suggestion of wistfulness for simpler times, times when families were close-knit units, times when the social event of the year was Commencement Day at Emory & Henry College.

"Everybody went," she says. "They went in buggies and wagons and on horseback. There were very few automobiles."

Hattye says she would raise chickens at her parents' home at the north end of the river bridge, sell them, and "go to your Granddaddy Sisk's store and pick out some dry goods in a nice pattern to sew myself a new dress. Every woman felt like she had to have a new dress for Commencement Day."

Another annual social event was the Laurel Springs Preachin'. "Seems like just about everybody in the county went," she recalls. "They'd take picnic baskets and eat on the grounds. There'd be two or three preachers, taking turn about."

The final social event, in the fall, was the Abingdon Fair. "My father, [Dan Johnson] would drive us into town in our two-seated surrey," she says. "I remember they had a riding ring there, and how pretty Laura Henry looked riding side-saddle on that pretty horse. She was a wonderful rider."

Hattye began her teaching career in 1918 in a little one-room school in Clinchburg, and continued until 1962 when she retired at Hayters Gap Elementary School.

"Oh, I did other things," she says. "I worked for a while in a department store in Roanoke, and in a silk mill there. And back here I sold Spirella corsets—every woman wore a corset in those days—and took orders for silk hose, the first silk hose in Hayters Gap."

Even after she retired from teaching she ran the county's cannery in Abingdon for 11 years. No sitting around and mildewing for this woman. However, the bulk of her life was spent in rural schools, beginning as a student in a little one-room building standing on the western edge of what was once my Granddaddy Sisk's meadow.

"There were no report cards in those days," she recalls. "When you finished your First Reader you were moved to second grade, and when you finished your Second Reader you were moved to third grade." Hattye credits the thoroughness of her schooling and the excellence of her teachers for her qualifying at Radford, and her subsequent teacher's certificate.

I asked her what she considered the most significant differences between public schools back then and those of today. "Well, for one thing, when I was a teacher I never had parents come to my school and get on me for disciplining their children," she says. "Students showed respect at school because they were taught respect at home. Too many parents today are sending undisciplined children to school expecting the teacher to do something they should have done."

For minor infractions, like talking in class, Hattye had a ready punishment. "I wrote a sentence on the blackboard, 'A bad combination is a small boy and a cigarette.' As punishment, I'd make a boy copy that sentence 100 times."

I'm sorry I didn't have Hattye for a teacher. Maybe today I wouldn't be on nighttime oxygen for emphysema following 43 years of heavy smoking.

Children today go home to television sets (which Hattye believes can be a bad influence), while in her day they went home to hard work on family farms. "But every weekend I'd send them home well entertained," she recalls. "Every Friday afternoon I'd read them a story with a moral to it, like 'The Little Engine that Could.' Books should never be replaced by television."

Hattye mentioned something I hadn't heard before—that there was an African-American school up in Tumbling Cove about five miles east of Hayters Gap. I knew that a black family by the name of Fullen had been among the original early settlers and early land owners there, but I hadn't heard about that school.

"Yes," she said, "and there was also a Baptist church down at the mouth of Tumbling Creek. Both blacks and whites were members of the congregation." The exact opposite of today. Today, there's integration in public schools but very little in houses of worship.

A lot of changes have occurred in the past 100 years. Hattye was born before the automobile and the airplane were invented, before electricity came to Hayters Gap, before the telephone. All monumental innovations. But have there been equally big changes in people themselves?

"If I had to pick one thing I'd say that back in my day we cared for each other, took care of each other. Today, the main concern seems to be how much money you can accumulate."

Saturday afternoon, several generations of family and friends will gather at Pleasant View Methodist Church (opposite Highlands Airport) to congratulate her and hope that her next one hundred will be as interesting as the first.

CB

245

A couple of days from now will mark a 50th anniversary for me. On Sept. 1, 1949, I walked into an old brick building on Shelby Street and began working as a reporter for a newspaper that was still in a state of parturition —Gene Worrell's *Virginia-Tennessean*. Imagine, 50 years later I am still writing for a Bristol newspaper. I don't know whether to congratulate myself on my longevity or to deplore my stagnation.

Seems like most of the big changes in my life have occurred within a one-week span. It was 22 years ago today that I finished loading a U-Haul in Chesapeake and set out for the mountain and a dramatically altered life style. And, with these other anniversaries, the Class of '39 at Bristol Tennessee High School held its 60th reunion a couple of Saturdays ago. The 60th, imagine that! It was the last class to graduate from the old building on Alabama Street.

Surprisingly, out of a class of 110, there are 53 known survivors. (Clean living will do it every time.) Of these, 27 attended a great get-together at the Bristol Country Club. Bernie Burleson, one of two surviving faculty members, also attended, and exhibited the same wit he had in his English classes at the old Tennessee High. Some things never change.

Actually, I didn't graduate with the Class of '39. Although I had started out with several of its members in the first grade at Fairmount grammar school, illness caused me to repeat a year. I blame it all on a boyhood chum, Frank DeFriece. Frank had talked me into taking a Red Cross Junior Lifesaving Course with him at the old YMCA. After strenuous swimming one evening in its heated pool, we emerged into frigid winter air. I suffered a chill that turned into a particularly virulent case of the flu, and was weeks recovering. So, I became a member of the Class of '40, the first to graduate from the new Tennessee High on Edgemont.

There's a distinct advantage in having membership in two classes. If one disavows me, I can always claim the other.

Memories, memories. This time of year brings a torrent, all marking the passage of years (as if looking in the mirror wasn't proof enough).

On the other hand, everyone's journey through life consists of a succession of memories, like beads on a string. Without them, what sense could we have of ourselves as individuals? My most nostalgic ones involve romantic encounters.

Back around 1950, a hit song on the radio was Nat King Cole's "Nature Boy," whose concluding lyrics, if I remember correctly, were:

"The greatest thing you'll ever learn

Is just to love, and be loved in return."

Reminiscing from the rather lofty vantage point of 78 years, I'll have to agree.

Other than my children, probably the most important components of my life have been words and women. One or the other has been dominant at times, but mostly there has been a pleasant commingling. Since I'm now too old for women, maybe I'm lucky to have words to fall back on— although I've yet to meet the syntax that could keep my feet warm on a cold night. If I'm ever told I have only 24 hours to live, I think I'll spend it writing thank-you notes to the women I've known. And why not? I can't think of a better way to make an exit than recalling the happy fragments of a life.

Am I a hopeless romantic? Oh, possibly, possibly. But I don't think I'm alone. A while back, I was looking in <u>The Oxford Dictionary of Quotations</u> to check the accuracy of a quote, and came across entries for "love." There were nearly 900 of them, more than any other category.

Modern Maturity, AARP's official magazine, has devoted its entire current issue to sex, including the cover story, "Great Sex: What's Age Got to Do with It?"

Ah, yes, the Viagra Vanities. To paraphrase Elizabeth Chase Akers:

"Backward, turn backward, O Time in thy flight,

And make me a stud again, just for tonight!"

Over the years, mankind has pondered the condition known as Old Age. Seneca put it tersely: "Old age is an incurable disease."

Anthony Powell wrote: "Growing old is like being increasingly penalized for a crime you haven't committed."

Jack Benny saw its humorous side: "Age is strictly a case of mind over matter. If you don't mind, it doesn't matter."

Bernard Baruch wrote that, "Old age is always 15 years older than I am." I would agree, except that I've reached the age where it's hard to find anyone 15 years older than I am.

There's a subtle transition between middle age and old age. The defining event is the shift between looking ahead and planning and dreaming, and looking back and bemoaning what has been left undone. It's a tacit acknowledgment that there's not much time left.

John Greenleaf Whittier said it best:

"For of all sad words of tongue and pen,

The saddest are these: 'It might have been!' "

CB

Living with Emphysema *December 6, 1999*

Here on the mountain, we observe Thanksgiving Day a day late. By gathering on Friday, family members can do the turkey bit in their own locality before heading for the hills. After we took our places around the fountain table, and my granddaughter, Lindsay, had said grace, my second granddaughter, Olivia, made a suggestion.

"Let's everybody tell what we're most thankful for," she said—an idea she'd picked up earlier that week in her first grade class in Roanoke. So, around the table we went, each citing a particular reason for being thankful. Well, all except 19-month-old, Eliza. She was too busy eating.

Most cited the warmth and love of family and friends, of being together around the festive table. I agreed, but something else came first. "Just being alive," I said.

All too true. I marvel over the fact I'm still here with enough energy left to moan and groan and complain. After all, I've been living with a progressive, incurable disease for many years. Compounding my wonder is the knowledge of how others have fared with emphysema—classmates, friends, relatives, neighbors.

I can name six people (all heavy smokers, of course) who came down with the affliction at pretty much the same time I did, two of them even later. All but one are now dead, including our next-door neighbor in Chesapeake. Another neighbor is on full-time oxygen after part-time use for only a year.

I went on night-time oxygen over six years ago. With only occasional exceptions, that's all I'm on today. How can such disparity be explained? Well, that's why I'm writing.

Statistically, several readers are sure to have emphysema. I want to share something that appears to have slowed the advance of my own condition, something not practiced, as far as I can learn, by those cited above.

I'm talking exercise. Specifically, walking—although perhaps equally important are daily tasks that demand a degree of physical exertion. Admittedly, I don't have the strength for some jobs. Like cutting and gathering firewood. My son, Tim, does that. But there are many other chores I force myself to do.

What I'm saying is, don't become a couch potato. If that happens, I'm convinced that months, if not years, are sliced off an emphysemiac's life. Generally, I take the dogs for only short walks. My usual one is to the top of our east ridge and back, a jaunt of not much over ten minutes. However, the other day, I decided to stretch it. Instead of back-tracking when I got to the top of the ridge, I went on down it—to the delight of the dogs, of course.

Down the ridge to the pines above our barn, then west to the pond, across the dam and up the steep slope of the ridge beyond, then up through the fields to the house. Ten years ago, I could probably have done it in half an hour instead of nearly an hour. But, then I wouldn't have been stopping to gasp for air. The significant thing is that I not only made it but actually felt better that evening.

Speaking of dogs, if you were one of the 70-plus people who turned out for the organizational meeting of the Animal Defense League of Washington County last month, the first regular meeting is scheduled for Wednesday at 7:30 p.m. at the Abingdon Fire Dept. building one block back from Campbell Funeral Home.

Even if you didn't attend the last meeting, now's the time to join. See you there!

છ

Love of Books   *December 22, 2003*

I'll bet if you have children and grandchildren you've been working on their Christmas "wish lists." It's the logical way to handle this annual hassle. I'm happy to report I'm practically through mine.

I'm also pleased that books dominated the lists. Even five-year-old Eliza had half a dozen on hers, including an illustrated dictionary. Most likely this was her mother's idea but I heartily approve. During my lifetime, I've probably used a dictionary more than any other book. Of course, when I got into computers and word processors 19 years ago, I began installing dictionaries on them.

A couple of months ago I came across the ultimate one. It's the "Oxford Pop-up Dictionary of the English Language." All you have to do is double-click on a word (while you're either reading or writing) and, bingo! It pops up on the screen with its definition, examples of usage, and how it came to enter the English language. An icon is also automatically established on your tool bar so you can use the dictionary even when the computer is idle. True, it doesn't give pronunciations, but it's still the handiest gadget I've encountered.

A love of books is instilled in childhood. My mother read every night to my brother and me, continuing until we started reading on our own. Then my wife picked up the thread with our children. So this year's wish lists didn't come as a surprise.

Among those selected by 14-year-old Lindsay (the Cannonball) was Roget's Thesaurus, the classic synonym-finder. Although I'd installed thesaurus software long ago, prior to that I'd used the book. I launched a shelf search so I could buy an identical copy. Finally found it. The inscription at its front caught my attention: "Christmas 1938." Which meant it had been on my wish list 65 years before Lindsay put it on hers.

During my search, I came across a number of books that had played significant roles in my life. In fact, some of them could be viewed as turning points. Among them was Two Little Savages, written and illustrated by a leading 19th century naturalist, Ernest Thompson Seton. The date of purchase was in its front: "Bought from Franklin Ramsey November 30, 1936. 10 cents." Which meant I'd used two-thirds of my lunch allowance to buy it.

Franklin Ramsey, a Tennessee High classmate, probably dined better than I did that day, but I was hungry for what was inside the book. It opened a door to a wealth of woodslore on plants and birds and trees and animals. Thereafter, instead of devoting my free time to studying girls (a normal proclivity for 17-year-old boys) I spent it out in the woods. Truth to tell, I might not be sitting on this mountain today were it not for that ten-cent purchase. Books, indeed, can change lives.

At least, that's the way it used to be for kids. Today, books have a lot of competition—television, DVDs, VCRs, boom-boxes. Television, of course, is the primary competitor. I'm probably one of the few fathers who denied his kids TV for over a year, although I'll have to admit it was inadvertent. There was no electricity in that drafty old farmhouse, but there were boxes of books stored in the woodshed loft.

Pam and Tim began reading them by the light of hissing Coleman lanterns. I was so impressed by this plunge into literature that, when we moved up to our new house, I banished the television set to a small junk room downstairs. Of course, several years later when the kids left home, I brought it up to this room. I'm too much of a news junkie to keep running up and down stairs.

All the kids and grandkids came in for this Thanksgiving weekend. One night, everyone had gone to bed when Lindsay came in and asked if I minded if she sat in the recliner. To watch television? Nope, to read a book.

Well, mercy, mercy, there may be hope for her generation after all.

CB

This column marks the beginning of its 18th year. That same time-frame would stretch from the day I was born to my senior year in high school. Hard to believe.

When the late Jim Baxley, then editor of the *Bristol Herald Courier*, invited me to try my hand at it I had no idea it would continue for so long. For that matter, I had no idea I would continue for so long. But who does? No man is promised tomorrow.

There've been times during the past year when I considered dropping the thing, thanks to a steady erosion of energy brought on by two deadly diseases. What made me continue? Well, you're partly to blame.

Time after time, someone has stepped up to me in an area supermarket and asked, "Are you the guy who writes the column in the newspaper?" After I've admitted my guilt, they generally have a comment about something in a recent one, or else cite topics they like best. It was during one of these supermarket introductions a couple of years ago that I encountered Elizabeth and Joe Szczesny, who probably qualify as No. 1 fans.

Elizabeth approached me and, after making sure of my identity, asked if she could give me a hug. Naturally, I acquiesced. She then introduced me to her husband, a former navy man.

They'd moved to the area in 1995, eight years after the column began appearing. Elizabeth wanted to read those eight years. Poor Joe was dispatched to make copies. He started at Emory & Henry College, copying microfiches from their files. Then he moved on to the public library in Abingdon, then the library in Bristol. One of the columns had been partially obliterated so he ended up at King College where he found a good copy. Now, that's the kind of readership that's kept me going.

In writing the columns, I'd never bothered to date them, much less make an index. When Elizabeth learned of this, she created one and e-mailed it to me. It not only contained the date of publication but also the headline that went with it. I've used it frequently. Last week, when I was writing a column on flu vaccine, I knew I'd written an earlier one on the same subject, but when? I turned to the index. Nov. 26, 2001, with the headline: "It's flu season—so where are the shots?"

Seventeen years. That's 884 columns. Well, not quite, for there'd been some weeks I'd missed. Not many, but some. How many? According to the index, seven in 17 years. Not bad.

I've gotten questions about how I write the thing—where I find topics, are they hard to write, how much time it takes, and so on. Whenever I bump into something interesting, I assume, rightly or wrongly, that readers will find it interesting, too—even insignificant, everyday events. Several have told me that when reading a column it's like I've written them a personal letter. Well, good.

A desire to communicate is common to most of the human race. It's an inbred trait and is probably the overriding reason I've kept on writing. Actually, I should be grateful that the column came along. In view of my senility and slowly deteriorating health, it's the only truly productive thing I have left.

I used to love being out in the woods gathering firewood at this time of year—looking up at a standing dead tree, judging its lean so I could adjust the angle of kerf; exulting when it crashed down just right; sitting on its bole enjoying the big silence following the screech of the chainsaw.

In the summer there was the garden—getting the smell and feel of the earth, looking proudly at the end products in freezer and root cellar.

Today, I've been reduced largely to the role of a shut-in, my activities limited to preparing meals and taking care of three worthless dogs.

Oh, well, at least I'm still able to prop myself up in front of a computer screen.

CB

Jack's home office, where he wrote his weekly column for more than 17 years.

"I've just finished watching a ruffed grouse, a hen, nervously cross my front lawn from the heavy timber in the west to the thickets on the east, shifting from a hesitant walk to a gliding run and then back to a walk again."

That was the opening paragraph of my first "A View from the Mountain" column. The date: October 19, 1987. Since that was 10 years ago yesterday, with this column I begin a second decade. Hard to believe, hard to believe. Where did the time go?

Most of that first column was dedicated to describing "a bumper year of watching wildlife on this remote mountain farm above Hayters Gap." Deer, I noted, had become a real problem in the garden. Instead of freezing my usual 200 servings of broccoli, I'd been able to put up exactly zero. Zilch. Nada.

In that and succeeding years, I experimented with just about every remedy in the book. Nothing worked. Nothing until this year when Tim and I surrounded the garden with an electrified wire. Eureka! Not a deer trespassed.

The next column described an October activity we always looked forward to—picking apples and carrying them over to Raymon Grace's for processing in his cider press. "Every year, I ask myself: What am I doing up in this apple tree at my age, shaking off apples that always hit me on the head . . . But I suppose when I don't climb that tree any more, then I'll be old."

Well, it's been several years since I climbed that big tree down by the barn, so I reckon I am now certifiably old.

Those early columns pretty much established a pattern that I still unconsciously follow—life here on the mountain, animal inhabitants, daily events, canine companions I've never been without, nostalgia. Oh, occasionally I'd wander beyond these borders, and still do. It generally happens when a topic of national interest injects a discordant note into my otherwise placid existence, and gets me riled to the point of blowing off steam.

Actually, I can think of very few subjects I haven't touched on in more than 500 columns. Which brings up one of the most common questions I get asked—where do I get the ideas for columns? Beats me. I wish I knew. I'd like to hang a bucket down in that well.

Occasionally, I've approached the 11th hour of my mid-week deadline without having a topic. The first time this happened was a bit unnerving, but after that, no sweat. In fact, I generally have a couple of columns laid out in my mind in advance.

Sometimes columns just happen. I recall one I wrote on songs I listened to on the Subaru's tape deck while trimming pine trees, and the memories that each evoked. I remember another column that was based on taking a friend from Blountville out to dinner, and then (at her suggestion) to an Abingdon discotheque. It was my first visit to such an establishment, and new experiences are always easy to write about. Moreover, I enjoyed it, and a writer's enjoyment always comes through loud and clear to the reader.

Which is another thing that ten years of column-writing has taught: You can't fake an emotion. No matter how hard you try to assume an attitude toward a subject, or disguise how you feel about it, the reader will see right through you. Honesty, therefore, is not only the best policy in everyday living, it is an absolute essential in column writing.

Bluntness may irritate the reader if it embodies an opinion differing from his own, but, so what? Nobody holds his nose to that page. He can always flip it over.

How long does it take to write a column? Well, it varies with the subject. There have been times when I've knocked one out in a couple of hours. There have been other times (and you can believe this or not) that I've spent several days working on something that takes only five minutes to read. And, occasionally, I've worked for hours on a subject only to give it up.

Why take all that bother when the pay's the same for any column? Well, I suppose it can be traced to a Scriptural admonition I adopted early in life: "Whatsoever thy hand findeth to do, do it with all thy might, for there is no work nor device nor knowledge nor wisdom in the grave whither thy goest."

Are there some things I enjoy writing about more than others? Of course. Not surprisingly, those columns are the ones readers also seem to enjoy—columns about dogs, nature, life on the mountain.

And how do I know that? Because you've told me with telephone calls and letters and after introducing yourselves in supermarket checkout lines—for which I am grateful. I'm therefore convinced that whatever popularity the column has enjoyed can be traced, in large part, to sharing those experiences.

It's now 2:30 a.m., and 40 degrees outside, but the moonlight is so incredibly beautiful that I think I'll take the dogs for a walk. Sorry you can't join me.

03 03 03

Jack wrote a total of 896 columns for the Bristol Herald Courier, beginning with his first on October 19, 1987. His final column appeared on March 6, 2005. Jack died March 9, 2005, at the age of 83. His dedication and commitment to his column is a tribute to his readers.

Jack's view from the mountain.

Jack Kestner's family at Mountainside, April 2006. Back row from left: Pam Kestner-Chappelear, Tim Kestner, and Lisa Kestner Quigley. Front: Olivia Chappelear, Eliza Quigley, and Lindsay Meredith.

To comment on this book or order a copy, contact:

Clinch Mountain Press
P.O. Box 117
Emory, Virginia 24327
(276) 944-5355
shearer@clinchmountainpress.net
www.clinchmountainpress.net